THE VEGAN INSTANT POT COOKBOOK

THE VEGAN INSTANT POT® COOKBOOK

wholesome, indulgent plant-based recipes

Nisha Vora

AVERY

AN IMPRINT OF PENGUIN RANDOM HOUSE
NEW YORK

AVERY

an imprint of Penguin Random House LLC
penguinrandomhouse.com

Most Avery books are available at special quantity discounts for bulk purchase for sales promotions, premiums, fund-raising, and educational needs. Special books or book excerpts also can be created to fit specific needs. For details, write SpecialMarkets@penguinrandomhouse.com.

INSTANT POT® and associated logos are owned by Instant Brands Inc. and are used under license.

Library of Congress Cataloging-in-Publication Data

Names: Vora, Nisha, author.
Title: The vegan Instant Pot cookbook : wholesome, indulgent plant-based recipes / Nisha Vora.
Description: New York : Avery an imprint of Penguin Random House, [2019] | Includes index.
Identifiers: LCCN 2019004732 | ISBN 9780525540953 (hardcover) | ISBN 9780525540960 (ebook)
Subjects: LCSH: Vegan cooking. | Smart cookers. | LCGFT: Cookbooks.
Classification: LCC TX837 .V67 2019 | DDC 641.5/6362—dc23
LC record available at https://lccn.loc.gov/2019004732

p.   cm.

Printed in the United States of America
1 3 5 7 9 10 8 6 4 2

Book design by Ashley Tucker

For Mom and Dad,
for your unconditional love
and for believing in my dreams

CONTENTS

INTRODUCTION

My love affair with food started in high school. What began as an effort to trade in school pizza lunches and Hostess cakes for healthier fare quickly turned into a lifelong passion for food. I began hosting eight-course feasts for family and friends, swapped out my *Seventeen* magazines for *Bon Appétit*, and nurtured a daily relationship with the Food Network. But as an academically inclined individual who thrived in the classroom (i.e., a nerd), food was just a hobby, never a possible career path.

After graduating from university with a double major in Political Science and Legal Studies, I took the next step in my neatly mapped out life: go to Harvard Law School and change the world. In law school, I learned how to solve tough problems creatively, how to master a new subject from scratch, and how to use a tool to effect change. Practicing law, however, was a very different story. As an associate at a big corporate law firm, I spent hours writing memos defending giant corporations, and even more hours feeling palpably anxious. I ate three meals a day (and countless snacks) at my desk and developed stress-induced ailments, from IBS to joint pain. After two very unhappy years, I made the first truly risky decision of my life: I traded in my high-paying, high-prestige job for a 40-liter backpack and cargo pants and embarked on a six-month backpacking trip around the world.

I returned from my international jaunt with three invaluable items: (1) the realization that life is too short to spend it doing something you hate (i.e., less desk job and more *eat, pray, love*); (2) a deep appreciation for global flavors and local cuisines; and (3) a sun-kissed tan.

Around the same time, I was introduced to the Instant Pot. I was working as a nonprofit lawyer in a meaningful but emotionally draining job, which left me too tired to cook most nights. On top of that, I had just moved into a quaint prewar (pre–Civil War) apartment that left much to be desired in the way of kitchen space. Sure, the Instant Pot wasn't a small device, but it was a multifunction device, which meant I could rid my counters of an enormous sous vide machine and a rarely used slow cooker.

As I rekindled my love for cooking, I still felt unfulfilled professionally, plagued by a nagging sense that my standards for my career—a job that I simply didn't hate—were far too low. I needed to be doing something that actually made me happy.

When I began my food blog and Instagram account in the spring of 2016, I was simply looking for a new craft to fill my spare time. But soon enough, I began spending all of my free time in the kitchen and started teaching myself everything I could about veganism and food photography. Luckily, the response to *Rainbow Plant Life* was great enough that it eventually persuaded me to make the second risky decision of my life: leave the law entirely and turn my long-standing hobby into a career.

The decision was not an easy one. I was a successful Harvard-educated lawyer. *You don't just turn your back on that*, many people told me. And I listened to them. At times, I felt embarrassed that I had given up on my first career before I turned thirty, that I had turned my back on my dream to change the world, that I was selfish enough to prioritize happiness. Other times, I felt self-conscious: without the security of easily introducing myself as a lawyer, it was no longer clear to the outside world that I was smart, hardworking, ambitious. Was I even smart, hardworking, and ambitious anymore? It certainly did not feel that way.

It would be many months before I accepted that I *didn't* turn my back on everything I knew. I simply gave myself permission to grow—to grow into a woman who was comfortable with her dreams and ideas changing over time; to grow into a career where I could channel my love for producing positive change, but in a different way; to grow into a new chapter of life where prioritizing happiness was not selfish but the product of hard work and cultivation.

And over the last few years, my passion for creating delicious vegan recipes and sharing them through vibrant food photography has been immensely rewarding. Reading messages from people who've been inspired to go vegan or cook more vegetables gives me the same inspiration I felt as an avid young law student ready to change the world. Constantly challenging myself to try new recipes or master a new area of cooking gives me the same motivation I felt when I was learning new subjects in school. And the daily conversations I have with omnivores and vegans alike encourage me to improve my recipes, write more thoughtfully, and produce better content that can inspire anyone to eat more plants and thereby improve their health and the health of this planet.

I am beyond grateful that the Rainbow Plant Life community has enabled me to write my very first cookbook! The process of writing this book was arduous, especially having to test (and eat) my Double-Fudge Chocolate Cake recipe more than a dozen times. But it was also the most rewarding thing I have ever done, and I am so excited to share it with you!

WITH HUGS AND (LIGHT) KISSES,

Nisha

THE INSTANT POT

There are few kitchen appliances that have transformed home cooking as much as the Instant Pot. For anyone familiar with this multifunction electric pressure cooker, this should come as no surprise. After all, what other appliance can churn out soups that have the depth of flavor associated with slow simmering in a fraction of the time? Can turn fibrous sweet potatoes into buttery goodness in just 5 minutes and pungent onions into sticky, caramelized jam? And pop out moist and tender cakes, homemade yogurts, and perfectly cooked beans with minimal work? (That was a rhetorical question. The answer is *no other appliances can do that.*)

If you're not familiar with the Instant Pot, your impression of pressure cookers might not be a positive one. Before the Instant Pot entered my life, I *hated* pressure cookers. As a child, my mother frequently used a stovetop pressure cooker, and it was my job to keep track of each whistle as it went off, informing her as she folded laundry or paid the bills that the sixth whistle had blown and it was now time to check on the rice. Inevitably, I always lost track after the second whistle, because, well, it was a boring pastime. I also vividly remember the day that the pressure cooker violently rattled on the stove until it exploded and left my mother with third-degree burns on her arms.

Unlike these stovetop pressure cookers of the past, the Instant Pot is both safe and easy to use. It has a foolproof safety mechanism that enables you to open it only when it is safe to do so. It has clearly labeled buttons like Pressure Cook and Sauté that remove any guesswork. And it has a digital countdown, so no need to set a timer in your head.

In fact, the only real hurdle to successful cooking in the Instant Pot is understanding the various buttons and settings. That's why I recommend reading the How to Use Your Instant Pot & Terminology (page 16) and Frequently Asked Questions (page 34), which will make the learning curve a lot less steep. Once you become familiar with the lingo, you'll realize that cooking with the Instant Pot is not too different from traditional cooking and, in many cases, much easier. You can sauté, steam, brown, braise, mash, and bake. You can make a pot of fluffy rice in 10 minutes or a pound of lentils in 15 minutes. And, you can leave a finished dish in the pot for hours and still come home to a warm meal.

I truly believe that this book can help transform the way you cook and, perhaps even more important, save you time. When the Instant Pot is taking care of your dinner, you'll discover newfound pockets of time. I trust that you'll use that time wisely, whether it's to squeeze in a workout, catch up on your favorite show, or spend time with friends and family.

Aside from magically granting you more free time, this cookbook will teach you how to whip up aromatic curries and soups, how to cook al dente pasta in 4 minutes or less, how to bake scrumptious cakes, and more, all in your Instant Pot. It contains seven chapters of recipes, along with a guide to deciphering Instant Pot terminology, helpful cook time charts, and tips for stocking a vegan pantry.

Many of these recipes are inspired by the cuisines I fell in love with during my travels, from Thai curries to Mediterranean-inspired grains and legumes. A few of these recipes are an ode to my mother's Indian home cooking and abound with fragrant spices that linger on the tongue. And some recipes are influenced by the seasons, whereas others are the product of my desire to marry comfort food with vegan food. Most of these recipes are simple enough for novice cooks but exciting and unique enough to serve at a dinner party that will wow your family and friends.

Why Vegan?

I became vegan in 2016 after what I can only describe as a weeklong binge on Netflix documentaries, and I've never looked back. Finding veganism has been one of the most rewarding decisions of my life. For one, I feel healthier: I am now winning a decade-long battle with IBS, my chronic migraines have all but disappeared, and my previously high cholesterol has dropped 50 points. I also feel happier knowing that I'm doing my small part to make this planet a happier, healthier place for both the animals and humans who live here.

Every recipe in this book is 100 percent vegan. Many of my recipes are inspired by vegetables, from the versatility of cauliflower in my Millet-Cauliflower Mash (page 135) and Tofu Cauliflower Tikka Masala (page 247) to the sweetness of carrots in my Ginger Carrot Miso Butter (page 67) and Creamy Carrot-Ginger Soup (page 251). But you will find much more than just vegetables here. I've made it my mission to develop creative ways to replicate my favorite foods without using meat or dairy, to show the world that eating a vegan diet does not require deprivation, and to prove just how damn delicious vegan food can be. In this book, you'll learn how to use nuts and legumes to make creamy concoctions, how to make grains taste decadent, and how to re-create classic comfort foods in the Instant Pot.

I am passionate about creating food that is both nourishing and indulgent, food that both tastes good and makes you feel good, and I hope that this book will provide you with the inspiration to use your Instant Pot to make drool-worthy plant-based meals with ease.

How to Use Your Instant Pot & Terminology

INSTANT POT MODELS

The primary Instant Pot models, in ascending order of fanciness, are the LUX, DUO, DUO Plus, and ULTRA.

LUX: A 6-in-1 pressure cooker. It does not have a low-pressure setting or a Yogurt setting.

DUO: a 7-in-1 pressure cooker that has both a high- and low-pressure setting and a Yogurt setting.

DUO PLUS: a 9-in-1 pressure cooker that has everything the DUO has, plus a Cake program, an Egg program, and a Sterilize setting.

ULTRA: a 10-in-1 "smart" pressure cooker that has everything listed above, along with highly customized programming, an LCD display that tracks your progress, and a central dial with added precision.

INSTANT POT SIZES

All of the models listed above come in three main sizes—3-quart, 6-quart, and 8-quart. A 6-quart capacity is sufficiently large for most needs, and all of my recipes were tested in 6-quart DUO or DUO Plus models. If you feed a large group on a regular basis, you may want to purchase an 8-quart model. I recommend a 3-quart model only if you regularly cook for just one person and have minimal storage space.

Given that the 6-quart model is the most popular size, most Instant Pot recipes you'll find online are also tested with a 6-quart model. If you are using an 8-quart model, the prescribed cook time should not change, as cook time is not based on the quantity of food but rather on the size, density, and makeup of the food. However, it will take more time for the 8-quart model to come to pressure and to release pressure, as there is more space to fill. You may also need to add a bit more liquid, depending on the recipe, as the 8-quart model requires a larger minimum amount of liquid (for instance, many recipes made in a 6-quart model require a minimum of 1 cup of liquid, but an 8-quart model might require 1½ cups of liquid for the same recipe).

FUNCTION KEYS

Depending on the model of your Instant Pot, you will have all of these function keys or most of them. All models have the major, most commonly used function keys.

PRESSURE COOK: This is the magic key—it's the most versatile setting and enables you to pressure cook and manually determine the pressure level and cook time. On older models, this is labeled as the Manual key. The Instant Pot defaults to high pressure (10.2–11.6 psi/239°–244°F), but you can use the Pressure Level button (or Pressure button on older models) to adjust it to low pressure (5.8–7.2 psi/229°–233°F). Use the +/− keys to adjust the cook time.

SAUTÉ: Use this function to sauté almost anything you'd cook in a skillet, such as browning aromatics and vegetables. You can adjust the temperature from Normal (320°–349°F) to Less heat (275°–302°F) or More heat (347°–410°F) by pressing the Sauté button again (or the Adjust button on older models). When the Instant Pot reaches the given working temperature, the display will read "HOT." When sautéing with lower-heat cooking oils such as olive oil, I find that it's best to add the oil and initial ingredients a few minutes after turning on the Sauté setting but before the display reaches "HOT" to prevent premature browning or burning. For higher-heat oils, you can wait until the display reaches "HOT" to add the first ingredients. You'll find many of these recipes begin on the Sauté setting before moving to the Pressure Cook setting: This method enables you to develop deep flavors and caramelization before pressure cooking.

STEAM: This is similar to pressure cooking at high pressure, but the Steam setting cooks at full power continuously, so direct contact between the food and the pot can cause burning or overcooking. That's why it's important to use a steamer rack or basket and add a sufficient amount of water in the inner pot. I use this setting to steam delicate vegetables (you can even set the cook time to 0 minutes for an instant steam) and to sterilize the Instant Pot.

RICE: Designed for white rice, this setting cooks automatically adjusts the cook time based on how much rice and water you add. Personally, when making plain white rice, I just use the Pressure Cook setting for 4 to 6 minutes with a natural pressure release.

SOUP: This setting defaults to cooking at high pressure for 30 minutes. The Instant Pot controls the pressure and temperature so that the liquid doesn't boil too vigorously, making it perfect for delicate soups.

BEAN/CHILI: This setting also defaults to cooking at high pressure for 30 minutes. For well-cooked, fully soft beans, you may need to adjust the setting to increase the cook time.

PORRIDGE AND MULTIGRAIN: These settings also default to high pressure and offer suggested cook times for various porridges and grains such as brown rice, respectively. A natural pressure release is advisable, as a quick pressure release of a large volume of grains can cause splattering through the vent. I typically just use the Pressure Cook setting to cook grains.

CAKE: Another setting that defaults to high pressure and offers suggested cook times. I typically just use the Pressure Cook setting to bake cakes.

YOGURT: I highly recommend using this setting to make homemade yogurt. As long as you follow a few critical steps, it's very simple and hands-off, and is cheaper than buying nondairy yogurt at the grocery store.

SLOW COOK: Use this setting as you would use an ordinary slow cooker, with normal mode being equivalent to most slow cookers. A tempered glass lid can be helpful for this setting.

MEAT/STEW AND EGG: Not applicable. You bought a vegan cookbook!

OPERATION KEYS

KEEP WARM/CANCEL: Keep Warm does exactly that and keeps the food warm between 145° and 172°F. I press this button before pressure cooking because it gives you a post-cooking timer, which is helpful for tracking how long the pressure has been releasing naturally. It's also handy if you won't be home when the cooking program ends but you want your food to stay warm. Depending on your model, your machine may automatically turn the Keep Warm function on when pressure cooking begins. Cancel enables you to end your selected cooking function at any time. With the DUO Plus or newer DUO models, Keep Warm and Cancel are distinct keys, but they are combined into one button on older models.

PRESSURE LEVEL: This button changes the pressure setting from high to low. On older models, use the Adjust button.

+/– BUTTONS: Use these buttons to increase and decrease the cook time, respectively.

DELAY START: Use this button when you want to delay the cooking start time. Select a cooking function, then press this button, using the +/– buttons to adjust the delayed hours and pressing this button again to adjust the delayed start in minutes. On older models, use the Timer button. I find this handy for cooking soaked beans—I soak the beans directly in the Instant Pot, select the cooking program and then Delay Start, after 8 hours of soaking, the cooking program automatically begins.

PRESSURE RELEASE

Sealing and Venting: The Pressure Release knob should be in the Sealing position for all pressure cook-style programs. If it's set to Venting, the Instant Pot won't come to pressure. On more than one occasion (okay, on like twenty-eight occasions), I have left the knob on Venting and have ended up ruining or over-cooking a meal. My advice: Get into the habit of turning the knob to Sealing immediately after securing the lid. If you have the ultra model, the Steam Release Valve seals automatically when you secure the lid. If the Quick Release button is in the up position, it is sealed.

Natural Pressure Release: This is how the Instant Pot depressurizes naturally. Once the cooking program ends, your Instant Pot may automatically turn off or it may default to the Keep Warm setting. Once depressurized, the float valve (the little metal pin) will drop down.

Quick Pressure Release: To release the pressure quickly, once the cooking program ends, carefully switch the Pressure Release knob from Sealing to Venting; a large cloud of steam will shoot out of the knob, which might seem intimidating, but you'll get used to it! You can use a pair of tongs or oven mitts to switch the knob if you'd like. Once the float valve drops, you will be able to open the pot. I use a quick release for most vegetables and other delicate ingredients to stop pressure cooking and avoid overcooking. I don't recommend it for foods with a high starch content (e.g., a big pot of beans or oatmeal) or very large quantities of liquid, as you may get sprayed with your dinner. To perform a quick release on the Ultra model, press down on the Quick Release button until it clicks and locks into the Venting position.

Combination Pressure Release: Many recipes call for allowing a natural release for a certain time period (e.g., 10 to 15 minutes) and then performing a quick release. This speeds things up a bit for high-volume liquids while reducing the risk of splattering from the knob.

OTHER TERMINOLOGY

SECURE THE LID: Close the lid and turn it clockwise until the lid arrow lines up with the "Close." If your Instant Pot is plugged in, you'll hear a chime that sounds like a bird chirping.

SILICONE SEALING RING: This ring lines the bottom of the lid and serves two functions: It allows the Instant Pot to reach pressure and prevents steam from escaping during cooking. It must always be securely in place when using a pressure cook function.

FLOATING VALVE: This is a safety mechanism that prevents you from opening the Instant Pot while it's at pressure. Located near the pressure release knob, it looks like a little metal pin and will be in a raised position when at pressure and in a dropped position when not at pressure.

ANTI-BLOCK SHIELD: Located on the underside of the lid near the sealing ring, this piece prevents food particles from clogging the pressure release valve. It should always be in place when using the Instant Pot.

CONDENSATION COLLECTOR: The little plastic cup that attaches to the back slot of the Instant Pot. It collects condensation that drips down from the lid and should be cleaned out occasionally.

Instant Pot Accessories & Other Essential Kitchenware

You can find most of these Instant Pot accessories and kitchen gadgets in well-stocked cookware stores or online, particularly on Amazon.

EXTRA SEALING RING: The silicone sealing ring has a tendency to absorb the smell of everything that goes into the Instant Pot (mine smells like cumin and maple syrup). Having two rings means you can reserve one for savory dishes and one for sweet dishes, especially if you buy color-coded rings (yes, those exist!). Plus, after six months of frequent use (or twelve to eighteen months of less frequent use), the ring tends to wear out and needs to be replaced.

EXTRA INNER POT: Using your inner pot as Tupperware but need to cook something new in the Instant Pot? A second inner pot comes to the rescue!

NONSTICK INNER POT: If you prefer to cook with minimal oil, a nonstick inner pot is useful, as the stainless steel inner pot typically requires a decent amount of oil when using the Sauté setting.

STAINLESS STEEL STEAMER RACK: The Instant Pot comes with a stainless steel steamer rack, which is necessary for pot-in-pot cooking (i.e., when you cook food inside of a pan that sits on top of the steamer rack inside the inner pot). If you have an older model, your steamer rack might be flat without handles, which makes it much more difficult to remove pots from inside the inner pot. I recommend purchasing a steamer rack with handles.

WIRE STEAMER BASKET: A steamer basket that fits your Instant Pot model is necessary for steaming vegetables and other delicate items that you don't want to boil. I prefer a deep, wide-rim mesh basket steamer.

TEMPERED GLASS LID: This is useful if you use the Slow Cook setting, or if you're sautéing something and either need to trap the steam or don't want sauce splattered on you but still want to see what's going on in the Instant Pot. Also, it turns the inner pot into a food storage vessel that you can leave in your fridge.

7-INCH ROUND PANS: 7-inch pans fit perfectly in a 6-quart Instant Pot and are essential for pot-in-pot cooking. I use a 7-inch springform pan with removable sides for cakes, cheesecakes, and even lasagna. I've had great results with the Hiware 7-inch nonstick springform pan. I also use a 7-cup round glass storage dish and/or 1½-quart ceramic soufflé-style dish for casseroles and bread puddings. If you have an 8-quart Instant Pot, you can use these 7-inch pans or 8-inch round pans.

OTHER CAKE PANS: If you want to make an adorable Bundt cake, like my Lemon Poppy Seed Bundt Cake (page 297), you'll need a 6-cup Bundt pan for the 6-quart Instant Pot models. And for baking banana bread and loaf cakes, you'll need a 7¾ × 3¾-inch loaf pan or silicone springform loaf pan.

POT HOLDER GRIPS: These clip on to the inner pot or pans inside the inner pot and make it easy to lift out hot pans and dishes.

FOIL SLING: This is not something you can purchase (to my knowledge). It's a homemade contraption that makes it easy and more stable to lift up hot and/or heavy pans out of the inner pot. Simply take a 20-inch length of heavy-duty foil and fold it lengthwise into thirds until you have a long strip. Place the foil sling underneath the steamer rack or pan and use the handles to both lower the steamer rack or pan into the Instant Pot and lift them out after cooking.

FOIL: Useful for said foil sling and for covering pans in the Instant Pot to prevent condensation from dripping onto the food.

PARCHMENT PAPER: Lining cake pans with parchment paper makes removal much easier. That way you can elegantly plate your cake instead of eating forkfuls directly from the pan.

FLAT-ENDED WOODEN SPATULA OR SILICONE SCRAPER: When you need to scrape up the browned bits after using the Sauté setting, either of these tools comes in handy.

FOOD PROCESSOR: An essential in any home kitchen, this is particularly useful for pureeing cooked ingredients (i.e., beans into hummus) and making salad dressings, sauces, vegan cheese substitutes, and dessert fillings.

HIGH-POWERED BLENDER OR IMMERSION BLENDER: Another kitchen essential, especially in a healthy, plant-based kitchen, a high-powered blender and/or immersion blender are particularly useful for pureeing soups and making sauces. With an immersion blender, you can puree directly in the inner pot of the Instant Pot.

My Approach to Cooking

Growing up, I loved watching the Food Network. The single most important principle I learned from these countless hours of instruction was how to layer flavors—how to combine, expand, and deepen the flavors in a dish with seasonings, spices, fats, liquids, and acids at different stages. Here is a distillation of those principles that are particularly apt for cooking with the Instant Pot.

SALT IS NOT THE ENEMY

The human body needs salt to survive. Most of our sodium intake comes from processed foods and drinks, not from homemade food cooked with salt. Accordingly, don't be afraid of seasoning food with salt!

LAYER SALT AS YOU GO

When you're using the Sauté function, add salt a little bit at a time at each stage of cooking to build flavors, instead of salting food at the end. Layering salt unlocks flavors and aromas at various stages and enables us to taste the inherent flavors in food. A dish that is salted at the end tastes salty; a dish that is salted throughout tastes well seasoned.

At first glance, you might see a recipe and think *"that seems like a lot of salt."* However, all of the recipes in this book, except for a few desserts, call for cooking with kosher salt, the least salty type of salt (more on that on page 29). And, the Instant Pot tends to sop up more flavor than traditional stovetop cooking, so a little extra salt is sometimes needed. Finally, the vast majority of the recipes in this book prescribe specific quantities of salt, though I do recommend tasting and adjusting the seasonings as you progress through the cooking process.

BEGIN WITH AROMATICS

It is very convenient to dump everything in the Instant Pot, turn on the Pressure Cook button, and walk away. And there are several recipes in this book that do just that. However, the Sauté button exists for a reason. Starting a recipe by sautéing aromatics (onions and garlic; maybe chile peppers and ginger, carrots and celery, or scallions and bell peppers) in oil imparts depth of flavor and unleashes flavor compounds that might otherwise lie dormant. Sure, it takes a few extra minutes, but it is always worth it.

SPICES AND HERBS ARE YOUR FRIEND

Spices and herbs, especially fresh herbs and whole spices, can elevate a basic dish into a sensual gastronomical experience that will delight and surprise your taste buds. Bay leaves subtly permeate soups and stews with a slightly bitter, tea-like aroma, while cumin seeds lend an earthy, musky fragrance and deep warmth. Fresh basil adds delicate yet pungent notes of anise and pepper to a finished dish, while freshly grated nutmeg infuses savory and sweet dishes alike with a spicy, bittersweet, herbal aroma. As with salt, I tend to use a slightly larger quantity of spices and herbs with Instant Pot cooking than with traditional stovetop cooking.

ADD SOME HEAT—IF YOU LIKE!

For me, chile peppers (in dried and fresh form) are an essential building block of flavor—they awaken the taste buds and offer an enchanting contrast between sweet and salty foods. However, since many people are sensitive to spicy food, my recipes offer suggestions on how to tone down the heat if you prefer. For fresh chiles, the heat is concentrated in the seeds and membranes, so removing those parts will significantly mitigate the heat. Jalapeño peppers are on the mild end of the chile pepper spectrum, so stick to those for a milder heat. If a recipe calls for crushed red pepper flakes or cayenne pepper, you can use a smaller quantity, or omit them entirely if you are very sensitive to spice. And finally, I try to stick to peppers that are commonly available at most supermarkets, but if you are a chile pepper aficionado, feel free to substitute with your favorite peppers!

FEAR NOT FAT

Fat is an essential element in cooking. It is what enables us to taste the full gamut of flavors and textures—from deep brown caramelized onions and flaky pie crusts to creamy pasta sauces and sharp vinaigrettes.

But if you want to minimize the amount of oil, a nonstick inner pot will be very useful when using the Sauté setting. I also recommend trying out one recipe and substituting half or all of the cooking oil with vegetable broth or water, and observe the results before replicating with another recipe.

DEGLAZE AS YOU GO

The brown gunk stuck to the bottom of your inner pot after a sauté session? Those are the caramelized bits from the food you've just cooked (most likely veggies since this is a meat-free cookbook). Deglazing the pan—which means adding a thin liquid such as vegetable broth, water, or wine to the hot pan and scraping up those browned bits with a wooden spatula or silicone scraper—helps those food remnants melt into the background and boosts the flavors in any savory dish.

Deglazing doesn't just amplify flavors, however. It's also a critical step in many Instant Pot recipes (after sautéing, before pressure cooking), particularly recipes that don't contain a large volume of liquid. If you leave a lot of browned bits on the bottom and don't add a lot of liquid, it can block the machine's heat sensor, resulting in that pesky "burn" notification. More on that on page 35.

DON'T FORGET THE ACID

Many of the savory recipes in this book end with a splash of acidity. Acid brings nuance and balance, offers contrast, and enlivens flavors, particularly in cooked dishes that are heavy or rich, such as those made in the Instant Pot. A splash of balsamic vinegar in a lentil soup, a squeeze of fresh lime juice in an Indian curry, and a splash of white wine in a creamy risotto—these seemingly minor additions not only perk up the freshness of a dish but also release aromas that might otherwise remain latent.

DIETARY RESTRICTIONS? I'VE GOT YOU COVERED

Some recipes in this book are decidedly healthier than others, but every single recipe is 100 percent vegan. I recognize that many people who eat a vegan or primarily plant-based diet might also eschew gluten, nuts, soy, and/or sugar, for allergy or health reasons, so every recipe specifies whether these allergens or ingredients are present.

Stocking Your Kitchen for Success

Here are some essentials that will help you master vegan cooking, especially with the Instant Pot.

PANTRY AND FRIDGE ESSENTIALS

NUTRITIONAL YEAST: A star ingredient in a vegan kitchen, nutritional yeast tastes much better than it sounds (deactivated yeast). It has a cheesy flavor and mouthfeel, making it the perfect ingredient in vegan cheese and egg substitutes, and even soups and savory porridges. It's fortified with vitamin B12, a vitamin not found in plant-based foods, so you can enjoy mac and cheese *and* do your body good.

TAMARI (GLUTEN-FREE SOY SAUCE): Tamari is a wheat-free soy sauce, and I use it instead of soy sauce because it has a richer yet more balanced flavor and imparts a deep umami flavor. I use reduced-sodium tamari so I can control the salty flavor more precisely. Tamari tends to be less salty than soy sauce, so if you substitute soy sauce, keep that in mind. Also, most varieties of tamari are gluten-free, whereas soy sauce is not.

VEGETABLE BROTH: Many Instant Pot recipes require a fair amount of liquid, and vegetable broth lends more flavor than water. The first chapter in this book contains a recipe for a rich vegetable broth that will add even more flavor to your dishes, but I typically use a store-bought, organic, low-sodium vegetable broth in most of my recipes with great results.

MISO PASTE: Made from fermented soybeans, miso paste is bursting with the rich, complex notes of umami. It is salty, savory, meaty, and nutty and adds a notable depth of flavor to dishes ranging from vegan cheeses to soups to risottos. All of my recipes call for white or yellow miso paste, which are the mildest and most versatile varieties.

NUTS AND SEEDS: I use nuts for various reasons. Raw cashews liquefy into creamy goodness and make both for luscious cheesecakes and rich cashew cream. Toasted almonds add a slight smoky flavor in savory dishes. Pine nuts and pecans add a buttery finish to crisp salads. Seeds are equally diverse, from toasted sesame seeds that add a nutty finish in Asian dishes to chia seeds that thicken jams and compotes. Nuts and seeds help make plant-based food taste rich and satisfying, and I always have a wide variety in my pantry. Since they can go rancid quickly, store large quantities in the fridge or freezer for a longer shelf life.

NUT AND SEED BUTTERS: Nut-based butters are important enough in a vegan's life to merit a separate section. I prefer store-bought varieties made with minimal ingredients (ideally, just nuts and salt), though if you have the time, feel free to make your own. The four varieties you'll find in this book are almond,

cashew, and peanut butter, along with tahini (sesame seed paste). Nut and seed butters are great in both sweet and savory dishes (I love using tahini and cashew butter for salad dressings) and lend a rich and creamy mouthfeel.

CANNED COCONUT MILK: This is the vegan secret behind many of the luxurious curries, creamy soups, and silky desserts in this book, as it perfectly mimics cream and milk in both savory and sweet dishes. You can find canned coconut milk in full-fat and "lite" varieties, and each recipe specifies which type to use. There is variation among brands—some have more of the thick coconut cream relative to the thinner liquid, whereas others are a bit grainy. As a general rule, try shaking the can at the grocery store, and if it feels like one solid mass (as opposed to a lot of liquid), you have a good can. For recipes where you need both the cream and liquid, you'll need to stir the can to evenly incorporate. And if a recipe calls for "coconut cream," that's the thick, solid portion, though you can also buy canned coconut cream separately. You may need to refrigerate the can of coconut milk in order to firm the cream up. I always keep a few cans in both my fridge and pantry so I can have either variety at the ready.

NONDAIRY MILK: I can't remember the last time I had dairy milk, so plant-based milk *is*, in my mind, milk. Most of the recipes that use plant-based milk call for almond milk, as it's the most readily available option, but nearly all of these recipes will work just as well with oat milk, soy milk, cashew milk, or coconut milk (coconut milk that comes in a carton is referred to as "drinking milk," while the canned variety is called "cooking milk").

CANNED TOMATOES AND TOMATO PASTE: Canned tomatoes—whether whole, diced, or crushed—are very useful in soups, stews, curries, and other Instant Pot recipes. And tomato paste, with its concentrated flavor, brings a rich umami flavor to savory dishes. Unfortunately, thick ingredients like crushed tomatoes and tomato sauce have a tendency to burn in the Instant Pot, so here are a few tips to avoid that: First, if you sauté ingredients before pressure cooking, scrape up those browned bits from the bottom of the pot before adding any thick sauces. Second, the thicker a sauce or tomato product is, the more liquid it needs to prevent scorching, so tailor accordingly if you modify a recipe. Third, add the thick, saucy ingredients at the end of the cooking process and let them sit on top of everything else without mixing in. (The directions in my recipes call out this step where necessary. I find that the tomatoes are less likely to mix into everything if you pour them as low and close to the pot as possible and not from high above.) Finally, some very viscous products like canned tomato sauce and jarred marinara sauce may simply need to be added after pressure-cooking, as in my Tofu Cauliflower Tikka Masala (page 247), or used in the pot-in-pot cooking method, as in my Breakfast Enchilada Casserole (page 77).

MUSTARD: I rely on Dijon mustard and whole-grain mustard as emulsifiers in vinaigrettes or when a sauce needs a little tangy kick. I use whole mustard seeds in Indian curries and dals.

CORNSTARCH AND ARROWROOT POWDER: Cornstarch and arrowroot powder are thickening agents, and I use them at the end of a recipe to thicken sauces and jams, or in desserts. Arrowroot is grain-free, more naturally processed, and produces a silkier mouthfeel and glossy appearance. In recipes where it's possible to use either, I've indicated so.

TOFU: I know, a lot of people hate tofu, but I am convinced that these haters have never had well-prepared tofu. Buy an organic variety to avoid GMOs, and learn when to use which variety: Silken soft tofu is for blending into creamy desserts or smoothies, and extra-firm and firm tofu are for sautéing and frying. The latter varieties should almost always be pressed to remove excess water and seasoned liberally. Once pureed or crumbled up, tofu mimics cheese remarkably well, and you'll find a few tofu-based cheese recipes in this book.

SALT AND SEASONINGS

KOSHER SALT: As I mention in the previous section, most of my recipes call for kosher salt, which is an inexpensive, coarse-grained salt, and I highly recommend it for cooking. I've tested all of the recipes in this book with Diamond Crystal kosher salt, which comes in a red box or container. I like using it because it has a light, flaky texture and dissolves very quickly, which makes it less likely that a dish will end up oversalted. In fact, even when I've been *very* generous with this salt, I have never oversalted a recipe, which is why I recommend it for perfectly seasoned food. I advise against using table salt, which is about twice as salty (by volume) as the kosher salt I use. It's heavily processed, adds no nuance in flavor, and honestly, it just tastes bad.

FINE SEA SALT: Since it's pricier than kosher salt, I reserve fine sea salt as a finishing salt or where I want a more delicate texture, as in desserts. (Keep in mind, fine sea salt is almost twice as salty as Diamond Crystal kosher salt.) I use a flaky sea salt for fancy garnishes.

KALA NAMAK (BLACK SALT): A Himalayan rock salt with a very pungent smell similar to eggs, I add a bit to tofu-based dishes when I want that distinctive eggy taste, though it is not necessary. You can find it in South Asian grocers or online.

SPICES AND HERBS

A well-stocked spice cabinet is an essential in any healthy kitchen. Spices and herbs, when used harmoniously, add a world of flavor, and without any calories. In many instances, fresh herbs are preferable to dried, as they taste better and have more flavor. Since pressure-cooked dishes are often robust and rich, many of my recipes end with fresh herbs, which bring a nice balance. I recommend stocking your pantry with your favorite spices

and experimenting with some new ones, especially whole spices. If you have an electric coffee or spice grinder or mortar and pestle, you can easily grind most whole spices. While there is nothing wrong with store-bought pre-ground spices, there is no comparison to the intoxicating aroma from freshly ground whole spices. To maximize shelf life, store spices in a cool, dry, dark place (not above the stove!) and in glass containers.

COOKING FATS

OLIVE OIL AND EXTRA-VIRGIN OLIVE OIL: A regular, organic olive oil is my go-to cooking oil. While you might be averse to cooking with olive oil due to its relatively low smoke point, its smoke point is higher than the Instant Pot's maximum temperature, so don't hesitate to use it. Reserve the nicer, pricier extra-virgin variety for vinaigrettes and certain baked goods or for drizzling on salads, grain bowls, cooked vegetables, dips, etc. I like a variety with slightly fruity, slightly grassy undertones. I specify which kind of olive oil to use in each recipe.

COCONUT OIL: Similar to olive oil, coconut oil's relatively low smoke point is still higher than the Instant Pot's maximum temperature. I use unrefined virgin coconut oil only when a coconut-y flavor is desired (e.g., a Thai or Indian curry or a coconut whipped cream). When a neutral taste is preferred, I use refined coconut oil. Coconut oil is solid at room temperature (unless your kitchen is warm, as in the summer), so if a dessert recipe calls for melted coconut oil, you'll want to bring the other liquid ingredients to room temperature so they don't seize up and solidify the melted oil.

GRAPESEED OIL AND SUNFLOWER OIL: These are my preferred oils for neutral-flavored, high-heat cooking, but you can substitute any neutral oil you prefer.

VEGAN BUTTER: I use this when a recipe will benefit from the rich buttery taste of, well, butter. I like Earth Balance (both original and soy-free varieties), as it has a nice, rich taste and works as a 1:1 substitute for butter in savory and (most) sweet recipes, and is widely available.

ACIDS

LEMON AND LIME JUICE: Look no further than nature for some of the best acidic ingredients. And when I say *nature*, I mean use *fresh* lemons and limes, not those little plastic green bottles of juice made with preservatives and citrus oil. Freshly squeezed tastes a million times better. To preserve the potent flavor, it's best to squeeze citrus juice right before you use it.

APPLE CIDER VINEGAR: This is my go-to neutral vinegar and it has a variety of applications. I use it in vinaigrettes, to finish beans and vegetables, and as an aid to leavening in baking.

BALSAMIC VINEGAR: This is the vinegar I use when a dish needs a touch of sweetness and richness. Many of my recipes call for a "high-quality" balsamic vinegar, and I know that makes me sound like a food snob, but hear me out. The cheap stuff doesn't add any complexity of flavor and just tastes sour and tangy. You're looking for an aged vinegar (aged for at least twelve years) that has a viscous, velvety, and glossy texture.

RICE VINEGAR: This is my acid of choice for most Asian-inspired recipes. Unlike the bolder vinegars found in Western cooking, rice vinegar has a subtle, delicately sweet flavor.

SWEETENERS

PURE MAPLE SYRUP: This is the sweetener I use most frequently. I always have a large jug of organic maple syrup on hand and use it in breakfasts and desserts or when a savory dish needs balance.

COCONUT NECTAR AND COCONUT SUGAR: These sweeteners come from the nutrient-rich sap from the flowers of a coconut tree and are unrefined alternatives to sugar that have a low glycemic index. Coconut nectar has a tropical scent and thick viscosity, and I reserve this pricy stuff when I want the texture of honey. Coconut sugar has a mild caramel flavor and is similar in texture to brown sugar, though a bit coarser. It doesn't behave the exact same way as refined sugar but can often be substituted in a 1:1 ratio.

AGAVE NECTAR: I typically reach for agave nectar when I want a liquid sweetener with a pleasant but neutral taste. If you avoid agave, each recipe that calls for it offers an alternative sweetener. When making substitutions, keep in mind that agave is a bit sweeter than white sugar, brown sugar, and maple syrup.

ORGANIC CANE SUGAR: Sometimes plain old sugar is necessary to achieve the right texture, particularly with baking. I always use organic cane sugar instead of standard granulated white sugar. For one, it's a bit less processed, and two, some white sugar is still processed with animal bone char, and buying organic is the only way to ensure that your sugar is vegan.

ORGANIC BROWN SUGAR: The same unfortunate truth about bone char applies to brown sugar, which is made by adding molasses to white sugar, so I always buy organic. Where possible, I provide a less refined sweetener alternative.

BEANS AND LENTILS

A well-stocked vegan pantry includes a variety of beans and lentils, which are packed with protein, fiber, and other nutrients. I used to eat exclusively canned beans (hi, yes, I'm lazy), but the Instant Pot makes it so much easier to cook them, and the flavor of home-cooked beans is incomparable. With the Instant

Pot, there's no need to soak the beans (though some recipes do suggest soaking to achieve the best texture and/or significantly reduce the cook time), no need to wait for hours of simmering, and no need to stress about burning the pot. But if beans make you toot (hey, it happens), soaking can aid with digestion. For the sake of convenience and/or ease, a few recipes do call for canned beans, but you can always use beans cooked from scratch.

Like beans, lentils are one of the healthiest foods on the planet, from soft red lentils that are perfect in curries and soups to elegant French green lentils that stay firm even in the high-pressure environment of the Instant Pot. For precise cook times for the most popular variety of beans and lentils, consult the Cook Time charts on page 38.

GRAINS

One of the most inexpensive staples in a plant-based diet is grains—preferably whole grains, but if I'm being honest, there's always room for pasta. From the chewy bite and earthy taste of farro to the nutty taste and delicate texture of millet, there is a vast array of delicious and nourishing whole grains, many of which are underrated and underutilized (yes, there is life beyond quinoa!). Cooking grains in the Instant Pot requires less time and less babysitting than on the stove, which means you can even squeeze in a workout while dinner cooks (or a nap, or watch a Netflix show, no judgment). For precise cook times for the most popular variety of grains, consult the Cook Time charts on page 37.

Frequently Asked Questions

Q: **How long does it take for the Instant Pot to come to pressure?**

A: The amount of time it takes for the Instant Pot to come to pressure will vary based on the amount of liquid, as well as the volume, temperature, and type of ingredients in a given recipe. A large pot of chili will take longer to pressurize than a small pot of rice. And the more liquid used, the longer it will take to come to pressure. The same applies to the temperature of the ingredients. Using warm vegetable broth instead of cold, for instance, will speed up the process. Adding a large quantity of frozen vegetables will slow down the process of building pressure.

Q: **How long does it take for the Instant Pot to release pressure naturally?**

A: As with coming to pressure, the amount of time it takes to release pressure will vary on the amount of food and liquid, as well as the type of ingredients. Generally, dishes with a large quantity of liquid or large volume will take longer to release pressure naturally. You can speed up the process by placing a wet kitchen towel on the metal portion of the Instant Pot lid.

Q: **My Instant Pot came to pressure but it just says ON and there's no timer countdown. What happened?**

A: Nothing to worry about! There will be some time lapse between the time the Instant Pot comes to pressure and when the countdown begins. For some dishes, it might be only 30 seconds, and for others, it might be a few minutes.

Q: **How do I adjust the cook time? How do I adjust the pressure setting? How do I adjust the heat level?**

A: To adjust the cook time, select a cooking function (i.e., Pressure Cook) and then use the +/– buttons to increase or decrease the cook time. To change the pressure setting on the DUO Plus or newer DUO models, use the Pressure Level button once you've selected a cooking program. On other models, use the Adjust button to switch between High and Low pressure settings. And to adjust the heat level when using the Sauté setting, on the DUO Plus or newer DUO models, simply hit the Sauté button again to reach More or Less heat; on most other models, use the Adjust button.

Q: **Many of your recipes say to use the Pressure Cook setting, but I don't have one! What do I use instead?**

A: On many models of the Instant Pot, including older versions of the Instant Pot DUO, the Pressure Cook setting is called the Manual setting—they are interchangeable.

Q: **The recipe says to pressure cook for 10 minutes, so why did it take longer than 10 minutes to cook?**

A: The Instant Pot's cook time countdown begins only once the machine has come to pressure, just like a traditional pressure cooker. The cook time (i.e., 10 minutes) does not include the time that the machine takes to pressurize, which will vary with each recipe.

Q: **How much liquid do I need to add to the Instant Pot?**

A: The amount of liquid needed varies on the type of ingredients used, including the volume of food and thickness of the liquid. Typically, the bare minimum liquid necessary (for a 6-quart model) is ½ cup, though some vegetables and fruits emit enough water that you can use less. Many recipes require at least 1 cup, or even 2 cups, of liquid.

Q: **My Instant Pot did not seal or my Instant Pot sealed but the display says "burn." What gives?**

A: There are several reasons why your Instant Pot might not have sealed or displays the "burn" notification.

- *What is your pressure release knob set to?*
  Solution: Verify the knob is set to Sealing, not Venting. I recommend getting in the habit of always turning the knob to the Sealing position as soon as you seal the lid.

- *Is your sealing ring properly installed? If it's missing, not perfectly in place, or worn out, the Instant Pot won't come to pressure and will likely start leaking.*
  Solution: Check the sealing ring and get in the habit of always checking it before you seal the lid. Also, clean the sealing ring after every use to remove debris that can prevent the ring from properly sealing.

- *Did you add enough liquid to the pot?*
  Solution: If not, quick-release the pressure, open the pot, and add a bit more liquid (if it won't ruin the recipe), and continue pressure cooking where you left off.

- *Did you brown lots of food on the Sauté setting (yum!), but forgot to deglaze the pan?*
  Solution: Quick-release the pressure, open the pot, and use a silicone scraper or flat-ended wooden spatula to scrape up any browned bits on the bottom. Oftentimes, those browned bits block the heat sensor, so scraping them up might solve the problem. Once you do that, continue pressure cooking where you left off.

- *Did you add a lot of thick liquids and not enough of a thin liquid? Some very thick liquids like tomato sauce and marinara sauce can cause the Instant Pot to burn.*
  Solution: For tips on avoiding this, see page 24.

Q: **Should I ever put the ingredients in the Instant Pot without the inner pot?**

A: Nope! Please don't do that.

Q: **Why can't I open my Instant Pot?**

A: When the Instant Pot is at pressure, a safety mechanism prevents you from opening the lid. You can open the lid only after all of the pressure has been released and steam no longer emerges. Once this happens, the floating valve will drop, indicating you are now able to open the lid.

Q: What is pot-in-pot cooking?

A: Pot-in-pot cooking (PIP, for short) is when you cook food in a pot set inside the inner pot. You can bake a cake or a casserole in the Instant Pot by mixing the ingredients in a separate pot (a springform cake pan, a Pyrex glass dish, etc.) and placing that pot on top of the steamer rack in the Instant Pot. You'll need to add some water to the bottom of the Instant Pot, which enables the cake or casserole to be steamed instead of directly pressure-cooked. It also makes for much easier cleanup.

Q: How do I clean my Instant Pot?

A: First things first, you should wash the sealing ring and antiblock shield underneath the lid after every use. Didn't know that? Don't feel bad—I only figured that out after I started writing this book. With regular use, you'll need to replace your sealing ring after six to eighteen months. The sealing ring, along with the inner pot, lid, and steamer rack are all dishwasher-safe (yay!). The Instant Pot hardware just needs to be wiped with a damp cloth.

Q: I really burned the heck out of my inner pot. Is it salvageable?

A: It just might be! I have scorched my inner pot more than a few times. My tried-and-true cleanup method is to sprinkle 2 tablespoons baking soda directly on the scorched bottom, add 4 cups water, and use the Pressure Cook/Manual setting at high pressure for 5 minutes with a quick pressure release. Drain the dirty brown water, rinse out the pot, and scrub it down with a sponge and some dish soap. Voilà!

Q: If I want to double a recipe, do I need to double the cook time? If I want to make only half of a recipe, do I need to reduce the cook time by half?

A: The cook time for each recipe depends on the thickness and density of the ingredients, rather than the weight, so doubling a recipe (or making just half of it) typically doesn't require a change in the cook time. Here are a few things to keep in mind. First, always stay below the Instant Pot's maximum capacity line. Second, when you add a greater volume of ingredients, the Instant Pot will take longer to come to pressure, and vice versa. Third, if doubling the recipe does affect the thickness of the ingredients (i.e., doubling a cake recipe but using the same cake pan), you will need to increase the cook time.

Cook Time Charts

These charts are written to be helpful guidelines, but not firm rules. That's because the precise cooking time for each food will depend on various factors—the weight and density of the ingredients, the temperature of the ingredients, how fresh the ingredients are, etc. If these ranges of time confuse or scare you, just start with the lower end of the range and then check for doneness. You can always add a few more minutes at the end if the food is not fully cooked. These cook times are designed to be used at high pressure, unless otherwise noted.

──────────────── GRAINS ────────────────

Name	Cook Time	Water:Grain Ratio
Amaranth	6 to 7 minutes	2:1
Barley, hulled	22 to 25 minutes	3:1
Barley, pearl	20 minutes	2:1
Brown rice	20 to 22 minutes	1¼:1
Buckwheat (groats)	3 minutes	1¾:1
Couscous	2 to 4 minutes	1¾:1
Couscous, Israeli/Pearl	3 minutes	1¼:1
Farro, pearled or semi-pearled	6 to 8 minutes	1¼:1
Millet	9 to 12 minutes	1¾:1
Oats, rolled	3 minutes	2:1
Oats, steel-cut	10 to 12 minutes	2½:1
Polenta (cornmeal)	8 to 10 minutes	4:1
Quinoa	1 minute	1¼:1
White rice	4 to 6 minutes	1:1
White rice, basmati	4 to 6 minutes	1:1
White rice, jasmine	4 to 6 minutes	1:1
Wheat berries	30 to 35 minutes	3:1
Wild rice	25 minutes	1½:1

For all types of rice and many grains, you'll want to allow a combination pressure release (at least 10 minutes natural release, followed by a quick release). For porridge-style grains, a complete natural pressure release works best. For delicate, quick-cooking grains, try a natural pressure release for 5 minutes before performing a quick pressure release. To prevent lots of foaming, don't fill the Instant Pot more than halfway when cooking a pot of grains.

Name	Cook Time (unsoaked beans)	Cook Time (soaked beans)
Baby lima beans	30 minutes	7 to 10 minutes
Black beans	22-25 minutes	8 to 10 minutes
Black-eyed peas	15 to 20 minutes	6 to 8 minutes
Cannellini (white kidney)	35 to 40 minutes	7 to 9 minutes
Chickpeas (garbanzo beans)	35 to 40 minutes	10 to 15 minutes
Kidney beans	30 minutes	7 to 9 minutes
Navy beans	20 to 25 minutes	9 to 12 minutes
Pinto beans	30 minutes	7 to 10 minutes

The cook time for beans will vary widely depending on how long the beans have been stored (fresher beans take less time to cook) and the temperature of the liquid (warm liquid takes less time to come to pressure). While there's no need to soak beans before cooking them in the Instant Pot, soaking does yield beans with the most even texture and fewer split beans (and aids with digestion for some). To soak 1 pound beans, cover with 8 cups water and soak overnight or for 8 to 10 hours. To prevent lots of foaming, don't fill the Instant Pot more than halfway when cooking a pot of beans.

Basic Recipe for Beans: Combine 1 pound beans + 6 cups water or vegetable broth + 2½ teaspoons kosher salt + freshly cracked black pepper in the Instant Pot. Use the Pressure Cook setting at high pressure according to the times listed above. Allow a natural pressure release or a combination pressure release (10 to 15 minutes natural release, followed by a quick release) to avoid getting bean splatter all over your face and clothes.

Name	Cook Time
Black beluga lentils	6 to 9 minutes
Brown lentils	6 to 10 minutes*
French green (Puy) lentils	6 to 8 minutes
Green lentils	6 to 10 minutes*
Red lentils	2 minutes
Split peas (green and yellow)	4 to 6 minutes
Yellow split lentils	2 to 3 minutes

To keep brown and green lentils on the firm side, use the lower end of the cooking time range. Black beluga and French green (Puy) lentils tend to hold their shape well, while red lentils and yellow split lentils get especially soft (great for soups and curries).

Basic Recipe for Lentils: Combine 1 cup lentils + 1¾ cups water or vegetable broth + ½ teaspoon kosher salt + freshly cracked black pepper in the Instant Pot. Use the Pressure Cook setting at high pressure according to the times listed above. Allow a natural pressure release or a combination pressure release (10 to 15 minutes natural release, followed by a quick release).

VEGETABLES

Name	Cook Time (Fresh)	Cook Time (Frozen)
Acorn squash, halved	5 to 7 minutes	n/a
Artichokes, whole and trimmed	8 to 12 minutes	10 to 14 minutes
Asparagus	1 to 2 minutes (low pressure)	2 to 3 minutes
Beans, green or wax	1 to 2 minutes (low pressure)	2 to 3 minutes
Beets, whole (large)	20 to 25 minutes	25 to 30 minutes
Beets, whole (small)	10 to 12 minutes	12 to 14 minutes
Bell peppers, chopped or sliced	1 to 2 minutes	2 to 3 minutes
Broccoli, florets	2 minutes (low pressure) or 0 minutes (high pressure)	2 to 3 minutes
Brussels sprouts, whole or halved	2 to 4 minutes	4 to 5 minutes
Butternut squash, chopped	5 to 7 minutes	7 to 9 minutes
Butternut squash, halved (2½ pounds)	10 to 13 minutes	n/a
Cabbage, chopped	2 to 3 minutes	3 to 4 minutes
Cabbage, wedges	3 to 4 minutes	4 to 5 minutes
Carrots, sliced or shredded	2 to 3 minutes	3 to 4 minutes
Carrots, whole or chunked	5 to 6 minutes	6 to 8 minutes
Cauliflower, florets	2 minutes	3 minutes
Celery, chopped	2 to 3 minutes	3 to 4 minutes
Collard greens	4 to 5 minutes	5 to 6 minutes
Corn (kernels)	1 to 2 minutes	2 to 3 minutes
Corn (on the cob, shucked)	2 to 3 minutes	4 to 5 minutes
Eggplant, chopped	2 to 3 minutes	n/a
Endive, whole	1 to 2 minutes	n/a
Green peas	1 to 2 minutes	2 to 3 minutes
Leafy geens (kale, spinach, beet greens), chopped	2 to 3 minutes	3 to 5 minutes
Leeks, chopped	2 to 3 minutes	3 to 4 minutes
Mixed vegetables, chopped (frozen blend)	n/a	0 to 1 minutes
Onions, sliced	2 to 3 minutes	3 to 4 minutes
Peas, sugar snap or snow (whole, in pod)	1 to 2 minutes	2 to 3 minutes
Potatoes, cubed	3 to 4 minutes	4 to 5 minutes

Name	Cook Time (Fresh)	Cook Time (Frozen)
Potatoes, fingerling	5 minutes	n/a
Potatoes, whole (6 to 7 ounces)	10 to 12 minutes	n/a
Pumpkin, large slices	8 to 10 minutes	10 to 14 minutes
Pumpkin, whole (3 to 4 pounds)	13 to 16 minutes	n/a
Rutabaga, chopped	4 to 5 minutes	5 to 6 minutes
Spaghetti squash, whole (2½ to 3 pounds)	7 minutes	n/a
Spinach	1 to 2 minutes	2 to 3 minutes
Sweet potatoes, cubed	3 to 4 minutes	4 to 5 minutes
Sweet potatoes, whole (large)	13 to 17 minutes	n/a
Sweet potatoes, whole (small)	10 to 12 minutes	n/a
Tomatoes, quartered or chopped	2 minutes	3 to 4 minutes
Tomatoes, whole	3 to 5 minutes	5 to 7 minutes
Turnips, chopped	3 to 4 minutes	4 to 5 minutes
Zucchini or summer squash, chopped	2 to 3 minutes	3 to 4 minutes

For most vegetables, you'll want to perform a quick pressure release to avoid overcooking. For delicate vegetables (e.g., asparagus, broccoli), I recommend starting out with the Steam setting at low pressure. When steaming vegetables, you'll need to pour 1 cup water in the inner pot and place the vegetables in a steamer basket. For frozen vegetables, there's no need to defrost them before cooking. Since there is great variability in the size of vegetables, use these cook times as a guideline and adjust accordingly.

1

PANTRY BASICS, SAUCES, AND DIPS

—

This chapter is filled with what I call flavor-boosters. There are pantry basics and sauces that give life to other dishes, from a hearty vegetable broth to a creamy cheesy sauce, as well as stand-alone dips that pack a lot more flavor than store-bought condiments and will take your snacking game to the next level.

MUSHROOM BROTH

makes about 9 cups	gluten-free, nut-free, no added sugar

When you first open your Instant Pot after cooking this mushroom broth, your senses will be overwhelmed with an intoxicating aroma, an aroma that can only be described as the purest essence of mushroom. It's like uncorking a perfectly aged bottle of Bordeaux and being met with a stunning sensual bouquet.

If you are a mushroom lover like I am, then you simply have to make this mushroom broth and use it in the Miso Mushroom Risotto (page 180). It takes an already delicious risotto over the top, infusing a deep umami flavor into each spoonful.

If savory tea is your thing, you can also drink this antioxidant-rich broth hot like a cup of tea. You can use it in lieu of water in noodle soups (especially udon noodle soup) or grains (especially barley), or in place of oil when sautéing vegetables. Or, for a quick meal idea, simmer the broth and add cubed tofu, baby bok choy, shiitake mushrooms, and rice noodles for a few minutes.

2 ounces dried mushrooms (shiitake, porcini, or a combination)

1 pound fresh mushrooms (any variety), diced

1 large yellow onion, roughly chopped

2 carrots, unpeeled and roughly chopped

6 garlic cloves, smashed

1 cup dry red wine (such as Pinot Noir)

3 bay leaves

6 to 8 sprigs fresh thyme

1 teaspoon whole black peppercorns

¼ cup reduced-sodium tamari or soy sauce

8 cups water

¼ teaspoon kosher salt

1. Place the dried mushrooms in a large bowl and submerge in warm water. Soak while preparing the other ingredients (for about 20 minutes). Drain the mushrooms.

2. Select the Sauté setting on the Instant Pot and after a few minutes, add the diced fresh mushrooms and onion. In order to prevent burning, stir frequently until the mushrooms begin releasing their liquid. Cook until the vegetables are softened and the mushrooms have reduced in size, 6 to 7 minutes.

3. Add the carrots, garlic, and wine. Cook, stirring, occasionally, until the liquid has mostly evaporated and the smell of alcohol has dissipated, 4 to 6 minutes.

4. Add the drained reconstituted mushrooms, bay leaves, thyme sprigs, peppercorns, tamari, water, and the salt. Stir to combine. Select the Cancel setting.

5. Secure the lid and set the Pressure Release to Sealing. Select the Pressure Cook setting at high pressure and set the cook time to 30 minutes.

6. Once the 30-minute timer has completed and beeps, allow a natural pressure release for 15 minutes and then switch the Pressure Release knob from Sealing to Venting to release any remaining steam.

7. Open the pot and, using oven mitts, remove the inner pot. Carefully strain the mushroom broth into a fine-mesh sieve set over a large bowl and discard the solids.

8. Allow the mushroom broth to cool to room temperature. Store in the refrigerator for 3 to 4 days or in the freezer for 3 months.

VEGETABLE BROTH

makes 11 to 12 cups	gluten-free, nut-free, soy-free, no added sugar

Many of the recipes in this book contain vegetable broth. And while every recipe has been designed to taste delicious using store-bought, organic, low-sodium vegetable broth, if you want to increase the deliciousness factor even more, I recommend using this easy, homemade broth when a recipe calls for vegetable broth. It adds a depth of flavor that you simply cannot get from a store-bought carton of broth.

I've included two different methods for making this vegetable broth: Method 1 is simpler, and Method 2 is tastier if you have a few extra minutes. In the latter method, the vegetables get browned and tender before the water is added, which yields a rich, complex flavor. If you use this broth instead of store-bought for a recipe in this book, you may want to ever so slightly decrease the amount of salt, as the deeper flavor means you don't need as much salt.

For the vegetable scraps, use whatever you have on hand—broccoli or cauliflower stalks, fresh herbs or their stems (such as parsley, cilantro, or dill), tough stalks from leafy greens, dried chile peppers, peels from potatoes or squash, and so on. The turmeric is optional and doesn't affect the taste, but I like to add it because, well, you can never have too many antioxidants.

1 tablespoon olive oil (for Method 2 only)

2 medium yellow onions, papery skin still on and roughly diced (14 to 16 ounces)

4 celery stalks, roughly diced (about 5 ounces)

3 large carrots, roughly diced (9 to 10 ounces)

1 cup roughly sliced mushrooms (3 to 3½ ounces)

2 to 3 cups vegetable scraps

3 bay leaves

6 garlic cloves, smashed

1½ teaspoons whole black peppercorns

10 to 12 sprigs fresh thyme

6 to 8 sprigs fresh rosemary

1½ teaspoons kosher salt

1 teaspoon ground turmeric (optional)

10 cups cold water

recipe continues

Method 1

1. Place the onions, celery, carrots, mushrooms, vegetable scraps, bay leaves, garlic, peppercorns, thyme, rosemary, salt, and turmeric (if using) in the Instant Pot. Add the water and stir to combine.

2. Secure the lid and set the Pressure Release to Sealing. Select the Pressure Cook setting at high pressure and set the cook time to 15 minutes.

3. Once the 15-minute timer has completed and beeps, allow a natural pressure release for 15 minutes and then switch the Pressure Release knob from Sealing to Venting to release any remaining steam.

4. Open the pot and, using oven mitts, remove the inner pot. Carefully strain the vegetable broth into a fine-mesh sieve sitting over a large bowl and discard the solids.

5. Allow the broth to cool to room temperature. Store in the refrigerator for 3 to 4 days or in the freezer for 3 months.

Method 2

1. Select the Sauté setting on the Instant Pot and let the pot heat up for a few minutes before adding the olive oil. Once the oil is hot, add the onions. Cook the onions, stirring occasionally, until they have deep brown spots, 7 to 8 minutes. Add the celery and carrots and cook until they start to soften, 4 to 5 minutes. Select the Cancel setting.

2. Add the mushrooms, vegetable scraps, bay leaves, garlic, peppercorns, thyme, rosemary, salt, and turmeric (if using) to the Instant Pot along with the water, and stir to combine. Secure the lid and set the Pressure Release to Sealing. Follow the remaining cooking directions outlined in Method 1 (steps 2 through 5).

VEGAN CHEESE SAUCE + VEGAN QUESO

makes 3½ to 4 cups	gluten-free, no added sugar

The last food I gave up before becoming 100 percent plant-based was cheese. I was, like many Americans, a cheese addict. In my quest to find substitutes, I learned that cashews can provide the creamy texture associated with cheese, that miso paste can deliver that irresistible umami taste, and that a generous amount of nutritional yeast can bring a cheesy, nutty mouthfeel.

While making vegan cheese may sound daunting, this sauce is actually very simple to make. Typically, nut-based cheeses require the nuts to be soaked overnight to soften them, but you can skip that step thanks to the powerful Instant Pot. Just be sure to blend the sauce for several minutes or it'll end up with small bits of unpulverized cashews.

This recipe calls for butternut squash, which lends a beautiful orange color, but if it's not available, you can substitute carrots. The taste will be slightly sweeter, but the cheese sauce will still be equally creamy and delicious. This sauce does thicken considerably as it rests, so you may want to thin it out with a bit of water or nondairy milk when reheating.

The Vegan Queso variation is the best queso or nacho-style sauce I've tried, and I'm confident you will become addicted to it. Delicious enough to eat by the spoon, but also really good in the Breakfast Enchilada Casserole (page 77), Tex-Mex Brown Rice and Lentils (page 199), and spooned on top of the Three-Bean Vegetable Chili (page 185). And, of course, drizzled on tortilla chips or sweet potato fries for nachos.

2 teaspoons olive oil, neutral-flavored oil, or cooking spray

1 cup diced butternut squash (4 to 5 ounces)

12 ounces Yukon Gold potatoes (2 medium), peeled and chopped

½ medium sweet onion, chopped

4 garlic cloves, peeled but whole

½ cup raw cashews

¾ cup nutritional yeast

2 tablespoons white or yellow miso paste

1½ teaspoons kosher salt, plus more to taste

2 tablespoons fresh lemon juice

1 cup canned "lite" or reduced-fat coconut milk, well stirred

recipe continues

1. Grease the inner pot with the oil or cooking spray to prevent sticking. Place the butternut squash, potatoes, onion, garlic, cashews, nutritional yeast, miso, salt, lemon juice, and lite coconut milk in the Instant Pot. Add 1 cup water and stir well to combine.

2. Secure the lid and set the Pressure Release to Sealing. Select the Steam setting at high pressure and set the cook time to 7 minutes.

3. Once the 7-minute timer has completed and beeps, perform a quick pressure release by carefully switching the Pressure Release knob from Sealing to Venting.

4. Open the pot and, using oven mitts, carefully pour the mixture into a high-powered blender (in batches if necessary). Remove the center cap from the blender lid (to vent steam), but cover the hole with a kitchen towel. Start at low speed and gradually work your way up to medium or medium-high and blend until the sauce is fully smooth, thick, and creamy, 2 to 3 minutes. If the sauce appears too thick, add 1 to 2 tablespoons water (or unsweetened plain nondairy milk), adding more as desired.

5. Alternatively, use an immersion blender directly in the Instant Pot for 2 to 3 minutes to puree all of the ingredients together, or until the cheese sauce is super smooth, thinning with a little additional water (or unsweetened plain nondairy milk) as desired.

6. Taste the cheese sauce for seasonings and add more salt as needed.

Vegan Queso

Add all of the ingredients for Vegan Cheese Sauce to the Instant Pot along with:

½ teaspoon smoked paprika
½ teaspoon chili powder
½ teaspoon ground cumin

Steam as directed.

After cooking, during the blending stage, add:

¼ cup sliced pickled jalapeños
¼ cup liquid brine from the jar or can of jalapeños
¼ cup salsa of your choice (mild, medium, or hot)

RESTAURANT-STYLE HUMMUS + THREE VARIATIONS

makes 3½ to 4 cups	gluten-free, nut-free, soy-free, no added sugar

The hurdle to making hummus from scratch is that few people want to deal with dried chickpeas (myself included). But, when you use the Instant Pot, it couldn't be simpler. No need to remember to soak the chickpeas overnight, no need to change the soaking liquid, no need to check the beans for doneness.

One of the secrets to ultra creamy hummus is skinning the chickpeas. As you can imagine, removing the skin from each chickpea, one by one, is a laborious task. This recipe has a "secret" to achieve that creamy texture without any of the manual labor: adding baking soda to the cooking water.

Baking soda increases the pH level of the water, making it less acidic. This can help break down the chickpeas, and along with the high pressure, it softens the chickpea skins so that they disintegrate during cooking. In case you didn't catch that, that means no work for you.

Like traditional hummus, this recipe relies exclusively on tahini instead of oil, so use the best-quality tahini you can find. Some tahini brands are chunky, which won't work here. You're looking for a smooth, creamy variety that stirs easily with a spoon.

8 ounces dried chickpeas (about 1 cup + 2 tablespoons)

1 teaspoon baking soda

2 teaspoons kosher salt, plus more to taste

¾ cup tahini

6 tablespoons fresh lemon juice (about 2 small lemons)

4 garlic cloves, roughly chopped

1½ teaspoons ground cumin

8 to 12 tablespoons ice water

OPTIONAL GARNISHES

Extra-virgin olive oil, smoked paprika, chopped Italian flat-leaf parsley

recipe continues

Roasted Red
Pepper Hummus

Restaurant-Style
Hummus

Harissa Hummus

Cilantro-Jalapeño
Hummus

1. Add the dried chickpeas to the Instant Pot and cover with 6 cups water. Stir in the baking soda and 1 teaspoon of the salt.

2. Secure the lid and set the Pressure Release to Sealing. Select the Pressure Cook setting at high pressure and set the cook time to 40 minutes.

3. Once the 40-minute timer has completed and beeps, allow a natural pressure release for 15 minutes and then switch the Pressure Release knob from Sealing to Venting to release any remaining steam.

4. Open the pot. The chickpeas should be very tender. Drain the chickpeas in a colander (discard the cooking liquid).

5. Transfer the chickpeas to a food processor and blend for 2 minutes until you have a thick paste-like puree, scraping down the sides with a silicone spatula as needed.

6. To the food processor, add the tahini, lemon juice, garlic, cumin, and the remaining 1 teaspoon salt. With the motor running, stream in the ice water, 1 tablespoon at a time, until the hummus is thick yet smooth and creamy. Taste for seasonings and add more salt, lemon juice, garlic, or cumin as needed. If the hummus is still too thick for your liking, add a tablespoon or two more of ice water.

7. Transfer the hummus to a serving bowl and cover with plastic wrap to keep it from drying out. Ideally, let it rest for 30 minutes before serving.

8. If desired, drizzle a generous amount of extra-virgin olive oil on top of the hummus and garnish with chopped parsley and smoked paprika. Store leftovers in the fridge in an airtight container for up to 1 week. Let the hummus come to room temperature before serving.

Variations:

Add these ingredients to the food processor:

❶ **Harissa Hummus:**
2 to 3 tablespoons harissa sauce or harissa paste

❷ **Cilantro-Jalapeño Hummus:**
1½ cups fresh cilantro + 4 fresh jalapeño peppers, chopped

❸ **Roasted Red Pepper Hummus:**
1 cup roasted red bell peppers, drained well and roughly chopped

GAME DAY BLACK BEAN DIP

serves 12 to 16	gluten-free, nut-free, soy-free, no added sugar

I'm not really into chips. Sure, I've eaten a whole bag of potato chips while at a party when it was the only vegan option available, but I don't ever find myself craving them. But, this dip, paired with some lightly salted tortilla chips . . . the combo is wildly addictive, even for a non-chip person like me!

Addiction aside, this protein-rich dip does make a great healthy snack option for game day, potlucks, or book clubs. And it couldn't be simpler to make—just dump everything in the Instant Pot, walk away, and then blend everything together. For ease, use an immersion blender directly inside the Instant Pot, or if you prefer an ultra smooth dip, transfer the mixture to a food processor or blender in batches and blend until thick and creamy.

Instead of making a dip, you can also serve the black beans whole. They're a little saucy, a little spicy, and a little smoky, and make the perfect filling for burritos, burrito bowls, or tacos. And the possible toppings are limitless, though my preference is to pair this dip with a spicy salsa and my Vegan Queso (page 49).

2 cups dried black beans

1 large yellow onion, diced

6 garlic cloves, minced

2 serrano peppers, finely diced (and seeded for a mild version)

1 cup loosely packed fresh cilantro, roughly chopped

1 (14.5-ounce) can crushed fire-roasted tomatoes

2 cups low-sodium vegetable broth

2 tablespoons olive oil

3 tablespoons fresh lime juice (about 1½ limes), plus more for finishing

2 teaspoons kosher salt, plus more to taste

2 teaspoons ground cumin

1 teaspoon chili powder

1 teaspoon dried oregano

1½ teaspoons smoked paprika

½ teaspoon ground coriander

⅛ teaspoon cayenne pepper (optional)

Freshly cracked black pepper to taste

OPTIONAL GARNISHES

Chopped cilantro, red onion, avocado, and/or jalapeños

Salsa of choice or hot sauce

Shredded vegan cheddar cheese or Vegan Queso (page 49)

1. Place the black beans in a colander and rinse with water. Add the rinsed beans to the Instant Pot and top with the onion, garlic, serranos, cilantro, crushed tomatoes, vegetable broth, olive oil, lime juice, salt, cumin, chili powder, oregano, smoked paprika, coriander, cayenne (if using), and black pepper and stir to combine.

2. Select the Bean/Chili setting at high pressure and set the cook time to 35 minutes.

3. Once the 35-minute timer has completed and beeps, allow a natural pressure release for 10 minutes and then switch the Pressure Release knob from Sealing to Venting to release any remaining steam.

4. Open the pot and, using an immersion blender, blend the bean mixture until it is thickened and creamy. This should take about 2 minutes. (Alternatively, transfer the mixture to a food processor or blender, in batches if necessary, and blend until smooth and creamy.)

5. Taste for seasonings and spice, adding more salt as needed. Finish with a squeeze or two of lime juice. If you want the dip to be a bit spicier, add a few drops of hot sauce or ¼ cup spicy salsa. Serve with tortilla chips.

FIERY ARRABBIATA SAUCE

makes about 7 cups	gluten-free, nut-free, soy-free option, no added sugar

The word *arrabbiata* means "angry" in Italian, referring to the spiciness of the peppers in this fiery tomato sauce. If you are a serious spicy food lover, you can make this sauce even "angrier" by adding more crushed red pepper flakes to your taste.

You'll notice that this recipe calls for using canned whole peeled tomatoes and crushing them by hand. I prefer using whole tomatoes in a sauce for two reasons: one, they are higher quality than precrushed or prediced tomatoes, and two, canned crushed tomatoes are too thick to be cooked in the Instant Pot without burning. Since the tomatoes are the star of this sauce, be sure to use high-quality San Marzano tomatoes.

If tomatoes are in season, you can use fresh tomatoes if you prefer. Dice 4 pounds tomatoes (easier yet, pulse them in a food processor until finely chopped), and add them after the crushed red pepper flakes. Fresh tomatoes will yield a lighter sauce with the taste and juice of fresh tomato, whereas canned tomatoes will create a deeper, more concentrated tomato flavor with an almost velvety texture.

Use this sauce in lieu of store-bought marinara in my One-Pot Bolognese Pasta (page 221) or Vegetable Lasagna with Basil Ricotta (page 205), as a pizza sauce, or even in a Bloody Mary.

2 (28-ounce) cans whole peeled San Marzano tomatoes

2 tablespoons extra-virgin olive oil, plus more for finishing

½ medium yellow onion, diced

1 small carrot, diced

4 garlic cloves, chopped

1 to 2 teaspoons crushed red pepper flakes, to taste (1 teaspoon for moderate heat, 2 teaspoons for spicy)

½ cup fresh basil, chopped + 2 tablespoons, finely slivered

1 sprig fresh oregano or 1 teaspoon dried oregano

¼ teaspoon kosher salt (½ teaspoon if using fresh tomatoes)

Freshly cracked black pepper

2 tablespoons tomato paste

1½ teaspoons reduced-sodium tamari or soy sauce (optional)

1 tablespoon high-quality balsamic vinegar

recipe continues

1. Pour the canned whole tomatoes into a large bowl (with the sauce) and crush the tomatoes with your hands by squeezing them through your fingers until no large pieces remain.

2. Select the Sauté setting on the Instant Pot and let the pot heat up for a few minutes before adding the olive oil. Once the oil is hot, add the onion and carrot. Cook until the vegetables are mostly softened, about 4 minutes.

3. Add the garlic and pepper flakes. Cook for 1 minute, stirring frequently to prevent burning.

4. Select the Cancel setting and pour in the crushed tomatoes, the ½ cup chopped basil, the oregano, salt, and black pepper to taste. Stir gently to combine all of the ingredients. Spoon the tomato paste on top but do not stir, to prevent burning.

5. Secure the lid and set the Pressure Release to Sealing. Select the Pressure Cook setting at high pressure and set the cook time to 10 minutes.

6. Once the 10-minute timer has completed and beeps, perform a quick pressure release by carefully switching the Pressure Release knob from Sealing to Venting.

7. Open the pot, remove the oregano sprig, and stir in the tamari (if using) and balsamic vinegar. Using an immersion blender, blend the sauce until it has a thick, chunky texture. (Alternatively, blend the sauce in batches in a high-powered blender. Be sure to remove the center cap from the blender lid to vent steam, but cover the hole with a kitchen towel.) Taste for seasonings and adjust accordingly.

8. When ready to serve, add the remaining 2 tablespoons basil and, if desired, a drizzle of extra-virgin olive oil.

9. Serve the sauce immediately, or allow the sauce to cool to room temperature, transfer to airtight containers, and refrigerate for up to 1 week. You can also freeze the sauce for up to 6 months. To reheat, warm the sauce gently in a saucepan, stirring until heated through, adding water as needed to thin.

CARAMELIZED ONION JAM

makes about 1½ cups	gluten-free, nut-free, soy-free option, refined sugar–free option

If you've caramelized onions before, you know that it can take upward of 30 minutes, much of which is spent babysitting the pan and hoping the onions don't burn.

Luckily, the high pressure from the Instant Pot helps solve this problem. It speeds up the rate at which caramelization and browning happen without the risk of burning. More simply put, the Instant Pot cooks whole onions down to sweet, luscious gooeyness in no time.

The addition of baking soda serves two functions in this recipe. First, it creates a high-pH environment, which speeds up the browning. Second, it causes the onions to break down even more, which is perfect for making onion jam. If you prefer not to use cornstarch or arrowroot powder, you can omit them if you're okay with a runnier jam.

While you can enjoy this jam anytime, it's perfect party fare that requires minimal work. Slice up a hearty loaf of bread (an olive bread would take this over the top), lather it with the onion jam, and top with a nut-based cheese, figs, and fresh basil. If you can't find vegan cheese where you live, add some toasted almonds or hazelnuts for a crunch and a drizzle of tahini.

¼ cup vegan butter (use a soy-free variety to keep soy-free) or olive oil

2 pounds yellow onions (about 4 large), cut into ⅛-inch-thick slices

1 teaspoon baking soda

Kosher salt or sea salt

Freshly cracked black pepper

4 garlic cloves, minced

1½ teaspoons chopped fresh rosemary leaves, or ½ teaspoon dried rosemary

½ teaspoon crushed red pepper flakes

2 tablespoons high-quality balsamic vinegar

2 tablespoons organic brown sugar or coconut sugar

1 tablespoon cornstarch or arrowroot powder

recipe continues

1. Select the Sauté setting on the Instant Pot and let the pot heat up for a few minutes before adding the butter. Once the butter is melted, add the sliced onions and baking soda and season very generously with salt (about ¾ teaspoon) and black pepper to taste.

2. Cook the onions, stirring frequently, until they begin to soften and reduce by half in volume, 4 to 5 minutes. Select the Cancel Setting.

3. Secure the lid and set the Pressure Release to Sealing. Select the Pressure Cook setting at high pressure and set the cook time to 25 minutes.

4. Once the 25-minute timer has completed and beeps, perform a quick pressure release by carefully switching the Pressure Release knob from Sealing to Venting.

5. Open the pot and stir in the garlic, rosemary, pepper flakes, vinegar, and brown sugar. Return the Instant Pot to the Sauté setting and bring the mixture to a boil, whisking frequently, until the onion jam is dark brown, about 5 minutes. When the mixture comes to a boil, stand back, as the jam might sputter up.

6. Meanwhile, in a small bowl, mix together the cornstarch or arrowroot with 1 tablespoon water until dissolved.

7. Stir the slurry into the onion jam and whisk until the jam gets a bit thicker, 2 to 3 minutes.

8. Once cooled, store the jam in a glass jar or airtight container in the fridge for 1 to 2 weeks.

TIP *Prefer your mojito in a chilled glass instead of a canning jar? To make a more traditional blueberry jam, omit the fresh mint and substitute lemon juice for the lime juice. Instead of adding lime zest, add the zest of 1 large lemon.*

BLUEBERRY MOJITO JAM

makes about 2 cups	gluten-free, nut-free, soy-free, refined sugar–free option

Made with antioxidant-rich blueberries, low-GI coconut nectar, and omega-3-rich chia seeds, this jam is basically a health food. I use coconut nectar because its gooey texture makes for a thick, jelled jam. You can also use organic cane sugar for similar results (or honey if you are not strictly vegan). To thicken the jam without using pectin, I rely on both chia seeds and arrowroot powder (or cornstarch).

Oh, and the mojito part? That was inspired by one of those frou-frou cocktails I ordered at a poolside bar in San Juan, Puerto Rico. I am normally a whiskey-on-the-rocks kind of old man (gal), but the chiseled bartender insisted I try the blueberry mojito, and who was I to decline his request? It had the slightly sweet yet refreshing taste of a classic mojito with a hypnotizing shade of purple. That same fresh lime-and-mint flavor gives this jam a bright twist.

3 medium juicy limes

2 pints fresh blueberries or 4 cups frozen blueberries

½ cup coconut nectar or organic cane sugar

12 sprigs fresh mint, tied tightly together with kitchen twine

2 tablespoons arrowroot powder or cornstarch

¼ cup chia seeds

1. Use a Microplane to grate the zest of 2 of the limes and set the zest aside. Next squeeze all of the limes to get 6 tablespoons lime juice.

2. Place the blueberries, coconut nectar, and 5 tablespoons of the lime juice in the Instant Pot and stir to combine. Tuck the bundle of fresh mint sprigs into the berries.

3. Secure the lid and set the Pressure Release to Sealing. Select the Pressure Cook setting at high pressure and set the cook time to 3 minutes.

4. Once the 3-minute timer has completed and beeps, allow a natural pressure release. Open the pot and discard the bundle of mint.

5. In a small bowl, whisk together the arrowroot or cornstarch with 2 tablespoons water until dissolved into a slurry. Add the slurry to the jam. Select the Sauté setting and bring the jam to a boil, whisking constantly until the jam has thickened, 3 to 5 minutes (arrowroot will require a few more minutes than cornstarch).

6. Select the Cancel setting and stir in the chia seeds, mixing well to incorporate. Add the lime zest and remaining 1 tablespoon lime juice. The jam will thicken once you add the chia seeds and will thicken considerably more as it cools to room temperature.

7. Once the jam has cooled, store in a glass jar or airtight container in the fridge for 1 to 2 weeks.

TIP *When it comes to coconut oil, an unrefined virgin coconut oil will bring a rich, coconutty taste to this dip, but if you prefer a more neutral taste, use refined coconut oil.*

GINGER CARROT MISO BUTTER

makes about 2 cups	gluten-free, nut-free, refined sugar–free

Smooth, creamy, and luxurious, this is the new (and improved) "I can't believe it's not butter." I love slathering this spread on a crusty hunk of seeded whole-grain bread (or a fluffy flax raisin bread from my local bakery), but it's also wonderful as a dip for crudités or served on top of grain bowls.

You might find the ingredient list to be an unusual combination, but the sweetness of the carrots and maple syrup blend harmoniously with the umami-packed miso paste and the spicy ginger. I use white or yellow miso paste because I love its subtle and slightly sweet flavor and it isn't so bold as to overwhelm the carrots, but still lends a rich, complex mouthfeel and indescribably unique flavor.

If you want the texture to be silky smooth like butter, transfer the cooked carrots and cooking liquid to a food processor along with the other ingredients. If you prefer to mix everything right in the Instant Pot, an immersion blender will do the trick. If using the latter method, stick to ground ginger, as the immersion blender will have a harder time pulverizing fresh ginger.

1 pound carrots (about 6 carrots)

½ cup low-sodium vegetable broth

3½ tablespoons white or yellow miso paste

1½ tablespoons pure maple syrup

3½ tablespoons coconut oil, melted (see Tip)

½ teaspoon ground ginger or 1 teaspoon finely grated or minced fresh ginger

Freshly cracked black pepper to taste

1. Peel and dice the carrots into ½-inch pieces. You should end up with 3 to 3½ cups carrots.

2. Place the carrots in the Instant Pot and add the vegetable broth.

3. Secure the lid and set the Pressure Release to Sealing. Select the Steam setting at high pressure and set the cook time to 3 minutes.

4. Once the 3-minute timer has completed and beeps, perform a quick pressure release by carefully switching the Pressure Release knob from Sealing to Venting.

5. Open the pot. There will be some vegetable broth remaining. Don't drain this liquid, as it will help bring the butter together. If you are using an immersion blender, leave the carrots and cooking liquid in the pot and add the miso, maple syrup, coconut oil, ground ginger, and pepper to taste. Blend all of the ingredients together until you have a smooth and spreadable texture. This process will take 2 to 3 minutes.

6. If you are using a food processor, transfer the carrots and the cooking liquid to a food processor and add the miso, maple syrup, coconut oil, ginger, and pepper. Blend until you have a completely smooth puree.

7. Store the miso butter in an airtight container in the fridge for up to 1 week.

2

BREAKFASTS

Whether you're on a 6 a.m. post-gym breakfast
regimen or more into a lazy, carb-heavy
Sunday brunch (or both; you can do both),
the delectable options in this chapter will
more than satisfy your cravings. There are
breakfast staples you'll have on repeat, creamy
porridges that will feed your soul, and jazzy
brunch options to please your weekend guests.

HOMEMADE COCONUT YOGURT

makes 3½ to 4 cups	gluten-free, nut-free option, soy-free, refined sugar–free

Transitioning to veganism was never hard for me, but I did miss being able to buy a container of yogurt at even the sparsest of supermarkets. Luckily, there is a growing selection of vegan yogurts, but making your own is a cheaper (and healthier) alternative.

To start, don't skip the sterilization step, which helps prevent harmful bacteria growth. When the Yogurt setting is done, if it smells funky or has a discolored film, the yogurt did not ferment properly and has gone bad (it will smell really bad). To ensure proper fermentation, the coconut milk needs to be at the right temperature when you add the probiotic powder. It's finicky, so you will need a thermometer when you boil it. If it's too hot, the yogurt won't culture and develop that delicious tangy taste; if it's too cold, the cultures won't be able to grow. The Yogurt setting takes a minimum of 8 hours to ferment, but I prefer a longer fermentation of at least 24 hours, even up to 36 hours for an irresistibly tart yogurt (my sweet spot is 32 hours). Just be sure you'll be home when the timer goes off, as letting the yogurt sit in the pot will cause it to spoil.

I've made this yogurt without the coconut cream, and while it is great, the extra coconut cream adds a luscious texture. The best thickening agent is a combination of tapioca starch and agar agar, a seaweed-derived alternative to gelatin (available online or in the "ethnic foods" aisle of high-end grocery stores). If you want to omit both of these, try fermenting for 36 hours, as the longer you ferment, the thicker the yogurt will become.

2 (13.5-ounce) cans full-fat coconut milk plus the solid coconut cream from another 13.5-ounce can (save the liquid for another use, such as smoothies)

2½ teaspoons agar agar flakes or 1 teaspoon agar agar powder

1¼ teaspoons tapioca starch

2 tablespoons pure maple syrup or coconut nectar

1 teaspoon pure vanilla extract

1¼ teaspoons probiotic powder (see Tip)

recipe continues

1. Sterilize the Instant Pot by pouring 2 cups cold water into the inner pot. Secure the lid and set the Pressure Release to Sealing. Select the Steam setting at high pressure and set the cook time to 1 minute. Once the timer has completed and beeps, perform a quick pressure release by carefully switching the Pressure Release knob from Sealing to Venting.

2. Discard the water and wipe down the inner pot and lid. Sterilize any tools, such as a whisk, by placing in boiling water for 10 minutes or running them in the dishwasher.

3. Pour the coconut milk and coconut cream into the sterilized inner pot. Select the Sauté setting and, once the cream has melted, add the agar agar flakes and tapioca starch and use a whisk to thoroughly combine. As the milk begins to boil, whisk constantly to dissolve the agar agar flakes and tapioca to prevent clumps from forming. Once it starts to boil and the temperature reaches 180°F, select the Cancel setting and whisk the mixture well. Depending on the temperature at which your coconut milk was stored, it should take 6 to 10 minutes to reach 180°F.

4. Using oven mitts, remove the inner pot and whisk in the maple syrup or coconut nectar and vanilla to combine. Allow the coconut milk to cool to 100°F. You can speed up the cooling process by placing the inner pot in a shallow pie plate or a rimmed baking sheet filled with an inch of cold water. With that method, it takes about 15 to 20 minutes to cool to 100°F. If possible, whisk the coconut milk mixture several times throughout the cooling process to prevent clumps.

5. Once the mixture has cooled to 100°F, add the probiotic powder a little at a time, whisking after each addition to prevent clumps. Return the inner pot to the Instant Pot and select the Yogurt setting and set the timer to 8 hours at a minimum, or 24 to 36 hours (see headnote). Secure the lid (the lid won't seal on the Yogurt setting).

6. Once the timer has completed, open the lid and check to ensure the yogurt has fermented. Taste the yogurt to make sure it has become tart enough to your liking, keeping in mind that you're tasting warm yogurt so it will taste much better once cooled. It's natural for homemade yogurt to have tiny clumps (especially if you didn't use the combination of agar agar and tapioca), so if you prefer a super smooth yogurt, just run an immersion blender through the yogurt for 1 to 2 minutes.

7. Pour the yogurt into glass jars with lids and refrigerate. The yogurt gets considerably thicker after chilling. Store in the fridge for 1 week.

TIP *Don't have probiotic powder? Just carefully open 5 to 6 probiotic capsules and measure out 1 teaspoon powder. If you are on a strict vegan diet, be sure to check that your probiotics are dairy-free and vegan.*

BASIC STEEL-CUT OATMEAL + THREE VARIATIONS

serves 4	gluten-free, nut-free option, soy-free, refined sugar–free

Steel-cut oats are superior to rolled oats (more fiber, more satiating, less processed), but cooking them with a traditional method is daunting. The Instant Pot helps you save time and enjoy oats in their purest form.

Just add three ingredients to the Instant Pot, give them a stir, and let the machine do its magic. In 12 minutes, you'll have oatmeal that is fully cooked but still has a bit of a bite. I like my oatmeal on the thicker side, but if you prefer a thinner version, you can either increase the amount of nondairy milk from 4 cups to 4½ cups, or decrease the amount of oats from 1½ cups to 1¼ cups. If you find the oatmeal too thick for your liking (it will thicken as it rests), just add some more nondairy milk when serving.

This recipe calls for almond milk, but you can use any nondairy milk of your choice. It comes out fabulous each time. If you use a sweetened milk beverage, taste it before adding any sweetener at the end.

Cooking spray or coconut oil, for the pot

1½ cups steel-cut oats (certified gluten-free if needed)

4 cups unsweetened plain almond milk or other nondairy milk (use soy or oat milk for a nut-free option)

Pinch of kosher salt or sea salt

3 tablespoons pure maple syrup or sweetener of choice (optional)

1. Lightly coat the inner pot of the Instant Pot with spray or oil to avoid sticking.

2. Add the oats, almond milk, and salt to the Instant Pot. If you are making one of the three variations on page 75, add in those ingredients and stir to combine.

3. Secure the lid and set the Pressure Release to Sealing. Select the Pressure Cook setting at high pressure and set the cook time to 12 minutes.

4. Once the 12-minute timer has completed and beeps, allow a natural pressure release for 20 minutes and then switch the Pressure Release knob from Sealing to Venting to release any remaining steam.

5. Open the pot and stir the oatmeal thoroughly. There may be some liquid on top, but once you stir it, the liquid will incorporate into the oatmeal and thicken up. Stir in the maple syrup or sweetener if desired. Or, if you are making one of the variations below, add in those additional ingredients and stir to combine. Transfer to bowls and serve as desired.

Spiced Apple-Walnut Oatmeal

Variations

❶ Spiced Apple-Walnut Oatmeal

Add to Instant Pot with the oats and almond milk:

1½ cups unsweetened applesauce

2 small apples, peeled, cored, and diced

1½ teaspoons ground cinnamon

½ teaspoon ground ginger

½ teaspoon ground cardamom

2 teaspoons pure vanilla extract

Stir into the oatmeal after pressure release:

3 tablespoons pure maple syrup

½ cup chopped walnuts

If desired, garnish with:

Apple slices, chopped walnuts, tahini

❷ Chocolate Peanut Butter Banana Oatmeal

Add to Instant Pot with the oats and almond milk:

2 tablespoons unsweetened cocoa powder

1½ teaspoons pure vanilla extract

½ teaspoon ground cinnamon

3 medium bananas, mashed

Stir into the oatmeal after pressure release:

¼ cup no-added-sugar peanut butter

1 tablespoon pure maple syrup (optional)

If desired, garnish with:

Dark chocolate, bananas, toasted coconut flakes

❸ Peaches and Cream Oatmeal

Add to Instant Pot with the oats and almond milk:

2 medium peaches, peeled, pitted, and diced

2 teaspoons pure vanilla extract

1 teaspoon ground cinnamon

Stir into the oatmeal after pressure release:

3 tablespoons organic brown sugar, coconut sugar, or pure maple syrup

Garnish with:

A splash of coconut milk or a dollop of nondairy yogurt

BREAKFAST ENCHILADA CASSEROLE

serves 4 to 6	gluten-free option, nut-free option, soy-free option, no added sugar

I love the ease of this dish. Simply sauté a few vegetables in an abundant amount of spices, and then layer them with enchilada sauce, canned beans and corn, and corn tortillas. And cheeze, of course. You cannot forget the cheeze. The cheeze or Vegan Queso really elevates this to the perfect Mexican-inspired comfort food. And no one will be mad if you use a little more than the prescribed amount of cheeze.

When I'm short on time, I use a store-bought organic enchilada sauce, but I do love my home-made red enchilada sauce, which takes only 10 minutes to prepare. If you're more into enchiladas verdes, feel free to substitute green enchilada sauce.

1½ tablespoons grapeseed oil or other neutral, high-heat cooking oil

8 scallions (white and light-green parts only), sliced

4 garlic cloves, minced

1 small zucchini or 1 small green bell pepper, diced

1 small red bell pepper, diced

1 teaspoon chili powder

1 teaspoon ground cumin

1 teaspoon dried oregano

1 teaspoon sweet or hot paprika

½ to 1 teaspoon kosher salt (depending on how salty your enchilada sauce is)

Freshly cracked black pepper

FOR ASSEMBLY

2 cups red enchilada sauce, store-bought or homemade (recipe follows)

1 (15-ounce) can black beans, drained and rinsed

1 (8.5-ounce) can sweet corn, drained and rinsed

2 (4-ounce) cans chopped or diced green chiles

6 to 8 (six-inch) corn tortillas, each cut into 6 strips

1 cup shredded vegan cheese (use a soy-free or nut-free variety as needed) or Vegan Queso (page 49; not soy-free or nut-free)

Cooking spray

OPTIONAL GARNISHES

Chopped scallions and/or cilantro, vegan sour cream, diced avocado

recipe continues

1. Select the Sauté setting and after a few minutes, add the oil. Once the display reads "HOT," add the scallions, garlic, zucchini, and red bell pepper. Cook, stirring frequently, to prevent burning, until the vegetables are almost tender, 3 to 4 minutes.

2. Add the chili powder, cumin, oregano, paprika, salt, and black pepper to taste, stirring to coat the vegetables. Stir constantly for 30 seconds until the mixture is fragrant and has dried out. Select the Cancel setting and, using oven mitts, remove the inner pot from the Instant Pot.

3. Assemble the enchilada casserole: Pour 2 to 3 tablespoons of the enchilada sauce into the bottom of a 7-cup round glass dish or a 1½-quart soufflé dish, spreading evenly. Top with one-third of the cooked vegetable mixture, one-third of the black beans, one-third of the corn, and one-third of the green chiles. Place one-third of the tortilla strips on top, fitting them to cover the diameter of the dish. Top the tortillas with one-third of the enchilada sauce and one-third of the shredded vegan cheese or the Vegan Queso.

4. Repeat the layers twice, ending with the cheese or queso. If you can't fit all of the tortilla strips, just leave a few out to avoid overstuffing. Rinse out the inner pot.

5. For easy removal of the glass dish from the Instant Pot, create a foil sling following the instructions on page 21. (Alternatively, you can use oven mitts to carefully remove the dish.) Pour 1½ cups of water into the inner pot of the Instant Pot. Spray a piece of foil with cooking spray and tightly cover the casserole dish, On the counter, place the covered dish on top of the steamer rack (with the handles facing up) and arrange the foil sling (if using) underneath the steamer rack. Carefully lower the steamer rack and dish into the inner pot using the foil sling or steamer rack handles.

6. Secure the lid and set the Pressure Release to Sealing. Select the Pressure Cook setting at high pressure and set the cook time to 10 minutes.

7. Once the 10-minute timer has completed and beeps, allow a natural pressure release. Open the pot and, using oven mitts, grasp the foil sling or steamer rack handles and carefully lift the dish out of the Instant Pot. Remove the foil cover and allow to sit for 5 to 10 minutes to allow the flavors to meld together. Garnish as desired.

Red Enchilada Sauce
Makes about 2 cups

- **1 (14-ounce) can whole peeled tomatoes**
- **3 garlic cloves, roughly chopped**
- **½ small white or yellow onion, roughly chopped**
- **1 chipotle pepper in adobo sauce**
- **1 tablespoon chili powder**
- **½ teaspoon ground cumin**
- **¼ to ½ teaspoon cayenne pepper, to taste**
- **¼ teaspoon kosher salt**
- **1 tablespoon grapeseed oil or other neutral cooking oil (optional)**
- **1 tablespoon flour (optional), gluten-free, all-purpose, or whole wheat**

In a high-powered blender, combine the tomatoes, garlic, onion, chipotle, chili powder, cumin, cayenne, salt, and ½ cup water and blend until the sauce is completely pureed. If you'd like to thicken the sauce, in a large saucepan or deep skillet, heat the oil and, once shimmering, whisk in the flour. Whisk constantly for 2 to 3 minutes. Gradually pour in the enchilada sauce, continuing to whisk until the sauce has thickened.

SAVORY TURMERIC BREAKFAST QUINOA

serves 4 to 6	gluten-free, nut-free, no added sugar

The idea for this dish came to me one cold winter day as I was eating lunch at a very hippie-friendly vegan café. I had a mushroom quinoa "risotto" in one hand and a turmeric coconut latte in the other hand, and I thought, Wouldn't it be cool if I could just combine these two dishes into one? Perhaps that doesn't sound as appetizing on paper as it did in my mind, but this resulting love child (recipe) is even better than I had expected.

The miso-tahini-tamari sauce adds a rich mouthfeel, the shiitake mushrooms lend a meaty, almost buttery flavor, and the full-fat coconut milk adds a subtle touch of milky sweetness. The combination is electric and makes it nearly impossible to put the spoon down.

You can use "lite" canned coconut milk or another type of unsweetened nondairy milk, though it won't have the exact same luxurious mouthfeel. If you can't find shiitake mushrooms, you can substitute cremini mushrooms. And feel free to round out this dish by adding more vegetables—broccoli or bok choy would complement these flavors perfectly.

2 tablespoons toasted sesame oil, plus more for finishing

1 large red onion, diced

1 red bell pepper, diced

Pinch of kosher salt or sea salt

1½ cups sliced shiitake mushrooms caps (about 4 ounces)

3 garlic cloves, minced

1-inch piece fresh ginger, grated or minced

1½ cups quinoa

1 (13.5-ounce) can full-fat coconut milk

1½ teaspoons ground turmeric

½ teaspoon freshly cracked black pepper

1½ tablespoons white or yellow miso paste

3 tablespoons tahini

1½ tablespoons reduced-sodium tamari or soy sauce

3 tablespoons hot water

1 tablespoon white or black sesame seeds

OPTIONAL GARNISHES

Chopped scallions or chives, crushed red pepper flakes, or Sriracha

recipe continues

1. Select the Sauté setting on the Instant Pot and let the pot heat up for a few minutes before adding the sesame oil. Once the oil is hot, add the onion and bell pepper. Season with the salt and cook until the onion begins to soften, 3 to 4 minutes.

2. Add the mushrooms, garlic, and ginger and cook for 2 minutes, stirring frequently to prevent burning. If the mixture looks dry, you can add a little more oil or a tablespoon of water to prevent burning.

3. Add the quinoa to the Instant Pot along with the coconut milk, turmeric, and black pepper. Select the Cancel setting and stir all of the ingredients together until well combined.

4. Secure the lid and set the Pressure Release to Sealing. Select the Pressure Cook setting at high pressure and set the cook time to 1 minute.

5. Meanwhile, in a small bowl, whisk together the miso, tahini, tamari, and hot water until you have a creamy, pourable sauce.

6. Once the 1-minute timer has completed and beeps, allow a natural pressure release for 10 minutes and then switch the Pressure Release knob from Sealing to Venting to release any remaining steam.

7. Open the pot and pour in the miso-tahini sauce and the sesame seeds, stirring to incorporate well. Transfer the quinoa to bowls and drizzle each with a bit of toasted sesame oil. Garnish as desired.

BUTTERNUT SQUASH BUCKWHEAT PORRIDGE

serves 4	gluten-free, nut-free, soy-free, refined sugar–free

If Thanksgiving were a breakfast and came in bowl form, this would be it. This porridge is cozy, comforting, and has all the flavors of fall. Except, unlike a Thanksgiving feast, it's healthy!

Though cooked like a traditional grain, buckwheat is a naturally gluten-free pseudo-grain. I use buckwheat because, like the butternut squash it is paired with, it is robust and slightly sweet with earthy, nutty notes. Buckwheat is sold in two forms—toasted (kasha) and raw (groats); you'll need the latter variety for this recipe. You can substitute a different grain if you prefer (millet would work great), but be sure to consult the Cook Time chart on page 37 and revise the recipe accordingly.

When grated, the butternut squash virtually melts into the hot porridge. Use the shredding disc on your food processor and cut the squash into large chunks that will fit in your food processor feed tube. Or, cut the squash into long rectangular shapes and carefully shred on the large-hole side of a box grater.

TIP *For the nondairy milk, I suggest something a little creamier than your standard almond milk, such as coconut milk ("drinking milk" from a carton, not a can), oat milk, macadamia nut milk, or cashew milk.*

1 cup raw buckwheat groats

2½ cups unsweetened plain nondairy milk (see Tip)

3½ cups peeled and shredded (see headnote) butternut squash (about 1 small squash)

¾ teaspoon freshly grated or ground nutmeg

1 tablespoon nutritional yeast

½ teaspoon kosher salt

Freshly cracked black pepper

¼ cup tahini, plus more to taste

2 tablespoons pure maple syrup, plus more to taste

OPTIONAL GARNISHES

Toasted pumpkin seeds

Roasted butternut squash

1. Place the buckwheat in a fine-mesh sieve and rinse under cold water. Shake to remove the excess water and place the buckwheat in the Instant Pot. Add the nondairy milk, butternut squash, nutmeg, nutritional yeast, salt, and pepper to taste.

2. Secure the lid and set the Pressure Release to Sealing. Select the Pressure Cook setting at high pressure and set the cook time to 5 minutes.

3. Once the 5-minute timer has completed and beeps, allow a natural pressure release.

4. Open the pot and stir. Select the Sauté setting and stir in the tahini and maple syrup. Cook until the porridge is thick and creamy, about 1 minute. Taste for seasonings and add more tahini or maple syrup to taste.

5. Garnish the porridge with pumpkin seeds and roasted butternut squash, if desired.

CHAI-SPICED RICE PUDDING

serves 4	gluten-free, nut-free option, soy-free, refined sugar–free

The one saving grace of winter is being able to enjoy cozy comfort foods without any guilt. Like this chai spiced rice pudding. It has the flavors of a warming cup of chai and the sweet richness of traditional rice pudding. For a luscious texture, I recommend using a rice that is labeled medium-grain rice, which has the perfect amount of starch to thicken the pudding while keeping it creamy but not sticky.

While this pudding is sweet enough for dessert, it's healthy enough for breakfast. Your options for topping are endless, but I love something crunchy like toasted nuts for a contrast in textures. It's also fabulous with stewed plums or the Roasted Grapes.

RICE PUDDING

1 cup medium-grain rice

1½ cups unsweetened plain almond milk or other nondairy milk (use soy or oat milk for a nut-free option)

1 cup canned full-fat coconut milk, well stirred

1 cup water

1 teaspoon pure vanilla extract

⅛ teaspoon kosher salt

2 teaspoons ground cinnamon

1 teaspoon ground ginger

½ teaspoon ground cardamom

½ teaspoon freshly grated or ground nutmeg

⅛ teaspoon ground cloves

2 tablespoons no-added-sugar almond butter

1 tablespoon pure maple syrup or coconut sugar

4 soft Medjool dates, pitted and roughly torn into pieces

ROASTED GRAPES (OPTIONAL)

1 bunch of seedless grapes

Olive oil

Kosher salt or sea salt

Fresh thyme leaves

recipe continues

1. If making the roasted grapes, preheat the oven to 450°F.

2. Make the rice pudding: Place the rice, almond milk, coconut milk, water, vanilla, salt, cinnamon, ginger, cardamom, nutmeg, cloves, almond butter, maple syrup, and dates in the Instant Pot and stir to combine.

3. Secure the lid and set the Pressure Release to Sealing. Select the Pressure Cook setting at high pressure and set the cook time to 10 minutes.

4. Meanwhile, prepare the roasted grapes: Spread the grapes out on a rimmed baking sheet. Drizzle with olive oil and sprinkle with salt and thyme leaves and gently toss with your hands. Bake until the grapes just begin to burst, 8 to 9 minutes.

5. Once the 10-minute timer on the Instant Pot has completed and beeps, allow a natural pressure release for 5 minutes and then switch the Pressure Release knob from Sealing to Venting to release the remaining steam.

6. Open the pot and stir the rice pudding thoroughly. There may be some extra liquid on top, but once you stir it, the liquid will incorporate into the rice and thicken up. Transfer the rice pudding to bowls and serve each bowl with the roasted grapes, if desired.

MINI MUSHROOM AND LEEK QUICHES

makes 4 mini quiches	gluten-free, nut-free, no added sugar

A traditional quiche can be hard to nail. You have to add the precise number of eggs (too many and your filling won't set, too few and your filling will be rubbery), blind bake the pie crust to avoid a soggy mess, remove the quiche from the oven before the center is set, and so on. Going crustless and replacing the eggs with tofu (and the oven with the Instant Pot) eliminates these pitfalls. And pressure-cooking also helps mimic the texture of an egg-based quiche—the center is a bit jiggly, but the edges are set.

Nutritional yeast and the pungent-smelling *kala namak* (also known as "black salt," though not black in color) give this dish a savory, umami, egg-like taste. One whiff of the pureed tofu filling and you'll swear you're cooking eggs. You can find *kala namak* in South Asian grocers or online, but if you can't find it (or think the smell of eggs is nauseating), just replace it with kosher salt.

The filling makes enough to fill four 6- or 8-ounce ramekins, making these quiches the perfect single-serving, protein- and fiber-rich breakfast.

TIP *Don't want to clean out the inner pot before pressure cooking the quiches? You can cook the filling in a skillet on the stovetop instead.*

1 (14-ounce) block firm tofu

MUSHROOM-LEEK FILLING

1½ tablespoons olive oil

1 leek, dark green tops discarded, thoroughly cleaned, trimmed, and diced

3 garlic cloves, minced

8 ounces mixed mushrooms, finely chopped (about 2½ cups)

½ teaspoon kosher salt

2 tablespoons finely chopped fresh chives

½ cup fresh basil, finely slivered

2 cups baby kale or baby spinach

QUICHE

½ cup unsweetened plain nondairy milk

2 tablespoons tahini

⅓ cup nutritional yeast

1 teaspoon black salt or kala namak (see headnote), plus more to taste

1 teaspoon dried thyme

½ teaspoon ground turmeric (optional but gives the quiche a golden color)

½ teaspoon freshly cracked black pepper

FOR SERVING (OPTIONAL)

Hot sauce or salsa, diced avocado, chopped chives or basil

recipe continues

1. Drain the tofu and cut it into 4 slabs. Place the tofu on a cutting board lined with paper towels. Place more paper towels on top of the tofu and weight them down with a few heavy cookbooks or a heavy skillet filled with a few cans of beans. Let sit for 10 minutes to press out some of the water.

2. Meanwhile, make the mushroom-leek filling in a skillet or the Instant Pot (see Tip): If using the Instant Pot, select the Sauté setting and let the pot heat up for a few minutes before adding the olive oil. Once the oil is hot, add the leek and garlic. Cook for 1 minute, stirring frequently, to prevent sticking.

3. Add the mushrooms and cook until most of the liquid cooks off, 3 to 5 minutes, adding the salt during the last minute of cooking. Stir in the chives, basil, and baby kale and cook until the greens are wilted, about 1 minute. Select the Cancel setting. Using oven mitts, remove the inner pot from the Instant Pot (or set the skillet aside).

4. Prepare the quiche: In a food processor or high-powered blender, combine the pressed tofu, nondairy milk, tahini, nutritional yeast, *kala namak*, thyme, turmeric (if using), and pepper. Blend until the mixture is completely pureed and creamy, scraping down the sides with a silicone spatula as needed. Taste for seasonings, and if you'd like a more "eggy" taste, add up to ½ teaspoon more *kala namak*.

5. Using a slotted spoon, transfer the mushroom-leek filling to a large bowl, leaving behind any liquid. Add the pureed tofu mixture, folding the ingredients together with a silicone spatula. Clean out the Instant Pot inner pot if you used it to cook the vegetables.

6. Dividing evenly, spoon the quiche mixture into four 8-ounce ramekins (4-inch diameter), filling them three-quarters full, or four 6-ounce ramekins (3½-inch diameter), filling them all the way up (don't worry, they won't rise). Cover each ramekin with a piece of foil.

7. Pour 1½ cups water into the inner pot of the Instant Pot and place the steamer rack in the pot with the handles facing up. Arrange two of the ramekins on top of the steamer rack in diagonal relation to one another, then carefully balance the two remaining ramekins on top of those. If your ramekins are on the smaller size, you'll be able to fit three on top of the steamer rack before having to stack the fourth.

8. Secure the lid and set the Pressure Release to Sealing. Select the Pressure Cook setting at high pressure and set the cook time to 20 minutes.

9. Once the 20-minute timer has completed and beeps, allow a natural pressure release.

10. Open the pot and, using oven mitts, carefully remove the ramekins. Pull up the foil to check for doneness. The edges should be firm and the centers should be a little jiggly. Serve the quiches with hot sauce, salsa, and/or avocado and garnish with fresh chives and basil, if desired.

OVERNIGHT SWEET POTATO FRENCH TOAST

serves 6	nut-free option, soy-free option, refined sugar–free option

I won't lie and tell you that my French toast is fat-free, sugar-free, and carb-free (you might as well stick with water), but as far as French toast is concerned, it falls into the realm of being able to "have your cake (French toast) and eat it, too." Sweet potato puree adds a creamy richness to the batter, but it's also a vegetable, so it's a win-win. The combo of nutritional yeast and chickpea flour lends a slight eggy flavor and texture without being overwhelming, but if you don't have chick-pea flour, feel free to substitute the flour of your choice.

In addition, this French toast is incredibly easy to prepare. The prep work takes 10 minutes at night, then in the morning you just pop it into the Instant Pot for 30 minutes. This low-effort, high-reward ratio makes it a great option for overnight guests or a holiday brunch, especially around Thanksgiving when you can use leftover cranberry sauce as a topping for that irresistible sweet-tart combo.

TIP *For French toast, you're looking for a tender, spongy bread that is still sturdy enough to soak up the batter without falling apart. A Pullman loaf and pane di casa are both great egg-free options, but if you prefer a chewier bite to your French toast, a loaf of French bread or sourdough will work; just be sure to soak the bread slices in the batter for at least 8 hours.*

Cooking spray or neutral-flavored oil

1 cup sweet potato puree, store-bought or homemade

1¼ cups unsweetened plain almond milk or other nondairy milk

¼ cup chickpea flour (also known as gram flour or besan)

2 tablespoons nutritional yeast

⅓ cup pure maple syrup or organic brown sugar

1½ teaspoons ground cinnamon

¼ teaspoon freshly grated or ground nutmeg

½ teaspoon ground ginger

¼ teaspoon kosher salt

1½ teaspoons pure vanilla extract

½ teaspoon aluminum-free baking powder

1½ teaspoons cornstarch or arrowroot powder

1 loaf Pullman bread or pane di casa (see Tip), about 12 ounces

1 tablespoon coconut sugar or organic brown sugar

¼ cup pecans, chopped (omit for a nut-free option)

1 tablespoon vegan butter, sliced into small pieces (use a soy-free variety to keep soy-free), or 1 tablespoon solid coconut oil, cut into pieces

1 to 2 teaspoons grated orange zest to taste

FOR SERVING

Raspberry or cranberry preserves, warmed up

Pure maple syrup

recipe continues

1. Lightly grease a 7-cup round glass dish or a 1½-quart soufflé dish with cooking spray or a bit of neutral oil.

2. In a blender, combine the sweet potato puree, almond milk, chickpea flour, nutritional yeast, maple syrup, cinnamon, nutmeg, ginger, salt, vanilla, baking powder, and cornstarch. Blend until the mixture is completely smooth.

3. Slice or tear the loaf of bread into ¾-inch pieces. You should end up with 6 to 7 cups. Place the bread pieces in a large bowl and pour the sweet potato mixture over the bread mixture and toss to coat all of the bread cubes thoroughly. Transfer the soaked bread to the greased glass dish, cover, and refrigerate overnight or for at least 6 hours.

4. The next morning, uncover the casserole and sprinkle the top evenly with the coconut sugar. Sprinkle the pecans and vegan butter or coconut oil over the casserole and into any crevices.

5. For easy removal of the dish from the Instant Pot, create a foil sling following the instructions on page 21. (Alternatively, you can use oven mitts to carefully remove the dish.)

6. Pour 1½ cups water into the inner pot of the Instant Pot. Spray a piece of foil with cooking spray and tightly cover the casserole dish. On the counter, place the dish on top of the steamer rack (with the handles facing up) and arrange the foil sling (if using) underneath the steamer rack. Carefully lower the steamer rack and dish into the inner pot using the foil sling or steamer rack handles.

7. Secure the lid and set the Pressure Release to Sealing. Select the Pressure Cook setting at high pressure and select the cook time to 30 minutes.

8. Once the 30-minute timer has completed and beeps, allow a natural pressure release.

9. Open the pot and, wearing oven mitts, grasp the foil sling or steamer rack handles and carefully lift the dish out of the Instant Pot. Carefully remove the foil cover without dropping condensation on the French toast.

10. Dollop each serving with a bit of orange zest and warmed raspberry or cranberry preserves. Serve with maple syrup if desired.

BROWN RICE CONGEE WITH MUSHROOM BROTH

serves 4	gluten-free, nut-free, no added sugar

I spent a month backpacking in Vietnam, and while the chaos of motorbike culture terrified me, I fell in love with the food. I ate a very simple rice pudding (*chao ga*) for breakfast nearly every morning, delighting in the warmth it brought to both my throat and my belly. As an American, I enjoyed the novelty of eating a savory porridge for breakfast. Plus, it was dirt cheap, so there's that.

Outside of Vietnam, this savory rice porridge is more commonly known as congee. It is rich and creamy and perfect comfort food. Traditionally, the rice is gently simmered in chicken broth (or vegetable broth or water) for an hour or two, but you can make it in an Instant Pot in a fraction of the time.

I use my homemade mushroom broth, which adds a rich earthiness and depth of flavor. I also replace half of the white rice with brown rice, which adds a slight nuttiness and, of course, more nutrients. A short-grain white rice, which tends to be stickier than long-grain varieties, will yield a velvety texture, almost like a risotto. I've included some of my favorite options for toppings, but feel free to use whatever you like best or have on hand.

1 tablespoon refined coconut oil or a neutral cooking oil such as grapeseed oil

4 garlic cloves, thinly sliced

2-inch piece fresh ginger, peeled, thinly sliced, and julienned

3½ ounces fresh shiitake mushrooms (see Tip), caps sliced (about 1½ cups)

½ cup short-grain white rice

½ cup short-grain or long-grain brown rice

4½ cups Mushroom Broth (page 44) or vegetable broth (see Tip)

1½ teaspoons kosher salt, plus more to taste

½ teaspoon ground turmeric

Freshly cracked black pepper

OPTIONAL TOPPINGS

Leftover vegetables (such as bok choy, spinach, or microgreens)

Fried shallots, roasted peanuts, or sesame seeds

TIPS *If you don't have fresh shiitake mushrooms, you can use dried shiitake mushrooms and rehydrate them in hot water for 20 minutes.*

For a lighter, less robust congee, you can substitute vegetable broth for the mushroom broth. If you use store-bought broth, you may want to add a pinch more of salt.

recipe continues

1. Select the Sauté setting on the Instant Pot and let the pot heat up for a few minutes before adding the oil. Once the oil is hot, add the garlic, ginger, and shiitake mushrooms. Cook, stirring frequently to prevent sticking, until the mushrooms are beginning to brown, about 3 minutes.

2. Add the white rice and brown rice and stir to coat in the oil and mushrooms. Pour in the mushroom broth, along with the salt, turmeric, and black pepper to taste. Stir to combine and select the Cancel setting.

3. Secure the lid and set the Pressure Release to Sealing. Select the Pressure Cook setting at high pressure and set the cook time to 30 minutes.

4. Once the 30-minute timer has completed and beeps, allow a natural pressure release.

5. Open the pot and stir the congee. Select the Sauté setting and press the Sauté button again until you reach Less heat. Bring the congee to a boil and simmer for a few minutes to absorb some of the extra liquid and thicken the porridge. If you prefer a thinner congee, skip this step and serve as is.

6. Season with salt and pepper to taste, as needed, and top with your desired garnishes.

PUMPKIN SPICE OATMEAL WITH COCONUT-WALNUT CRUMBLE

serves 6	gluten-free, soy-free, refined sugar–free

I can count the number of times I've cooked steel-cut oats on the stove on two fingers (yes, it's been exactly twice). I'm simply too impatient to wait 30 minutes for oats while having to frequently check them for tenderness. With the Instant Pot, however, you can dump in all of your ingredients, push a button, and simply walk away. Of course, if you make the Coconut-Walnut Crumble, you can't technically walk away, but it takes just 2 minutes to prepare and I promise you, it's worth it. When you return to the kitchen, you'll be treated to the flavors of pumpkin pie in the form of a creamy, milky porridge.

As the Instant Pot depressurizes, the oats will absorb the liquid and become perfectly tender. I use almond milk here, but any nondairy milk will do, such as soy milk or oat milk.

If you have leftovers, simply reheat the oatmeal on the stove or in the microwave, but you may need to thin out the oatmeal with additional nondairy milk, as the oats will thicken while resting.

Cooking spray or coconut oil, for the pot

1½ cups steel-cut oats (gluten-free if needed)

4 cups unsweetened plain almond milk or other nondairy milk

1 (15-ounce) can unsweetened pumpkin puree

1 teaspoon pure vanilla extract

1 tablespoon pumpkin pie spice, store-bought or homemade (recipe follows)

COCONUT-WALNUT CRUMBLE

¾ cup raw walnuts, chopped

¾ cup unsweetened shredded coconut

3 tablespoons pure maple syrup

3 tablespoons coconut oil, melted

1½ teaspoons pumpkin pie spice, store-bought or homemade (recipe follows)

⅛ teaspoon kosher salt or sea salt, plus more to taste

recipe continues

1. Lightly coat the inner pot of the Instant Pot with cooking spray or coconut oil.

2. Add the oats, almond milk, pumpkin puree, vanilla, and pumpkin pie spice to the Instant Pot. Stir to combine.

3. Secure the lid and set the Pressure Release to Sealing. Select the Pressure Cook setting at high pressure and set the cook time to 12 minutes.

4. Meanwhile, make the coconut-walnut crumble: In a bowl, stir together the walnuts, coconut, maple syrup, melted coconut oil, pumpkin pie spice, and salt until you have a sticky crumble. Taste for seasonings and adjust accordingly. I like a noticeable taste of salt to balance the sweetness of the maple syrup.

5. Once the 12-minute timer has completed and beeps, allow a natural pressure release for 20 minutes and then switch the Pressure Release knob from Sealing to Venting to release any remaining steam.

6. Open the pot and stir the oatmeal thoroughly. There may be some extra liquid on top, but once you stir it, the liquid will incorporate into the oatmeal and thicken up. Transfer the oatmeal to bowls and serve each bowl with the coconut-walnut crumble.

Pumpkin Pie Spice
Makes 4 to 5 tablespoons

3 tablespoons ground cinnamon
1½ tablespoons ground ginger
1 teaspoon freshly grated or ground nutmeg
1½ teaspoons ground cloves

In a small bowl, mix together the cinnamon, ginger, nutmeg, and cloves, stirring to combine thoroughly.

BAKED BEANS ON TOAST

serves 10 to 12	nut-free

These beans are thick, rich, and coated in a sweet and savory glaze-like sauce. There's a bit of tanginess from the (vegan) Worcestershire sauce and balsamic vinegar, and a hint of smokiness from the smoked paprika. The blackstrap molasses adds that rich, sweet-but-not-too-sweet depth of flavor. And don't forget the bread! Traditionally, Brits serve these beans on sandwich-style bread and slather on some butter. I usually prefer a crusty bread (and vegan butter) instead, but I do see the appeal of a softer bread to soak up that gooey, thick sauce.

You can eat this humble meal any time of day, but I like it for breakfast because it has enough fiber and protein to help me stay full for hours, especially if I eat it with a hearty whole-grain bread. If beans on toast sounds weird to you, serve these beans at your next barbecue or potluck.

1 pound dried navy beans

1½ tablespoons plus 1½ teaspoons kosher salt, plus more to taste

2 cups low-sodium vegetable broth

3 tablespoons organic brown sugar, coconut sugar, or date sugar

¼ cup blackstrap molasses, plus more to taste

1 teaspoon smoked paprika

1 tablespoon whole-grain or Dijon mustard

1 tablespoon olive oil

1 large yellow onion, finely chopped

4 garlic cloves, finely chopped

3 bay leaves

Freshly cracked black pepper

½ cup canned tomato sauce

3 tablespoons vegan Worcestershire sauce, store-bought or homemade (recipe follows)

2 tablespoons tomato paste

1 tablespoon balsamic vinegar, plus more to taste

FOR SERVING

Bread of your choice

Extra-virgin olive oil or vegan butter

Chopped fresh Italian flat-leaf parsley (optional)

recipe continues

1. In a large bowl or the inner pot of the Instant Pot, combine the beans, 8 cups water, and 1½ tablespoons of the salt and let soak for at least 10 hours and up to 12 hours. (Soaking the beans in plenty of salted water is key to softening their skins.) Drain and rinse the beans.

2. When you are ready to cook the beans, in a large measuring cup, stir together the vegetable broth, brown sugar, molasses, smoked paprika, and mustard.

3. Select the Sauté setting on the Instant Pot and let the pot heat up for a few minutes before adding the olive oil. Once the oil is hot, add the onion. Cook until the onion is browned, 4 to 6 minutes. Add the garlic and cook until it starts to turn golden, about 1 minute.

4. Pour ½ cup of the broth-molasses mixture into the pot. Use a wooden spoon or spatula to scrape up any browned bits on the bottom of the pot. Cook 2 to 3 minutes to slightly thicken the mixture.

5. Add the soaked beans, bay leaves, black pepper to taste, the remaining 1½ teaspoons salt, and the remaining broth-molasses mixture. Stir to combine and select the Cancel setting.

6. Secure the lid and set the Pressure Release to Sealing. Select the Pressure Cook setting at high pressure and set the cook time to 35 minutes.

7. Once the 35-minute timer has completed and beeps, allow a natural pressure release.

8. Open the pot and check to see if the beans are tender. If they are still a bit firm, secure the lid and cook the beans for another 5 to 10 minutes on the Pressure Cook setting at high pressure and allow the pressure to release naturally for 10 minutes. Discard the bay leaves.

9. Once the beans are cooked to your liking, select the Sauté setting and add the tomato sauce, Worcestershire sauce, tomato paste, and vinegar. Simmer the beans uncovered, stirring occasionally, until the sauce is thick and gooey, 5 to 10 minutes. The beans will also thicken while resting.

10. While the beans heat, prepare your toast. I like to drizzle my toast with extra-virgin olive oil and heat it up in a grill pan, or spread it with a pat of vegan butter and heat it up in a skillet.

11. Taste the beans and adjust the seasonings to your liking, adding more salt, molasses, or vinegar as desired. Top your toast with the beans and garnish with chopped parsley if desired.

Vegan Worcestershire Sauce
Makes about ⅓ cup

- ¾ cup apple cider vinegar
- 3 tablespoons organic brown sugar
- ⅓ cup reduced-sodium tamari or soy sauce
- ¾ teaspoon onion powder
- ¼ teaspoon ground cloves
- ¼ teaspoon ground cinnamon
- ½ teaspoon freshly cracked black pepper

Add the vinegar, brown sugar, tamari, onion powder, cloves, cinnamon, and pepper to a medium saucepan over medium-high heat. Bring to a boil, then reduce the heat to medium-low and simmer until the sauce has reduced by nearly half and has thickened considerably, 15 to 20 minutes. Store leftovers in a covered glass jar for up to 3 months.

COCONUT-MILLET PORRIDGE

serves 4	gluten-free, nut-free option, soy-free, no added sugar

If you're not familiar with millet, it is an underrated ancient grain that's rich in protein and alkaline in nature, which is beneficial for digestive health. And while it starts out as a nutty grain, when it gets cooked down with coconut milk, it transforms into a creamy porridge. It's the kind of porridge that will soothe your belly and heart and help you stay warm (and full) on cold winter days. This porridge is perfectly tasty on its own, but if you feel like dressing it up, I've included some of my favorite porridge toppings below.

MILLET

1 cup millet

1 (13.5-ounce) can "lite" or reduced-fat coconut milk

2¼ cups unsweetened plain almond milk or other nondairy milk

1½ teaspoons pure vanilla extract

1½ teaspoons ground cinnamon

¼ teaspoon ground ginger

4 large soft Medjool dates, pitted and finely chopped

¼ cup unsweetened shredded coconut

TOPPING OPTIONS

1 ounce 90% dark chocolate, chopped + 1 small banana, sliced + 2 tablespoons hemp seeds

¼ cup chopped pistachios + ¼ cup chopped dried apricots + 2 tablespoons chia seeds

2 tablespoons Mixed Berry Compote (page 287) + ¼ cup chopped walnuts + 2 tablespoons cacao nibs

1. Select the Sauté setting on the Instant Pot and, after a few minutes, add the millet to dry-toast. Toss occasionally until the millet is a shade darker, 5 to 7 minutes. Toasting unleashes millet's inherent nuttiness.

2. Carefully pour in the coconut milk and 1¼ cups of the almond milk. The mixture will briefly bubble. Add the vanilla, cinnamon, ginger, and dates. Stir to combine and select the Cancel setting.

3. Secure the lid and set the Pressure Release to Sealing. Select the Pressure Cook setting at high pressure and set the cook time to 12 minutes.

4. Once the 12-minute timer has completed and beeps, allow a natural pressure release.

5. Open the pot and stir to combine the porridge. The porridge will be very thick at this point. Add ½ cup of the remaining almond milk, stirring until the porridge is creamier and looser. Add another ½ cup milk as needed until you achieve your desired consistency. Then stir in the shredded coconut. Transfer the porridge to bowls and add your toppings of choice.

> **TIP** *If you want to lighten up this porridge, swap out the canned coconut milk and use 3½ cups of almond milk to cook the millet. To thin out the porridge, add about 1 additional cup of almond milk after cooking until you reach your desired consistency.*

SPICY GOLDEN MYLK

serves 4	gluten-free, nut-free option, soy-free, refined sugar–free

Growing up, turmeric was an essential ingredient in my family's medicine cabinet. Whenever I was sick, my mom would make me drink *haldi doodh*, which translates to "turmeric milk" in English. And once, when my sister sprained her ankle, my aunt lathered her swollen ankle in a thick turmeric paste, insisting that Eastern medicine would cure all. (From my sister's perspective, a bit of Western Advil would have also been helpful.)

This golden mylk harnesses turmeric's powerful anti-inflammatory and antioxidant properties. But turmeric isn't the only superstar in this beverage. Ginger, chile peppers, and cinnamon also contribute to this mylk's nutrient-rich profile, and the habanero pepper gives it a kick (if you're not keen on very spicy foods, use a serrano pepper instead and omit the seeds). The black pepper helps you get all the benefits of the turmeric by dramatically increasing its bioavailability. If you can't find fresh turmeric, you can use one-third the amount of ground turmeric, though the flavor and texture will be slightly different.

I like to drink this nourishing, no-fuss golden mylk first thing in the morning or on a cold afternoon when I need a pick-me-up but don't want any caffeine.

4 cups unsweetened plain almond milk or other nondairy milk

¼ cup pure maple syrup

4 cinnamon sticks

1 habanero pepper, thinly sliced (seeded and membranes removed for less heat; see headnote)

¼ cup grated fresh turmeric (from about one 4-inch piece)

¼ cup grated or minced fresh ginger (from about one 4-inch piece)

½ teaspoon freshly cracked black pepper

1. Combine the almond milk, maple syrup, cinnamon sticks, habanero, turmeric, ginger, and black pepper in the Instant Pot. Pour in 2 cups of water and stir to combine.

2. Secure the lid and set the Pressure Release to Sealing. Select the Pressure Cook setting at *low pressure* and set the cook time to 5 minutes.

3. Once the 5-minute timer has completed and beeps, allow a natural pressure release for 10 minutes and then switch the Pressure Release knob from Sealing to Venting to release any remaining steam.

4. Open the pot. Set a fine-mesh sieve over a large glass jug or jar and strain the mylk into the jug or jar. Discard the cinnamon sticks and any large pieces of ginger, turmeric, or chile. Once cooled, store in the fridge for up to 1 week.

3

SATISFYING SIDES

From creamy beans to hearty grain salads, these dishes are perfect for batch cooking and meal prep, and help round out the dinner table when feeding a crowd. Many of these dishes are hearty enough to work as a main course, such as the Mediterranean Lentil Salad (page 137), or can easily turn into one with the addition of a green salad or a hunk of bread.

BASIC (BUT OH-SO-DELICIOUS) INDIAN DAL

serves 4 to 6	gluten-free, nut-free, soy-free, no added sugar

Some people consider the lifeblood of India to be the sacred Ganges River. I, however, consider the lifeblood of India to be dal. Dal has been an integral part of India's culinary history for centuries, served at almost every meal. It's inexpensive, nourishing, and readily available, making it widely consumed by both the poor and rich, the rural and the urban. Dal begins with a very basic ingredient—a type of lentil, split pulse, or bean—but with a harmonious infusion of spices, herbs, and aromatics, it transforms from the simple to the exquisite, from the humble to the extraordinary.

Lentils cooked al dente are common in the West, but Indians typically cook lentils until they develop a thick, stew-like consistency. And the Instant Pot does a fabulous job of turning lentils and water into creamy morsels bathing in a velvety stew.

The final step in most dal recipes, including this one, is the *tadka*, and that's where the magic happens. Spices are tempered in hot oil until deeply fragrant and then poured over the cooked dal, adding an incredible depth of flavor to each bite.

TIP *You can find yellow lentils (split yellow mung beans or yellow mung dal) in most grocery stores these days, as well as online or in Indian grocery stores. If they're not available, you can substitute red lentils.*

1½ cups yellow lentils (split yellow mung beans) (see Tip)

3 tablespoons unrefined virgin coconut oil

1 large yellow onion, chopped

5 garlic cloves, minced

1½-inch piece fresh ginger, grated or minced

2 serrano peppers (seeded and membranes removed for less heat), diced

1 teaspoon ground cumin

1 teaspoon ground coriander

1 teaspoon ground turmeric

1 teaspoon garam masala

½ teaspoon Indian red chile powder or ¼ teaspoon cayenne pepper (omit for a mild version)

2 bay leaves

4 cups water

1 teaspoon kosher salt, plus more to taste

2 large or 3 small tomatoes, chopped, or 1 (14.5-ounce) can diced tomatoes

2 shallots, thinly sliced

½ teaspoon black mustard seeds or brown mustard seeds

1 teaspoon cumin seeds

3 dried red chile peppers (optional)

Juice of ½ lime, plus more to taste

½ cup fresh cilantro, roughly chopped

FOR SERVING

White rice

Indian bread such as naan, roti, or dosa

recipe continues

1. Soak the lentils in cold water for 15 minutes and then drain them.

2. Select the Sauté setting on the Instant Pot and let the pot heat up for a few minutes before adding 1 tablespoon of the coconut oil, followed by the onion. Cook until the onion is translucent, 3 to 4 minutes.

3. Add the garlic, ginger, and serranos, and cook for 1 to 2 minutes, stirring frequently to prevent sticking.

4. Add the ground cumin, coriander, turmeric, garam masala, chile powder (if using), and bay leaves and stir vigorously for 30 seconds until very aromatic.

5. Select the Cancel setting and pour in the water, using a wooden spoon to scrape up any browned bits on the bottom of the pot. Add the soaked and drained lentils, salt, and tomatoes. Stir to combine.

6. Secure the lid and set the Pressure Release to Sealing. Select the Pressure Cook setting at high pressure and set the cook time to 10 minutes.

7. Once the 10-minute timer has completed and beeps, allow a natural pressure release for 10 minutes and then switch the Pressure Release knob from Sealing to Venting to release any remaining steam.

8. While the pot is depressurizing, make the *tadka*. Heat a medium skillet on the stove over medium-high heat. Add the remaining 2 tablespoons coconut oil and, once shimmering, add the shallots. Stir and cook until the shallots turn golden and are beginning to crisp, 2 to 3 minutes. Add the mustard seeds, cumin seeds, and dried red chiles (if using). Cook, stirring frequently, until the seeds are beginning to pop, 30 to 60 seconds. Remove from the heat.

9. Open the pot and discard the bay leaves. Carefully pour the *tadka* over the dal. Stir to combine well. Add the lime juice and cilantro and taste for seasonings, adding more salt or lime juice as needed.

10. Serve the dal with rice and/or your choice of Indian bread.

FLUFFY GARLIC MASHED POTATOES

serves 6	gluten-free, nut-free, soy-free, no added sugar

I've been making mashed potatoes for family holidays since I was fifteen years old. Using the Instant Pot is, without a doubt, the easiest method I've tried yet. Typically, I spend up to an hour waiting for the potatoes to reach a boil, then check every few minutes for fork-tenderness. And the potatoes usually don't cook evenly. Now I swear by the Instant Pot for making mashed potatoes, as it's foolproof, stress-free, and takes a fraction of the time.

Russet potatoes are your best bet for light and fluffy mashed potatoes, as they are a high-starch potato. You can also use medium-starch Yukon Gold potatoes, which have less inherent fluffiness but more flavor. Want the best of both worlds? Use half Yukon Golds and half russets for light, fluffy mashed potatoes with a hearty potato flavor.

For fluffy and smooth potatoes, use a ricer or food mill. A handheld potato masher is your next best bet, followed by an electric handheld mixer, but I strongly recommend against throwing the potatoes in a food processor—it'll leave you with a sticky, gummy mess.

2½ pounds russet potatoes and/or Yukon Gold potatoes (see headnote)

6 large garlic cloves, roughly chopped

2½ teaspoons kosher salt, plus more to taste

6 tablespoons vegan butter (use a soy-free variety to keep soy-free), plus more to taste

⅓ cup canned "lite" or reduced-fat coconut milk

Freshly cracked black pepper

OPTIONAL GARNISHES

Finely chopped fresh herbs, such as rosemary, thyme, chives, or Italian flat-leaf parsley

Extra-virgin olive oil, for drizzling

recipe continues

1. Scrub, peel, and dice the potatoes into 1- to 1½-inch pieces and place in the inner pot of the Instant Pot. Add the garlic and 1 teaspoon of the salt. Cover the potatoes with enough water to completely cover the potatoes, 4 to 5 cups.

2. Secure the lid and set the Pressure Release to Sealing. Select the Pressure Cook setting at high pressure and set the cook time to 5 minutes for russet potatoes or 6 minutes for Yukon Gold potatoes (6 minutes if using a mixture of both).

3. Once the timer has completed and beeps, perform a quick pressure release by carefully switching the Pressure Release knob from Sealing to Venting.

4. Open the pot and transfer the potato-garlic mixture to a colander. The potatoes should be very fork-tender and nearly falling apart. Let the potatoes rest for 5 minutes to dry out.

5. If you are using a ricer or a food mill, set it over the inner pot or a large bowl and pass the potato-garlic mixture through. If you are using a potato masher or an electric handheld mixer (on low speed), return the potato-garlic mixture to the inner pot or a large bowl and mash. Add the vegan butter, coconut milk, and remaining 1½ teaspoons salt. Fold gently with a silicone spatula to combine, or, if using an electric handheld mixer, whip lightly until the potatoes are smooth and creamy.

6. Add more salt, vegan butter, and/or pepper to taste. I usually add about ½ teaspoon more salt. If desired, garnish with chopped fresh herbs and a drizzle of extra-virgin olive oil.

ISRAELI COUSCOUS AND LENTILS

serves 4 as a main dish, 8 as a side dish	nut-free, soy-free, no added sugar

There are many reasons why I love this recipe and think you will, too. For starters, it's a dump-everything-in recipe that requires no hands-on cooking. I think that's reason enough, but I have more reasons to share. Second, it's hearty enough to feel like a main dish thanks to the protein-packed lentils but still feels light and refreshing, in part due to the grassy flavor of fresh dill. And finally, this recipe yields a lot of food, so it's an ideal weekly-meal-prep-with-individual-containers situation. Or if you're feeling generous, you can bring it to a potluck, summer picnic, or barbecue.

I use French green lentils in this salad (and most lentil-based salads) because they hold their shape during cooking. Typically, there is no need to soak lentils, but soaking them here reduces the cook time to just 3 minutes, allowing you to cook the lentils at the same time as the Israeli couscous.

This is one of those dishes that gets better the next day, as the lentils and couscous will have had a chance to thoroughly absorb the flavors of the vinaigrette and herbs.

COUSCOUS AND LENTILS

1 cup French green (Puy) lentils

1 medium yellow onion, diced

2 red, yellow, or orange bell peppers, diced

2 carrots, diced

6 garlic cloves, minced

1 cup Israeli or pearl couscous

3½ cups low-sodium vegetable broth

2 teaspoons kosher salt

Freshly cracked black pepper

2 bay leaves

Handful of fresh thyme sprigs

TO FINISH

2½ tablespoons extra-virgin olive oil

1½ tablespoons red wine vinegar

1 small bunch of fresh dill (about 1 cup), finely chopped

1 cup fresh Italian flat-leaf parsley, finely chopped

15 pitted green olives, sliced

1 pint cherry tomatoes, halved or quartered

Kosher salt and freshly cracked black pepper

recipe continues

1. Soak the lentils in water to cover for 8 hours or overnight. Drain the lentils.

2. Place the soaked and drained lentils, onion, bell peppers, carrots, garlic, couscous, vegetable broth, salt, pepper to taste, bay leaves, and thyme sprigs in the Instant Pot and stir well to combine.

3. Secure the lid and set the Pressure Release to Sealing. Select the Pressure Cook setting at high pressure and set the cook time to 3 minutes.

4. Once the 3-minute timer has completed and beeps, allow a natural pressure release for 10 minutes and then switch the Pressure Release knob from Sealing to Venting to release any remaining steam.

5. Open the pot and discard the bay leaves and thyme sprigs.

6. Transfer the couscous-lentil mixture to a large bowl and allow to come to room temperature.

7. To the couscous-lentil mixture, add the extra-virgin olive oil, vinegar, dill, parsley, olives, tomatoes, and salt and pepper to taste. Stir to combine and taste for seasonings, adding more salt and pepper as needed, or a splash more vinegar for acidity.

CHINESE TAKEOUT-STYLE TOFU AND BROCCOLI

serves 4	gluten-free, nut-free

There are three keys to making tofu taste delicious. First, select the right variety. Tofu comes in many forms, but the extra-firm variety—with its spongy, dense texture and low water content—is best for frying, as in this recipe. Second, unless you are using a soft or silken tofu, you'll almost always want to press out the excess water in tofu. This drastically improves the texture, helps the tofu hold its shape when cooked, and enables more flavor to seep into the tofu. Finally, don't be stingy with seasonings, whether it's spices, aromatics, or sauces. Tofu is a blank canvas and easily takes on the flavors it's given.

For the tofu skeptics in my life, I often recommend trying this Chinese takeout-style tofu. It's a little crispy on the outside, soft and tender in the inside, and saturated with lots of bold flavors like ginger, Sriracha, and toasted sesame.

Since broccoli cooks very quickly in the Instant Pot, this recipe calls for pressure-cooking the tofu for a few minutes before adding the broccoli. To make this a complete, balanced meal, serve alongside rice or your favorite grain.

MARINATED TOFU

1 (14-ounce) block extra-firm tofu

3 tablespoons reduced-sodium tamari or soy sauce

2 teaspoons Sriracha or similar chili-garlic sauce

1 teaspoon toasted sesame oil

2 teaspoons rice vinegar

GINGER-CHILI SAUCE

¼ cup reduced-sodium tamari or soy sauce

¼ cup agave nectar or coconut nectar (or maple syrup, but that will have a more robust, less neutral flavor)

2 tablespoons water

1½ tablespoons Sriracha or similar chili-garlic sauce

1 tablespoon toasted sesame oil

1 tablespoon rice vinegar

1½-inch piece fresh ginger, grated or finely minced

FOR FINISHING

1½ tablespoons grapeseed oil or other neutral, high-heat cooking oil

2 medium heads broccoli, cut into small florets (about 4 cups)

2 tablespoons cornstarch

FOR SERVING

White rice or brown rice

recipe continues

1. Marinate the tofu: Drain the tofu and cut into 4 slabs. Place the tofu on a cutting board lined with paper towels. Place more paper towels on top of the tofu and weight them down with a few heavy cookbooks or a heavy skillet filled with a few cans of beans. Let sit for at least 30 minutes or ideally 1 hour, changing the paper towels in between to drain all of the moisture. Cut the tofu into ¾-inch cubes.

2. Place the tofu in a gallon-size zip-top bag and add the tamari, Sriracha, sesame oil, and vinegar. Toss to combine and let the tofu rest in the marinade for 5 minutes, massaging occasionally.

3. Meanwhile, make the ginger-chili sauce: In a medium bowl, whisk together the tamari, agave nectar, water, the Sriracha, sesame oil, vinegar, and ginger until well combined.

4. Finish the dish: Select the Sauté setting on the Instant Pot and let the pot heat up for a few minutes before adding the grapeseed oil. Once the display reads "HOT," use a slotted spoon or fork to carefully transfer the marinated tofu to the pot. Cook the tofu for 1½ minutes undisturbed. Use a spatula to flip and cook the tofu until it starts to brown on all sides, 3 to 4 minutes total. Add the ginger-chili sauce and stir to combine. Select the Cancel setting.

5. Secure the lid and set the Pressure Release to Sealing. Select the Pressure Cook setting at high pressure and set the cook time to 3 minutes.

6. Once the 3-minute timer has completed and beeps, perform a quick pressure release by carefully switching the Pressure Release knob from Sealing to Venting.

7. Open the pot. Add the broccoli florets to the tofu and stir with the sauce to combine. Secure the lid and set the Pressure Release to Sealing. Select the Pressure Cook setting to low pressure and set the cook time to 1 minute. Once the 1-minute timer has completed and beeps, carefully perform another quick pressure release.

8. In a small bowl, stir together the cornstarch with ¼ cup water, whisking until combined without any lumps. Select the Sauté setting and press the Sauté button again until you reach Less heat. Add the cornstarch slurry to the Instant Pot and gently stir to combine. Cook, stirring gently, until the sauce thickens, 2 to 3 minutes.

9. Serve the tofu and broccoli over rice.

TIP To crush sesame seeds, you can use a mortar and pestle or a spice grinder; pulse them in a food processor 6 to 8 times until the seeds are crushed; or, move the flat side of a large chef's knife over the seeds and press down to crush them.

SPICY SESAME EDAMAME

serves 4	gluten-free, nut-free

I really like all of the recipes in this book. But of course I do have a few favorite recipes, and this is one of them.

This dish is equal parts spicy and sweet, with notes of nuttiness from the sesame seeds and sesame oil. Its tantalizing aroma will excite your senses, and the heat of the chile peppers will pleasantly linger on your tongue. If you have a high tolerance for spicy food, I do recommend using two serrano peppers because the heat is well balanced by the other flavor profiles. For most palates, however, one serrano pepper works best. And if you're sensitive to spicy food, I recommend removing the chile's seeds and membranes.

1 pound frozen shelled edamame

1 tablespoon agave nectar or coconut nectar (or maple syrup, but it will have a more robust, less neutral flavor)

1 tablespoon tahini

Grated zest of 1 medium lime

1½ tablespoons fresh lime juice

3 tablespoons reduced-sodium tamari or soy sauce

1½ tablespoons white or black sesame seeds, crushed

1 tablespoon toasted sesame oil

1 tablespoon grapeseed oil or other neutral, high-heat cooking oil

1 bunch of scallions (about 6), thinly sliced

4 garlic cloves, chopped

1 to 2 serrano peppers, diced (see headnote)

¾ cup fresh cilantro, roughly chopped

¼ cup unsweetened shredded coconut

1. Pour 1½ cups water into the inner pot of the Instant Pot. Lower a steamer basket into the Instant Pot and add the edamame to the basket.

2. Secure the lid and set the Pressure Release to Sealing. Select the Pressure Cook setting at high pressure and set the cook time to 1 minute.

3. Meanwhile, in a small bowl, whisk together the agave nectar, tahini, lime zest, lime juice, tamari, crushed sesame seeds, and sesame oil. Set the dressing aside.

4. Once the 1-minute timer has completed and beeps, perform a quick pressure release by carefully switching the Pressure Release knob from Sealing to Venting.

5. Open the pot and, using oven mitts, carefully lift the steamer basket and set aside. Lift out the inner pot and discard the cooking water.

6. Return the inner pot to the Instant Pot. Select the Sauté setting and, after a few minutes, add the grapeseed oil. Once the display reads "HOT," add the scallions, garlic, and serranos. Cook until the garlic begins to turn golden, 2 to 3 minutes.

7. Return the steamed edamame to the pot and pour in the dressing. Stir to combine for 1 minute, ensuring all of the beans are coated with the dressing.

8. Transfer the edamame to a serving bowl and add the cilantro and shredded coconut. Gently toss to combine and serve warm or at room temperature.

CLASSIC CREAMY POLENTA

serves 4 to 6	gluten-free, nut-free, soy-free, no added sugar

I've always found the idea of making polenta using a traditional cooking method to be too daunting. In fact, the first time I tried making polenta was in the Instant Pot, and I was delighted to discover I could have the buttery, creamy goodness of this traditional Italian cornmeal porridge with minimal effort and very little stirring (no standing over a stove for 45 minutes!).

Traditionally, polenta is cooked in water, which allows the flavor of corn to take center stage, though savory vegetable broth brings a richer mouthfeel. This recipe for polenta is quite creamy as is, but if you want even more richness, stir in the optional "lite" coconut milk at the end and a sprinkling of vegan parmesan cheese. Use cornmeal that is labeled "polenta" or any medium or coarsely ground cornmeal (if you prefer a smoother polenta, stick to medium-grind cornmeal). Just stay away from finely ground cornmeal and instant polenta, as they tend to develop a pasty texture during cooking and lack that deep corn flavor.

When it comes to toppings, polenta is a natural bed for so many savory comfort foods and you can top it with anything you'd put on or in pasta. It's phenomenal with The Best Damn Ratatouille (page 173), a great way to scoop up the sauce in my Gigantes Plaki with Herbed Tofu Feta (page 131), or perfect with Caramelized Onion Jam (page 63).

Cooking spray or olive oil, for the pot

4 cups water or low-sodium vegetable broth, at room temperature

1 teaspoon kosher salt, plus more to taste

¼ teaspoon freshly cracked black pepper, plus more for serving

1 cup polenta (see headnote)

2 tablespoons extra-virgin olive oil

2 tablespoons vegan butter (use a soy-free variety to keep soy-free) or extra-virgin olive oil

A large handful of fresh thyme sprigs

A large handful of fresh oregano sprigs

¼ cup nutritional yeast

¾ cup canned "lite" or reduced-fat coconut milk (optional)

½ cup vegan parmesan cheese (optional)

recipe continues

1. Coat the inner pot of the Instant Pot with cooking spray or olive oil to minimize sticking. Select the Sauté setting on the Instant Pot and after a few minutes, add the water, salt, and pepper. Once the water is warm to the touch, gradually add the polenta, whisking after each addition. Bring the polenta mixture to a simmer and whisk again to combine all of the ingredients. Select the Cancel setting.

2. Secure the lid and set the Pressure Release to Sealing. Select the Pressure Cook setting at high pressure and set the cook time to 9 minutes.

3. Meanwhile, heat a large skillet over medium heat and add the extra-virgin olive oil and vegan butter (or simply use a total of ¼ cup extra-virgin olive oil). Once melted and frothy (or shimmering if just using oil), add the thyme and oregano sprigs. Allow the herbs to cook for a bit, tossing them around occasionally, until the oil is bubbling and smells very fragrant, 2 to 3 minutes. Discard the herbs using a slotted spoon.

4. Once the 9-minute timer has completed and beeps, perform a quick pressure release by carefully switching the Pressure Release knob from Sealing to Venting.

5. Open the pot and whisk the polenta until it is thick and creamy. Stir in the herb-infused oil-butter mixture and nutritional yeast. Whisk to incorporate all of the ingredients. Taste for seasonings and adjust accordingly, adding more salt as needed. If desired, stir in the coconut milk and vegan parmesan. Serve with freshly cracked black pepper.

TIP *Soft polenta solidifies in the fridge, so if you want creamy leftovers, heat the polenta on the stove over low heat or in the microwave with ¼ to ½ cup water or broth until it reaches your desired consistency, whisking well before serving. Or, better yet, take the solidified polenta, cut it into squares, and fry them in a little olive oil for a crispy snack.*

ROSEMARY AND GARLIC WHITE BEANS

makes about 7 cups	gluten-free, nut-free, soy-free, no added sugar

When you're looking for an easy side dish or protein fix that's hearty and flavorful, these beans are the answer. The first layer of flavor comes from rosemary, which infuses the beans with a uniquely piney aroma and earthy pungency. Next comes a whopping 10 cloves of garlic, which might sound like a lot, but a pound of beans swells to 7 cups when cooked. This bountiful amount of garlic makes each bite fragrant and sharp (just be sure to keep the post-dinner kissing to a minimum).

In addition to the bold flavors, I love the soft, creamy texture of the cannellini beans. While it's not necessary to soak beans when using the Instant Pot, if you have the time, I recommend soaking them, as I find that the beans cook more evenly and with fewer split skins (it also significantly reduces the cook time). The beans might appear a bit soupy when you first uncover the pot, but they thicken up quite a bit as they rest.

I keep a batch of these beans in the fridge for a quick pre- or post-workout snack and to serve alongside grain bowls and salads, but my favorite way to serve them is piled on top of a hunk of bread (obviously) and drizzled with extra-virgin olive oil.

1 pound dried cannellini beans (2¼ to 2½ cups)

2 tablespoons olive oil

¾ cup diced shallots (about 3 shallots)

2 tablespoons fresh rosemary leaves, roughly chopped

10 garlic cloves, roughly chopped

3½ to 5½ cups low-sodium vegetable broth or water (the larger quantity if using unsoaked beans)

2 bay leaves

1 tablespoon dried oregano

2½ teaspoons kosher salt

½ teaspoon freshly cracked black pepper

½ cup fresh Italian flat-leaf parsley, finely chopped (optional)

recipe continues

1. If you have time to soak the beans, place them in a large bowl and cover with 8 cups cold water. Soak for 8 hours or overnight. Drain the beans and rinse with fresh water.

2. Select the Sauté setting on the Instant Pot and, after a few minutes, add the olive oil, followed by the shallots. Cook until the shallots are starting to brown, about 2 minutes. Add the rosemary and garlic and stir occasionally until the garlic is soft and lightly golden, 1 to 1½ minutes. Select the Cancel setting.

3. Add the drained beans, 3½ cups broth (5½ cups for *unsoaked* beans), bay leaves, oregano, salt, and pepper, stirring well to combine.

4. Secure the lid and set the Pressure Release to Sealing. Select the Bean/Chili setting at high pressure and set the cook time to 9 minutes for soaked beans (or 55 minutes for *unsoaked* beans).

5. Once the timer has completed and beeps, allow a natural pressure release.

6. Open the pot, stir the beans, and discard the bay leaves. Taste for seasonings and adjust accordingly. Transfer to a serving dish and garnish with chopped parsley, if desired. Once cooled, store leftovers in a glass jar or airtight storage container for 1 week.

FRIJOLES
(MEXICAN-STYLE PINTO BEANS)

makes about 7 cups	gluten-free, nut-free, soy-free, no added sugar

Frijoles is simply the Mexican word for beans, and in Mexico, there are hundreds of different ways to prepare them. I keep my version of frijoles simple but flavorful with pinto beans and flavoring agents like onions, jalapeños, garlic, chili powder, and cilantro.

Spoon these beans into tortillas for tacos or burritos, serve with rice for an inexpensive yet satisfying meal, or turn them into a soup by adding more vegetable broth at the end. And don't forget the toppings: I love scallions and avocado, and a vegan cheddar cheese takes them over the top.

You'll note that the recipe calls for quick-soaking the beans for 15 minutes. I find that this quick soak helps the beans cook more evenly and results in fewer split skins, ensuring that some beans aren't falling apart while other beans are still firm.

1 pound dried pinto beans (about 2½ cups)

1 tablespoon olive oil

1 medium yellow onion, diced

1 red bell pepper, diced

2 teaspoons kosher salt, plus more to taste

Freshly cracked black pepper

2 jalapeño peppers, diced

4 garlic cloves, minced

4 cups low-sodium vegetable broth

1 tablespoon chili powder

2 teaspoons ground cumin

1½ teaspoons dried oregano

1½ teaspoons smoked paprika

¼ to ½ teaspoon cayenne pepper (optional for spicy), to taste

2 bay leaves

1 (14.5-ounce) can crushed fire-roasted tomatoes

½ cup fresh cilantro, roughly chopped

OPTIONAL GARNISHES

Chopped tomatoes and/or avocado

Shredded vegan cheddar cheese or Vegan Queso (page 49)

recipe continues

1. Place the beans in a large bowl and cover with a generous amount of cold water. Soak for 15 minutes. Drain the beans in a colander and rinse with fresh water.

2. Select the Sauté setting on the Instant Pot and let the pot heat up for a few minutes before adding the olive oil. Once the oil is hot, add the onion and bell pepper. Season with a pinch each of salt and black pepper and cook for 4 to 5 minutes, stirring occasionally. Add the jalapeños and garlic and cook for 1 minute, stirring frequently to prevent burning. Select the Cancel setting.

3. Add the soaked and drained pinto beans, vegetable broth, chili powder, cumin, oregano, smoked paprika, cayenne (if using), bay leaves, 2 teaspoons salt, and black pepper to taste. Stir well to combine. Top the mixture with the crushed tomatoes but do not stir, allowing the tomatoes to sit on top (this prevents the tomatoes from blocking the Instant Pot's heat sensor and burning).

4. Secure the lid and set the Pressure Release to Sealing. Select the Bean/Chili setting at high pressure and set the cook time to 50 minutes.

5. Once the 50-minute timer has completed and beeps, allow a natural pressure release.

6. Open the pot, stir the beans, and discard the bay leaves. Add the cilantro and taste for seasonings, adding more salt as needed. Garnish the beans as desired.

GIGANTES PLAKI
WITH HERBED TOFU FETA

serves 6	gluten-free, nut-free, no added sugar

Several years ago, I traveled to Greece with my mother and sister, where I spent my days savoring crisp white wine, the Aegean Sea, and a variety of Greek specialties including this dish.

Gigantes plaki are giant Greek beans baked in tomato sauce and lots of herbs until creamy and tender. This dish is typically served as a side dish but it's satisfying enough to work as a main dish, especially if you make the protein-packed tofu feta. And as with many Greek foods, it's even more delicious served alongside a slice of rustic bread.

I love *gigante* beans because their large size makes them feel particularly hearty and when they're cooked, they become creamy yet still hold their shape well. You can find *gigantes* in Mediterranean stores, specialty food markets, or online. If you cannot find them, substitute large lima beans or butter beans.

The herbed tofu feta is incredibly easy to make and takes this dish over the top. The hardest part is waiting for it to marinate in the fridge. Serve leftover feta in salads, on top of pizza, stuffed in tomatoes or zucchini, or on roasted potatoes. If you don't make the tofu feta, I recommend adding an additional ½ teaspoon kosher salt to the beans while they cook.

GIGANTE BEANS

2 cups dried gigantes (Greek giant beans) or other large white beans (see headnote)

2 teaspoons kosher salt, plus more to taste

2 tablespoons olive oil

1 large Spanish onion, diced

5 garlic cloves, thinly sliced

1 teaspoon crushed red pepper flakes

⅓ cup dry white wine (such as Pinot Grigio or Sauvignon Blanc)

3 cups water

3 bay leaves

1½ teaspoons dried oregano

½ teaspoon freshly cracked black pepper

1 (28-ounce) can crushed San Marzano tomatoes

2 tablespoons tomato paste

FOR SERVING

½ to 1 cup Herbed Tofu Feta (optional; recipe follows)

¼ cup chopped fresh Italian flat-leaf parsley

1 tablespoon fresh lemon juice

recipe continues

1. Prepare the beans: Soak the *gigantes* in 6 cups water with 1 teaspoon of the salt for at least 12 hours, or up to 16 hours. Drain the beans.

2. Select the Sauté setting on the Instant Pot, and after a few minutes, add the olive oil, followed by the onion. Cook until the onion is translucent, 4 to 5 minutes. Add the garlic and pepper flakes and cook, stirring frequently, for 1 minute.

3. Pour in the wine and cook until it has almost evaporated, 3 to 4 minutes. Add the soaked beans and toss to coat for 30 seconds. Add the water, bay leaves, oregano, black pepper, and remaining 1 teaspoon salt (or 1½ teaspoons if not making the tofu feta). Stir to combine and select the Cancel setting.

4. Secure the lid and set the Pressure Release to Sealing. Select the Bean/Chili setting at high pressure and set the cook time to 25 minutes.

5. Once the 25-minute timer has completed and beeps, allow a natural pressure release for 10 minutes and then switch the Pressure Release knob from Sealing to Venting to release any remaining steam.

6. Check the beans with a fork—they should be mostly but not completely tender (if they are not, cook for 5 more minutes and allow a natural pressure release for 5 minutes). Using a soup ladle, scoop out ¾ to 1 cup of the liquid and discard. This helps keep the beans thick and saucy.

7. Add the crushed tomatoes and tomato paste and stir well. Secure the lid and set the Pressure Release to Sealing. Select the Bean/Chili setting at high pressure and set the cook time to 5 minutes. Allow a natural pressure release for 5 minutes and then switch the Pressure Release knob from Sealing to Venting to release any remaining steam.

8. Open the pot and discard the bay leaves. Serve the beans topped with herbed tofu feta and chopped parsley. Squeeze the lemon juice on top.

Herbed Tofu Feta
Makes about 2½ cups

1 (14-ounce) block extra-firm tofu

3 tablespoons white or yellow miso paste

⅓ cup apple cider vinegar or red wine vinegar

¼ cup fresh lemon juice (about 1½ medium lemons)

2 tablespoons extra-virgin olive oil

4 garlic cloves, crushed through a press

2 tablespoons nutritional yeast

1 tablespoon dried oregano

½ teaspoon onion powder

½ teaspoon crushed red pepper flakes (optional)

½ teaspoon kosher salt

½ teaspoon freshly cracked black pepper

1. Drain the tofu and cut into 4 slabs. Place the tofu on a cutting board lined with paper towels. Place more paper towels on top of the tofu and weight them down with a few heavy cookbooks or a heavy skillet filled with a few cans of beans. Let sit for at least 1 hour, changing the paper towels in between to drain all of the moisture. Cut the pressed tofu into small cubes.

2. In a bowl, whisk together the miso, vinegar, ⅓ cup water, the lemon juice, olive oil, garlic, nutritional yeast, oregano, onion powder, pepper flakes (if using), salt, and black pepper until well combined.

3. Place the tofu in a large glass jar or container and pour on the marinade. Mix well and refrigerate for at least 2 hours or up to 48 hours. Tofu feta will stay good for 5 to 7 days.

MILLET-CAULIFLOWER MASH

serves 6 to 8	gluten-free, nut-free, soy-free, no added sugar

The Instant Pot takes cruciferous cauliflower and crunchy millet and instantly turns them into a bed of soft, pillowy mash. In the winter, I make a batch of this and serve it with roasted veggies and tahini. You can also serve it alongside a big green salad or cooked greens like the Citrus Kale and Carrots (page 167), top it with a stew or saucy beans such as the Rosemary and Garlic White Beans (page 125), or pair it with The Best Damn Ratatouille (page 173).

1½ tablespoons olive oil

2 medium leeks, dark green tops discarded, thoroughly cleaned, trimmed, and diced

3 garlic cloves, minced

1 cup millet

2¼ cups low-sodium vegetable broth

1 medium cauliflower (2 to 2½ pounds), cut into florets

2 teaspoons kosher salt, plus more to taste

Freshly cracked black pepper

2 to 3 tablespoons tahini

1 teaspoon apple cider vinegar or distilled white vinegar

½ cup fresh Italian flat-leaf parsley, chopped

OPTIONAL GARNISHES

Chopped chives and extra-virgin olive oil

1. Select the Sauté setting on the Instant Pot and let the pot heat up for a few minutes before adding the olive oil. Once the oil is hot, add the leeks. Cook until the leeks are tender, 2 to 3 minutes. Add the garlic and cook for 1 minute, stirring frequently to prevent burning.

2. Add the millet and toss for 30 to 60 seconds to coat the grains. Pour in the vegetable broth, followed by the cauliflower, salt, and pepper to taste. Select the Cancel setting.

3. Secure the lid and set the Pressure Release to Sealing. Select the Pressure Cook setting at high pressure and set the cook time to 10 minutes.

4. Once the 10-minute timer has completed and beeps, allow a natural pressure release.

5. Open the pot and stir to combine the ingredients. Using an immersion blender, carefully blend the millet-cauliflower mixture until the texture is similar to thick mashed potatoes. (Alternatively, you can transfer the mixture to a food processor or blender or use a potato masher.)

6. Drizzle in 2 tablespoons tahini and the vinegar, stir to incorporate, and taste for seasonings. I usually add a third tablespoon of tahini and a bit more salt at this point. Top with chopped parsley and garnish as desired. Serve warm.

MEDITERRANEAN LENTIL SALAD

serves 4 as a main dish, 8 as a side dish	gluten-free, soy-free, refined sugar–free

This salad is an ode to one of my favorite chefs, Yotam Ottolenghi. His pairing of vegetables, legumes, and grains—married with ingredients like fresh herbs, toasted nuts, and dried fruit—is always elegant and exquisite, and opens your palate up to a world of plant-based possibilities. And his generous and creative use of spices and herbs invites you to reimagine and reexperience Mediterranean and Middle Eastern flavors.

This salad calls for handfuls of parsley, cilantro, and mint, but you can use other tender herbs if you like (basil would be lovely). Rinse the herbs and pat dry, remove the leaves from the stems, discard the stems, and add the leaves whole to the salad or coarsely chop them. The fresh herbs add a deep complexity and aroma to this salad.

I love using French green lentils in salads because they hold their shape even when cooked under the high pressure of the Instant Pot. You can substitute standard green or brown lentils (though they will come out a bit mushier). Finally, if you can't find dried figs, you can substitute chopped dates, currants, or golden raisins.

LENTILS

1 cup French green (Puy) lentils

1¾ cups low-sodium vegetable broth or water

6 sprigs fresh thyme

2 garlic cloves, minced

1 bay leaf

1 teaspoon dried oregano

½ teaspoon cumin seeds

½ teaspoon kosher salt

½ teaspoon freshly cracked black pepper or whole black peppercorns

SALAD

½ cup fresh Italian flat-leaf parsley, leaves only

½ cup fresh mint, leaves only

½ cup fresh cilantro, leaves only

¼ cup sliced or slivered almonds

3 large carrots

½ small red onion, very thinly sliced

4 ounces baby arugula (about 4 cups)

½ cup dried Black Mission figs, quartered, or Medjool dates, chopped

¼ cup pistachios, chopped

2 tablespoons white sesame seeds

Citrus-Cumin Vinaigrette (recipe follows)

recipe continues

1. Make the lentils: Add the lentils, broth, thyme, garlic, bay leaf, oregano, cumin seeds, salt, and pepper to the Instant Pot and stir to combine.

2. Secure the lid and set the Pressure Release to Sealing. Select the Pressure Cook setting at high pressure and set the cook time to 6 minutes.

3. Meanwhile, prepare the salad: Roughly chop the parsley, mint, and cilantro leaves. Or, if you prefer, you can leave the leaves whole.

4. Heat a skillet over medium heat and spread out the almonds. Let them sit for 1 to 2 minutes until they start to get brown and fragrant. Stir the almonds around in the pan, stirring every 30 seconds or so until they are nicely browned and have a toasted flavor. Pour out of the skillet into a large salad bowl to cool.

5. Run a Y-shaped vegetable peeler down the length of the carrots to create ribbons. Place them in the salad bowl with the toasted almonds. Add the chopped herbs, red onion, and arugula.

6. Once the 6-minute timer on the Instant Pot has completed and beeps, allow a natural pressure release for 10 minutes and then switch the Pressure Release knob from Sealing to Venting to release any remaining steam.

7. Open the pot, stir the lentils, and discard the bay leaf and thyme sprigs. Using a slotted spoon, transfer the lentils to the salad bowl with the salad ingredients, leaving any remaining liquid in the pot. Toss all of the ingredients together with tongs or two large spoons. Top the salad with the dried figs, pistachios, and sesame seeds.

8. When ready to serve, drizzle the salad with the citrus-cumin vinaigrette and season to taste with additional salt and pepper.

Citrus-Cumin Vinaigrette
Makes about 5 tablespoons

1 tablespoon fresh lemon juice
1 garlic clove, finely minced
1 teaspoon pure maple syrup
1 teaspoon Dijon or whole-grain mustard
½ teaspoon kosher salt
Freshly cracked black pepper to taste
½ teaspoon ground cumin
½ teaspoon sweet paprika
¼ teaspoon ground coriander
⅛ teaspoon ground cinnamon
3 tablespoons extra-virgin olive oil

In a small bowl, combine the lemon juice, garlic, maple syrup, mustard, salt, pepper, cumin, paprika, coriander, and cinnamon and whisk to combine. Stream in the olive oil while whisking to emulsify the dressing. Taste for seasonings and adjust accordingly. (Alternatively, you can add all of the ingredients to a glass jar, secure the lid, and shake vigorously until well combined.)

WILD RICE SALAD
WITH LEMON-SHALLOT VINAIGRETTE

serves 8	gluten-free, soy-free, refined sugar–free

I knew this salad was a winner when my partner eagerly shoved large spoonfuls down his throat. My partner does not like earthy tastes (wild rice is very earthy), he does not like dried fruit (he believes it has no place in savory food; he is simply wrong); and he doesn't care for kale (I know, he is a silly man).

One of my favorite parts of this salad is the dried sour cherries, which have a chewy bite and a unique sweet-sour flavor. If you cannot find dried cherries, you can use dried cranberries and soak them in hot water for 20 minutes to plump them up. Most store-bought dried cranberries are sweeter than cherries, so don't go overboard. I also adore the pine nuts in this recipe, but I know those tiny little things can be very pricy, so feel free to use chopped toasted almonds instead. The freshness of the herbs balances the earthy bold-ness of the rice, and the lemony vinaigrette adds a delightful zing that brings everything together.

I like to serve this as a side dish, but add some lentils or beans, and you have yourself a satisfying main course. Leftovers will stay good in the fridge for 2 to 3 days, but let the salad come to room temperature before serving.

2 cups wild rice (about 12 ounces)

3¼ cups low-sodium vegetable broth

½ cup walnuts, roughly chopped

½ cup pine nuts or almonds

½ cup fresh cilantro, leaves only

½ cup fresh Italian flat-leaf parsley, leaves only

1 cup fresh basil leaves

1 small bunch of Tuscan (lacinato) kale (about 5 ounces)

½ cup dried sour cherries

½ cup dried apricots, chopped

LEMON-SHALLOT VINAIGRETTE

Grated zest of 1 large lemon

¼ cup fresh lemon juice

1 tablespoon pure maple syrup

2 teaspoons Dijon mustard

3 tablespoons diced shallots

2 garlic cloves, finely minced

6 tablespoons extra-virgin olive oil

Kosher salt or sea salt and freshly cracked black pepper

recipe continues

1. Place the wild rice in a fine-mesh sieve and rinse under cold water. Shake to drain and add the rice to the inner pot of the Instant Pot. Add the vegetable broth and stir to combine.

2. Secure the lid and set the Pressure Release to Sealing. Select the Pressure Cook setting at high pressure and set the cook time to 25 minutes.

3. Meanwhile, heat a medium or large skillet over medium-low heat. Add the walnuts and pine nuts and leave them for 1 minute until they start to get brown and fragrant. Stir the nuts around in the pan frequently to avoid burning and toast them until they are nicely browned and have a toasted flavor. Remove from the pan and set aside to cool.

4. Roughly chop the cilantro and parsley leaves. Make a chiffonade of basil by stacking the leaves on top of each other, rolling them up, and slicing thinly into strips. Strip the kale of its stems and ribs (or trim them using a knife) and slice the leaves into thin strips.

5. In a large salad bowl, combine the herbs, kale, walnuts and pine nuts, dried cherries, and dried apricots.

6. Make the lemon-shallot vinaigrette: In a bowl, combine the lemon zest, lemon juice, maple syrup, mustard, shallots, and garlic and whisk to combine. Stream in the olive oil while whisking to emulsify the dressing. Season with a generous amount of salt and pepper to taste. If the vinaigrette tastes a bit too acidic or sour for your taste, add 1 or 2 more teaspoons maple syrup.

7. Once the 25-minute timer has completed and beeps, allow a natural pressure release for 10 minutes and then switch the Pressure Release knob from Sealing to Venting to release any remaining steam.

8. Open the pot and give the rice a stir. There may be a little liquid left over, which is normal. Using a slotted spoon, transfer the rice to the large salad bowl with the rest of the salad ingredients, discarding any liquid as necessary. Toss all of the ingredients together with tongs or two large spoons. Pour on the vinaigrette and toss thoroughly. Taste for seasonings and adjust accordingly.

4

VEGETABLES

A vegan cookbook would not be complete without
a chapter dedicated to vegetables, so here it is.
But you won't find steamed broccoli or boiled
potatoes here. In a vegan world, vegetables get
elevated from neglected stepsisters to the
stars of the show, and these recipes will teach
you how to make vegetables shine—from
transforming crunchy carrots into rich buttery
goodness to making greens taste indulgent.

SPAGHETTI SQUASH PASTA PUTTANESCA

serves 4	gluten-free, nut-free, soy-free, no added sugar

Spaghetti squash is low-carb, but its noodle-ish strands mimic pasta in a surprisingly satisfying way. And there's a scandalous Italian fable behind the garlicky, umami-rich puttanesca sauce (legend has it the aromatic sauce was created by ladies of the night to lure in customers).

I love this recipe because it's ridiculously easy to make and packed with flavor, which makes for a winning combo. The combination of capers, caper brine, and olives creates a complex salty flavor that permeates each bite. Traditional puttanesca sauce is made with black olives, but feel free to substitute green olives (my preference). Also, try to pick a squash that weighs under 3½ pounds, or you might have trouble fitting both halves into a 6-quart Instant Pot.

TIP *Cutting the spaghetti squash crosswise instead of lengthwise will yield longer "pasta" strands. I find that it's easiest to run a sharp paring knife along the squash instead of trying to cut it with a large knife in one fell swoop.*

1 medium spaghetti squash (2½ to 3 pounds)

2 tablespoons olive oil

1 small yellow onion, diced

6 garlic cloves, minced

1 to 2 teaspoons crushed red pepper flakes, to taste

2 teaspoons dried oregano

1 cup cherry tomatoes or grape tomatoes, sliced

½ to 1 teaspoon kosher salt (depending on how salty your olives are)

½ teaspoon freshly cracked black pepper

1 (14.5-ounce) can crushed tomatoes, preferably San Marzano

¼ cup capers + 1 tablespoon caper brine

½ cup olives (preferably oil-cured), sliced

OPTIONAL GARNISHES

¼ cup pine nuts (not nut-free)

¼ cup vegan parmesan cheese

⅓ cup fresh Italian flat-leaf parsley, chopped

1. With a sharp knife, halve the spaghetti squash crosswise (see Tip). Using a spoon or melon baller, scoop out the seeds and sticky gunk in the middle of each half.

2. Pour 1 cup water into the inner pot of the Instant Pot and place the steamer rack in the pot with the handles facing up. Arrange the squash halves, cut side facing up, on top of the steamer rack.

3. Secure the lid and select the Pressure Cook setting at high pressure and set the cook time to 7 minutes.

4. Once the 7-minute timer has completed and beeps, perform a quick pressure release by carefully switching the Pressure Release knob from Sealing to Venting.

5. Open the pot and check the doneness of the squash using a fork. It should be tender but not mushy. If you want the squash to be more tender, secure the lid and cook on the same setting for 1 to 2 minutes longer and perform a quick pressure release.

6. Open the pot and, using oven mitts, carefully lift the steamer rack out of the Instant Pot and pour out the water that has collected in the squash cavities. Wrap each squash half in a kitchen towel so you can comfortably handle it while still hot. Using the tines of a fork, separate the cooked strands into spaghetti-like pieces and set aside in a bowl.

7. Pour the water out of the inner pot and return it to the Instant Pot. Select the Sauté setting and let the pot heat up for a few minutes before adding the olive oil. Once the oil is hot, add the onion and cook for 3 minutes. Add the garlic, pepper flakes, and oregano and cook for 1 minute.

8. Add the sliced tomatoes, salt, and black pepper and cook until the tomatoes are softened, about 2 minutes.

9. Pour in the crushed tomatoes, capers, caper brine, and olives and bring the mixture to a boil. Select the Cancel setting and then re-select the Sauté setting and press the Sauté button again until you reach Less heat. Cook for 2 to 3 minutes to allow the flavors to meld.

10. Stir in the spaghetti squash noodles and cook for 1 to 2 minutes to warm everything through.

11. Transfer the dish to a serving platter. If desired, garnish with pine nuts, vegan parmesan, and chopped parsley.

SWEET POTATOES
WITH SRIRACHA CASHEW SAUCE

serves 4	gluten-free

All of the ingredients in this dish meld harmoniously to create a side dish that's a little spicy, a little sweet, and full of bold flavors. If you can't find cashew butter, feel free to substitute almond butter or peanut butter. If you use peanut butter, the flavor will be a bit more intense and peanutty (not surprising), so you may want to use a little less peanut butter.

I've had the best results with large sweet potatoes (8 to 9 ounces) that I cut into 4 thick wedges. Cooking the wedges at low pressure for 5 minutes yields tender sweet potatoes that are still firm enough to hold up to the creamy sauce.

2½ pounds sweet potatoes, 8 to 9 ounces each

SRIRACHA CASHEW SAUCE

¼ cup no-added-sugar creamy cashew butter

2 tablespoons water

1½ tablespoons Sriracha or similar chili-garlic sauce (use less for a milder version)

1½ tablespoons rice vinegar or fresh lime juice

1 tablespoon pure maple syrup or agave nectar

1 tablespoon reduced-sodium tamari or soy sauce

1 tablespoon toasted sesame oil

1-inch piece fresh ginger, grated or minced

3 garlic cloves, crushed through a press

GARNISHES

1 tablespoon white or black sesame seeds

½ cup fresh cilantro, roughly chopped

3 scallions (white and light-green parts only), thinly sliced

1. Peel the sweet potatoes and cut each one into 4 large wedges. Try to cut them as evenly in size as possible to ensure even cooking. Place the potato wedges in a steamer basket.

2. Pour 1¼ cups water into the inner pot of the Instant Pot and place the steamer basket in the pot.

3. Secure the lid and set the Pressure Release to Sealing. Select the Steam setting at *low pressure* and set the cook time to 5 minutes.

4. Meanwhile, make the Sriracha cashew sauce: For a very smooth sauce, add the cashew butter, water, Sriracha, vinegar, maple syrup, tamari, sesame oil, ginger, and garlic to a blender and puree until creamy. For a slightly chunkier sauce, place the cashew butter in a microwave-safe medium bowl and microwave for 20 to 30 seconds until it's very smooth. Then add the remaining ingredients except for the water and whisk until combined. Add the water and whisk to thin out the sauce.

5. Once the 5-minute timer has completed and beeps, perform a quick pressure release by carefully switching the Pressure Release knob from Sealing to Venting.

6. Open the pot and, using oven mitts, carefully lift the steamer basket out of the Instant Pot and set aside. Remove the inner pot and pour out the cooking water, then return it to the Instant Pot.

7. Select the Sauté setting and press the Sauté button again until you reach Less heat. Once the pot is warm, pour in the Sriracha cashew sauce and gently stir using a silicone spatula for 1 minute. Add the cooked sweet potatoes to the sauce and gently stir for 1 to 2 minutes to coat them in the sauce, taking care to not mush the potatoes.

8. Remove the potatoes from the heat and gently toss with the sesame seeds, cilantro, and scallions. Serve immediately.

LEMONY ASPARAGUS WITH GREMOLATA

serves 2 to 4

gluten-free, nut-free, soy-free, refined sugar–free

Though you can likely find spindly stalks of imported asparagus year-round in many supermarkets, asparagus is a spring treasure and is intensely more flavorful when eaten in season. It is tender and sweet (yes, sweet!) with crisp vegetal notes. I add a punchy vinaigrette and citrusy gremolata, which offer strong, bold flavors without overpowering the asparagus.

To trim the woody bottoms of asparagus, hold the asparagus with two hands and find the natural break point. Instead of snapping right there, I cut an inch or so below that. This method involves less waste, of both food and money (the king of spring ain't cheap). I find that medium spears work best in the Instant Pot. The very thin stalks are too delicate for pressure cooking and the fat stalks are too fibrous.

TIP *Have leftover gremolata or want to double the recipe? Sprinkle it on leftover cooked vegetables, add it to a marinade or a salad dressing, or toss it with hot pasta.*

GREMOLATA

1 cup loosely packed fresh Italian flat-leaf parsley leaves

3 garlic cloves, peeled

2 small or 1 extra-large organic lemon

ASPARAGUS

1½ pounds asparagus, trimmed (see headnote)

LEMONY VINAIGRETTE

1½ tablespoons fresh lemon juice

1 teaspoon pure maple syrup

1 teaspoon Dijon mustard

2 tablespoons extra-virgin olive oil

Kosher salt or sea salt and freshly cracked black pepper

OPTIONAL GARNISH

2 to 3 tablespoons slivered almonds, to taste (not nut-free)

recipe continues

1. Make the gremolata: Finely chop the parsley. Using a Microplane, grate the garlic directly over the parsley and then zest the lemon(s) on top. Mix the garlic and lemon into the parsley and chop the parsley until finely minced.

2. Cook the asparagus: Pour 1 cup water into the inner pot of the Instant Pot. Arrange the asparagus in a steamer basket or place them on top of the steamer rack. Lower the steamer basket or steamer rack (handles facing up) into the Instant Pot.

3. Secure the lid and set the Pressure Release to Sealing. Select the Steam setting at *low pressure* and set the cook time to 2 minutes.

4. Meanwhile, prepare the lemony vinaigrette: In a bowl, combine the lemon juice, maple syrup, and mustard and whisk to combine. Slowly drizzle in the olive oil and continue to whisk. Season generously with salt and pepper to taste.

5. Once the 2-minute timer has completed and beeps, perform a quick pressure release by carefully switching the Pressure Release knob from Sealing to Venting.

6. Open the pot and, using oven mitts, carefully remove the steamer basket or steamer rack from the Instant Pot.

7. Transfer the asparagus to a serving platter, drizzle with the vinaigrette, and sprinkle on the gremolata. Taste for seasonings and add more salt or pepper as needed. If desired, finish the asparagus with slivered almonds.

COUSCOUS AND CHICKPEA–STUFFED BELL PEPPERS

makes 4 stuffed peppers	nut-free, soy-free, no added sugar

You might be wondering why you should make stuffed peppers in your Instant Pot instead of in your oven. First of all, you don't have to turn on your oven, which is a wonderful relief in the summer. Second, traditional recipes call for parboiling the peppers before baking and other extra steps, while this meal comes together in no time (well, some time, but very little time). And Instant Pot peppers turn out juicy and plump every time.

For the filling, I love using Israeli couscous, a soft but chewy grain that is objectively superior to its cousin, regular couscous. But, if you want to make this recipe as easy as possible, use any grains that are leftover in your fridge. My favorite alternative is brown rice, but quinoa would also work (and orzo, though technically not a grain, is also delicious here).

A 6-quart Instant Pot will comfortably fit 4 large peppers or 5 small-to-medium ones. Depending on their size, you might have a little extra stuffing, but I am pretty sure you won't mind because it makes an incredibly tasty snack.

4 large bell peppers

STUFFING

1½ cups cooked Israeli (pearl) couscous (see Tip) or other cooked grain (see headnote)

4 garlic cloves, finely minced

1¾ cups cooked chickpeas or 1 (15-ounce) can chickpeas, drained and rinsed

1 (6-ounce) jar marinated artichokes, drained and chopped

¼ cup pitted green olives, sliced

1 teaspoon ground cumin

1 teaspoon dried oregano

1 teaspoon dried thyme

½ teaspoon sweet or hot paprika

1 scant teaspoon kosher salt

½ teaspoon freshly cracked black pepper

¼ cup fresh lemon juice (about 1½ medium lemons), plus more to taste

¼ cup tahini

½ cup loosely packed fresh Italian flat-leaf parsley, chopped

½ cup loosely packed fresh dill, finely chopped

FOR SERVING

¼ cup fresh basil, finely slivered

1 to 2 tablespoons tahini, to taste

¼ cup Herbed Tofu Feta (page 131; not soy-free) (optional)

recipe continues

1. Slice off the top off each bell pepper. Remove and discard the stem, membranes, and seeds.

2. Make the stuffing: In a large bowl, combine the cooked couscous, garlic, chickpeas, artichokes, olives, cumin, oregano, thyme, paprika, salt, black pepper, lemon juice, tahini, parsley, and dill. Stir well to combine. Taste the mixture for seasoning and adjust accordingly, adding more lemon juice, tahini, or salt as needed.

3. Place the bell peppers on a flat surface and fill each pepper with the couscous and chickpea filling to the top, but do not overstuff.

4. Pour ½ cup water into the inner pot of the Instant Pot and place the steamer rack in the pot with the handles facing up. Arrange the four stuffed peppers on top of the steamer rack.

5. Secure the lid and select the Pressure Cook setting at high pressure and set the cook time to 6 minutes.

6. Once the 6-minute timer has completed and beeps, perform a quick pressure release by carefully switching the Pressure Release knob from Sealing to Venting.

7. Open the pot and, using oven mitts, carefully lift the steamer rack out of the Instant Pot and transfer the peppers to a serving platter. To serve, top the peppers with the basil and drizzle the tahini on top. If desired, crumble a tablespoon of tofu feta onto each bell pepper.

TIP *To cook Israeli or pearl couscous in the Instant Pot, add 1 tablespoon of oil on the Sauté setting and then add 1 cup Israeli couscous and stir to coat for 1 minute. Add 1¼ cups vegetable broth or water and stir to combine. Use the Pressure Cook setting at high pressure and cook for 3 minutes. Allow a natural pressure release for 5 minutes, then perform a quick release. Fluff with a fork and season to taste with salt and pepper.*

GARLICKY BROCCOLI
WITH ORANGE ZEST AND ALMONDS

serves 4 to 6	gluten-free, soy-free, no added sugar

This is one of the simpler recipes in this book, but it is also one of my favorites. I make it whenever broccoli is on sale at my local grocery store, or whenever my body subtly (or not so subtly) tells me that it needs some green food.

It takes less than 20 minutes from start to finish, and despite its simplicity, the flavors are addictive. Broccoli goes from meh to craveworthy with the addition of flash-fried garlic, fresh orange zest, and slightly smoky roasted almonds.

And possibly the best part? Despite the powerful strength of the Instant Pot, this broccoli stays crisp-tender and bright green, thanks to the low-pressure function on the Steam setting. No soggy brown mush here!

6 cups broccoli florets (about 2 pounds broccoli or 3 large broccoli heads)

1½ tablespoons olive oil

8 garlic cloves, thinly sliced

2 shallots, thinly sliced

½ teaspoon crushed red pepper flakes, plus more to taste

Grated zest and juice of 1 medium orange (about ¼ cup juice)

½ teaspoon kosher salt, plus more to taste

Freshly cracked black pepper

¼ cup roasted or toasted almonds or walnuts, chopped

¼ cup fresh basil, finely slivered

1. Pour 1 cup water into the bottom of the inner pot of the Instant Pot. Place the broccoli florets in a steamer basket and lower into the inner pot.

2. Secure the lid and set the Pressure Release to Sealing. Select the Steam setting at *low pressure* and set the cook time to 2 minutes.

3. Prepare an ice bath for the broccoli by filling a large bowl of cold water with ice. This helps retain the broccoli's bright green color and prevents overcooking.

4. Once the 2-minute timer has completed and beeps, perform a quick pressure release by carefully switching the Pressure Release knob from Sealing to Venting.

5. Open the pot and, using oven mitts, carefully lift the steamer basket out of the Instant Pot and transfer the broccoli to the ice bath. Once cooled, drain the broccoli and pat dry.

6. Select the Sauté setting on the Instant Pot and, after a few minutes, add the olive oil, followed by the garlic. Cook for 30 seconds, tossing frequently to prevent burning. Add the shallots and pepper flakes and cook for 1 minute.

7. Add the drained broccoli, ¼ cup orange juice, the salt, and black pepper to taste. Toss the ingredients together and cook for 1 minute. Taste for seasonings and add more orange juice, pepper flakes, or salt as needed.

8. Transfer the broccoli to a serving platter and top with the chopped almonds, 2 teaspoons of the orange zest, and the basil.

Variation

For an herbed tahini dressing (upgrade!), place all of
the tahini dressing ingredients (minus the water and
capers) in a food processor with the dill and parsley
and blend until smooth. With the motor running,
gradually pour in the water until thick but pourable.
Stir in the capers, pour the dressing into the Instant
Pot, and finish the recipe as instructed.

WARM TAHINI FINGERLING POTATO SALAD

serves 6	gluten-free, nut-free, soy-free, no added sugar

For most of my life, the only potato salad I knew was the traditional mayo-laden stuff that I had been served out of gallon-size plastic buckets at barbecues. But when I became vegan, a world of condiments beyond mayonnaise began to open up. Like tahini. Tahini makes for a creamy yet light potato salad, one that is full of healthy fats and won't weigh you down. With the addition of capers, dill, and fresh lemon zest, you get a taste of freshness and summer in each bite.

2 pounds fingerling potatoes, unpeeled

TAHINI DRESSING

⅓ cup tahini

2 garlic cloves, crushed through a press

2 teaspoons grated lemon zest

3 tablespoons fresh lemon juice

2 teaspoons Dijon or whole-grain mustard

1 teaspoon kosher salt, plus more to taste

½ teaspoon crushed red pepper flakes (optional)

Freshly cracked black pepper

¼ cup warm water, plus more as needed

2½ tablespoons capers, drained

FOR FINISHING

¼ cup fresh dill, chopped finely

½ cup fresh Italian flat-leaf parsley, chopped

½ cup very thinly sliced red onion (about 1 small)

1. Pour 2 cups water into the inner pot of the Instant Pot. Place the fingerling potatoes in a steamer basket and lower into the inner pot.

2. Select the Steam setting at high pressure and set the cook time to 5 minutes.

3. Meanwhile, make the tahini dressing: In a medium bowl, whisk together the tahini, garlic, lemon zest, lemon juice, mustard, salt, pepper flakes, and black pepper to taste. Whisk in the water to thin, then add up to 2 additional tablespoons of warm water as needed, until it is pourable but still thick. You don't want it to be too thin. Stir the capers into the tahini dressing.

4. Once the 5-minute timer has completed and beeps, perform a quick pressure release by carefully switching the Pressure Release knob from Sealing to Venting.

5. Open the pot and, using oven mitts, remove the steamer basket and let the potatoes cool for 10 minutes or until you're able to handle them comfortably. Then slice the potatoes in half.

6. Pour the water out of the inner pot and return it to the Instant Pot. Select the Sauté setting and press the Sauté button again until you reach Less heat. After a few minutes, pour in the dressing and gently stir using a whisk or silicone spatula for 30 seconds. Add the sliced potatoes, dill, parsley, and red onion and stir gently until the potatoes are evenly coated. This dish is best served immediately, but if you refrigerate leftovers, allow them to come to room temperature and finish with fresh lemon juice.

SICILIAN-STYLE CHARD AND WHITE BEANS

serves 4 to 6	gluten-free, soy-free, no added sugar

As you read this recipe, you might see the 1-minute cook time and think—cooking leafy greens in just 1 minute, that must be a typo! But the Instant Pot has the word "instant" in its name for a reason.

In fact, the only hurdle to making this dish is properly washing the chard, which hides a lot of dirt in its nooks and crannies. Using a salad spinner makes it easy: Chop the leaves into ribbons, place them in the spinner, and fill it up with water. Let the leaves soak in the water momentarily and then pull the basket out, discarding the dirty water. Then run the salad spinner, discard the water, and repeat several times to remove all of the dirt.

Once you get through the washing phase, just enjoy the delicious Sicilian-inspired flavors: pungent red onions and garlic married with spicy red pepper flakes, sweet golden raisins alongside salty olives and capers, nutty cannellini beans and buttery pine nuts, and zingy lemon zest.

2 bunches of Swiss chard (or rainbow chard), thick bottom stems discarded, leaves sliced into 1-inch-wide ribbons (you should end up with 16 to 20 ounces of leaves)

2 tablespoons olive oil

4 garlic cloves, thinly sliced

1 large red onion, cut into ⅜-inch-thick slices

½ teaspoon kosher salt, plus more to taste

½ teaspoon crushed red pepper flakes

⅓ cup low-sodium vegetable broth

½ cup golden raisins

1½ cups cooked cannellini beans or 1 (15-ounce) can cannellini beans, drained and rinsed

⅓ cup toasted pine nuts or chopped toasted almonds

10 pitted green olives, sliced

2 tablespoons capers, drained

Grated zest of 1 large lemon

recipe continues

1. Thoroughly wash and dry the chard leaves (see headnote).

2. Select the Sauté setting on the Instant Pot and let the pot heat up for a few minutes before adding the oil. Once the oil is hot, add the garlic. Cook, tossing frequently to prevent burning, until the garlic is lightly golden, 1 to 2 minutes.

3. Add the onion and season with the salt and pepper flakes. Cook for 2 minutes, tossing occasionally, then select the Cancel setting.

4. Add the chard leaves, vegetable broth, and raisins. Using a large spoon, mix together the ingredients as much as you can. Press down the pile of chard with the spoon to ensure the mixture is below the Instant Pot's maximum capacity line.

5. Secure the lid and set the Pressure Release to Sealing. Select the Pressure Cook setting at high pressure and set the cook time to 1 minute.

6. Once the 1-minute timer has completed and beeps, perform a quick pressure release by carefully switching the Pressure Release knob from Sealing to Venting.

7. Open the pot and transfer the cooked vegetables to a large bowl. Add the cannellini beans, toasted nuts, olives, capers, and lemon zest. Toss to combine and serve.

MAPLE CARROTS
WITH GINGER-ALMOND CREAM

serves 3 to 4	gluten-free, refined sugar–free

Melt-in-your mouth. Buttery. Irresistible. These are all very good adjectives to describe these carrots. If you have picky eaters or vegetable-averse individuals in your household, this is exactly what you should serve them to make them fall in love with veggies. Or, what you should serve to guests whom you'd like to impress.

Naturally sweet, these carrots get taken to the next level with pure maple syrup, which adds a rich sweetness and delicate glaze. The sweetness is balanced by the rich mouthfeel of the vegan butter, a touch of umami from the soy sauce, and a deep nuttiness from the almond butter and toasted sesame seeds. While I do love whole roasted carrots, they can take up to 45 minutes in the oven, so I welcome the minimal cook time in the Instant Pot.

TIP *To toast white sesame seeds, place them in a dry skillet over medium heat for 3 to 5 minutes, stirring frequently to prevent burning. (Alternatively, you can toast them in the oven on a rimmed baking sheet at 350°F for 5 minutes, then shake the baking sheet and toast until golden, another 3 to 5 minutes.)*

1½ pounds carrots, scrubbed and peeled

2 tablespoons vegan butter or olive oil

1 tablespoon pure maple syrup

½ teaspoon garlic powder

½ teaspoon kosher salt

Freshly cracked black pepper

GINGER-ALMOND CREAM

2 tablespoons no-added-sugar creamy almond butter

2 teaspoons rice vinegar

1 teaspoon pure maple syrup

1 teaspoon reduced-sodium tamari or soy sauce

1-inch piece fresh ginger, grated or finely minced

¼ cup water

FOR SERVING

¼ cup fresh cilantro, finely chopped

2 teaspoons white sesame seeds, toasted (see Tip), or black sesame seeds, untoasted

recipe continues

1. If you have carrots that are relatively uniform in width and not too fat, simply trim the ends and tops so that they fit lying flat in the inner pot of the Instant Pot. For carrots that are much fatter on the top and much skinnier at the bottom, halve the carrots crosswise, then slice the fat tops lengthwise and keep the skinnier bottoms whole.

2. Select the Sauté setting on the Instant Pot and, after a few minutes, add the vegan butter. Once the butter has melted, add the carrots, toss around in the butter, and cook for 2 minutes.

3. Add the maple syrup, garlic powder, salt, and pepper to taste and toss to coat the carrots evenly. Select the Cancel setting.

4. Secure the lid and set the Pressure Release to Sealing. Select the Pressure Cook setting at high pressure and set the cook time to 3 minutes (if your carrots are very fat, you'll want to increase the cook time to 4 minutes).

5. Meanwhile, make the ginger-almond cream: In a bowl, whisk together the almond butter, vinegar, maple syrup, tamari, ginger, and water until smooth.

6. Once the 3-minute timer has completed and beeps, perform a quick pressure release by carefully switching the Pressure Release knob from Sealing to Venting.

7. Open the pot and, using a slotted spoon, transfer the carrots to a serving dish. Keep the liquid remaining in the pot and add all of the ingredients for the ginger-almond cream to the pot. Select the Sauté setting and press the Sauté button again until you reach Less heat. Whisk the ingredients together and cook until you have a thick but pourable sauce, 1 to 2 minutes. Using oven mitts, remove the inner pot and pour the cream on top of the carrots. Garnish with cilantro and sesame seeds.

SWEET AND SPICY BRAISED RED CABBAGE

makes about 7 cups	gluten-free, nut-free, refined sugar–free option

Cabbage is a wonderfully underrated, delicious vegetable. Plus, it's inexpensive and a highly nutritious superfood. The Instant Pot quickly transforms this cruciferous veggie from crunchy and tough to tender and sweet in only a few minutes, just as if you had slowly braised it on the stove. And with the addition of ingredients like apples, dried cherries, apple cider vinegar, and crushed red pepper flakes, the result is a harmonious balance of sweet, salty, spicy, and acidic.

This dish is also incredibly beautiful, like an edible bowl of ruby-toned jewels. Serve warm alongside the Lentil Shepherd's Pie (page 191) or any other chilly-weather comfort food, or serve as a cold side dish (I love it on a bed of brown rice, Israeli couscous, or bulgur).

1 tablespoon olive oil

1 medium red cabbage (2 to 2¼ pounds), roughly chopped

1¼ teaspoons kosher salt

2 large carrots, grated

1 Granny Smith apple, unpeeled and grated

1¼ cups low-sodium vegetable broth

¼ cup apple cider vinegar

1½ tablespoons reduced-sodium tamari or soy sauce

1 tablespoon organic brown sugar or coconut sugar

½ cup dried sour cherries

1 teaspoon crushed red pepper flakes, to taste

2 teaspoons white sesame seeds

1. Select the Sauté setting on the Instant Pot and let the pot heat up for a few minutes before adding the olive oil. Once the oil is hot, add the cabbage. Add ½ teaspoon of the kosher salt and cook, stirring occasionally, until the cabbage begins to brown, about 4 minutes.

2. Top the cabbage with the carrots and apple, then pour in the vegetable broth, vinegar, and tamari and add the brown sugar, dried cherries, pepper flakes, and the remaining ¾ teaspoon salt. Stir well to combine and select the Cancel setting.

3. Secure the lid and set the Pressure Release to Sealing. Select the Steam setting at high pressure and set the cook time to 3 minutes.

4. Once the 3-minute timer has completed and beeps, perform a quick pressure release by carefully switching the Pressure Release knob from Sealing to Venting.

5. Open the pot and taste the cabbage for seasonings, adding salt or pepper flakes as needed.

6. Transfer the cabbage to a serving dish and garnish with the sesame seeds. Store leftovers in an airtight container in the fridge for up to 5 days.

CITRUS KALE AND CARROTS

serves 4	gluten-free, nut-free, soy-free, no added sugar

Initially, I was skeptical about pressure-cooking kale. The cooked kale dishes I had previously tried were always underwhelming—entirely unsalted or too salty, skimpy on flavor, and watery in texture. I'm proud to say that this dish is none of those things.

The Instant Pot quickly and easily turns kale from fibrous to tender, and with the addition of sweet carrots and a bright, zippy citrus dressing, the final result is an unexpectedly light and summery side dish with bright flavors. I am partial to Tuscan kale (also known as lacinato or dinosaur kale), but use whichever variety you prefer, or even a bag of prewashed, chopped kale. Serve on the side with my Vegetable Paella (page 209) or any time you're in the mood for greens that don't require thorough chewing. Or as I like to say, let them eat kale!

KALE AND CARROTS

2 tablespoons olive oil

2 medium yellow onions, diced

8 garlic cloves, chopped

6 medium carrots, sliced into ½-inch-thick half-moons

1 teaspoon kosher salt, plus more to taste

Freshly cracked black pepper

12 to 16 ounces Tuscan (lacinato) kale (1 very large bunch or 2 small bunches), thick stems removed, leaves sliced into 1-inch pieces

⅓ cup low-sodium vegetable broth

6 sprigs fresh thyme

CITRUS DRESSING

Grated zest and juice of 1 small orange

1 tablespoon balsamic vinegar

½ teaspoon Dijon or whole-grain mustard

¼ teaspoon kosher salt, or to taste

Freshly cracked black pepper

FOR SERVING

2 tablespoons hemp seeds

recipe continues

1. Prepare the kale and carrots: Select the Sauté setting on the Instant Pot and let the pot heat up for a few minutes before adding the olive oil. Once the oil is hot, add the onions. Cook until the onions are just beginning to soften, about 3 minutes. Add the garlic and carrots with a pinch each of salt and pepper and cook until the carrots are slightly softened, 4 to 5 minutes.

2. Add the sliced kale, packing it down, followed by the vegetable broth, thyme sprigs, 1 teaspoon salt, and pepper to taste. Use a long-handled spoon to toss the mixture together as much as you can and to push down the kale to ensure it is below the Instant Pot's maximum capacity line. Select the Cancel setting.

3. Secure the lid and set the Pressure Release to Sealing. Select the Steam setting at high pressure and set the cook time to 3 minutes.

4. Meanwhile, make the citrus dressing: In a small bowl, combine the orange zest, orange juice, vinegar, mustard, salt, and pepper and whisk until smooth. If you have any orange pulp in your dressing and would like to remove it, strain it through a fine-mesh sieve.

5. Once the 3-minute timer has completed and beeps, perform a quick pressure release by carefully switching the Pressure Release knob from Sealing to Venting.

6. Open the pot and discard the thyme sprigs. Using a slotted spoon, transfer the kale and carrots to a serving dish, leaving behind any remaining liquid. Top with the citrus dressing and hemp seeds, stirring gently to coat.

ROOT VEGETABLE MASH

serves 8	gluten-free, nut-free, soy-free, no added sugar

Although I'm a firm believer in the importance of serving mashed potatoes at Thanksgiving, I also like to offer an alternative to those who avoid white potatoes, like this root vegetable mash. While this buttery mash makes an excellent side dish any time of year, it is particularly perfect during the holidays, when stove and oven space are at a premium.

The Instant Pot transforms these vegetables into a silky, buttery puree that gets a deeply complex, sweet flavor from roasted garlic. Traditionally, garlic is roasted whole in the oven (drizzled with olive oil, wrapped in foil, and roasted at 400°F for 40 to 45 minutes), but this recipe calls for "roasting" the garlic in the Instant Pot (steaming, technically) and finishing it under the broiler for a few minutes to get it browned and caramelized. If you have the time, feel free to roast the garlic in the oven, but you can get the same results in less time using the Instant Pot.

1 head garlic, unpeeled

1 tablespoon olive oil, plus more for roasting garlic

1 medium yellow onion, roughly chopped

1 pound carrots (about 6), peeled and cut into large cubes

1 pound sweet potatoes, peeled and cut into pieces slightly larger than the carrots

1 small head cauliflower, roughly chopped into florets

1 large sprig fresh rosemary

6 sprigs fresh thyme

1¼ teaspoons kosher salt, plus more to taste

Freshly cracked black pepper

⅓ cup low-sodium vegetable broth

2 tablespoons vegan butter (use a soy-free variety to keep soy-free) or extra-virgin olive oil

recipe continues

1. Slice off the top of the garlic head to just expose the cloves. If you are roasting the garlic in the oven, skip Steps 2 through 5.

2. Pour 1 cup water into the inner pot of the Instant Pot and place the steamer rack in the pot with the handles facing up. Place the head of garlic on top of the steamer rack. Meanwhile, turn on your oven's broiler.

3. Secure the lid and set the Pressure Release to Sealing. Select the Pressure Cook setting at high pressure and set the cook time to 10 minutes.

4. Once the 10-minute timer has completed and beeps, allow a natural pressure release for 10 minutes and then switch the Pressure Release knob from Sealing to Venting to release any remaining steam.

5. Open the pot and transfer the garlic to an ovenproof dish or rimmed baking sheet, drizzle the exposed flesh with a bit of olive oil, and put it under the broiler for 5 minutes to caramelize.

6. Pour the water out of the inner pot and return it to the Instant Pot. Select the Sauté setting and let the pot heat up for a few minutes before adding the olive oil. Once the oil is hot, add the onion. Cook until the onion is lightly browned, 4 to 5 minutes.

7. Select the Cancel setting and add the carrots, sweet potatoes, cauliflower, rosemary, and thyme. Squeeze the roasted garlic cloves directly into the Instant Pot and season with ¾ teaspoon of the salt and pepper to taste. Pour the vegetable broth on top and stir all of the ingredients to combine.

8. Secure the lid and set the Pressure Release to Sealing. Select the Pressure Cook setting at high pressure and set the cook time to 5 minutes.

9. Once the 5-minute timer has completed and beeps, perform a quick pressure release by carefully switching the Pressure Release knob from Sealing to Venting.

10. Open the pot and add the vegan butter and remaining ½ teaspoon salt. Using an immersion blender, blend all of the ingredients together until you have a smooth texture. If you'd like a super smooth texture, transfer all of the ingredients to a food processor and blend. Taste for salt and adjust accordingly. Serve warm.

THE BEST DAMN RATATOUILLE

serves 8	gluten-free, nut-free, soy-free, no added sugar

According to my partner, this is "the best damn ratatouille" he's ever had. Thus, the recipe title! Aside from its deliciousness, it is also very healthy, as it's made exclusively with vegetables, heart-healthy olive oil, and herbs.

Be sure that your tomatoes are juicy and in season. I particularly love using heirloom tomatoes during the summer, as they lend a complex sweetness and succulence. If flavorless, mealy water bombs are the only available form of tomato at your supermarket, I recommend using high-quality canned diced tomatoes instead.

You can toss this ratatouille with pasta or spread it on toasted bread for a mouthwatering crostini, but I really recommend serving it over the Millet-Cauliflower Mash (page 135) or Classic Creamy Polenta (page 123) for some rustic Italian comfort food.

1 pound eggplant, cut into ¾-inch cubes

1 tablespoon kosher salt, plus more to taste

¼ cup olive oil

1 large sweet onion, diced

8 garlic cloves, chopped

2 medium summer squash or zucchini, cut into pieces roughly the same size as the eggplant

2 medium red or yellow bell peppers, cut into pieces roughly the same size as the eggplant

½ to 1 teaspoon crushed red pepper flakes, to taste

½ teaspoon freshly cracked black pepper

1 cup fresh basil leaves

2 tablespoons capers, drained

1 bay leaf

6 sprigs fresh thyme

1 pound heirloom or Campari tomatoes, roughly chopped, or 1 (14.5-ounce) can diced San Marzano tomatoes

2 tablespoons tomato paste

½ tablespoon high-quality balsamic vinegar

½ cup fresh Italian flat-leaf parsley, finely chopped

recipe continues

1. Place the eggplant cubes on a cutting board or plate and sprinkle with 1 tablespoon salt. Toss to evenly coat, then place the eggplant in a colander to drain.

2. Select the Sauté setting on the Instant Pot and let the pot heat up for a few minutes before adding the oil. Once the oil is hot, add the onion. Cook until the onion is soft and almost translucent, 4 to 5 minutes. Add the garlic, squash, and a pinch of salt and cook until the vegetables are slightly softened, about 3 minutes.

3. Add the bell peppers, pepper flakes, black pepper, and ½ cup of the basil (leaves kept whole). Cook for 4 minutes, tossing occasionally. Transfer the vegetable mixture to a bowl and set aside.

4. Add the remaining 2 tablespoons olive oil to the Instant Pot, followed by the drained eggplant. Stir gently and frequently to prevent the eggplant from sticking to the bottom of the pot. Cook until the eggplant is soft and starting to turn golden, 4 to 5 minutes. Select the Cancel setting.

5. Return the vegetable mixture to the Instant Pot, along with the capers, bay leaf, and thyme sprigs. Stir all of the ingredients to combine. Top the mixture with the tomatoes and tomato paste, but do not stir, allowing the tomatoes and tomato paste to sit on top (this prevents the tomatoes from blocking the Instant Pot's heat sensor and burning).

6. Secure the lid and set the Pressure Release to Sealing. Select the Pressure Cook setting at high pressure and set the cook time to 9 minutes.

7. While the ratatouille is cooking, make a chiffonade of the remaining ½ cup basil by stacking the leaves on top of one another, rolling them up, and slicing thinly into strips.

8. Once the 9-minute timer has completed and beeps, perform a quick pressure release by carefully switching the Pressure Release knob from Sealing to Venting.

9. Open the pot and check the ratatouille—it should be a bit soupy and the vegetables should be very tender. Discard the thyme sprigs and bay leaf.

10. Select the Sauté setting on the Instant Pot and bring the ratatouille to a boil to reduce the liquid and thicken the sauce. This should take 5 to 8 minutes.

11. Select the Cancel setting and stir in the vinegar, parsley, and sliced basil. Taste for salt and adjust accordingly. Use a slotted spoon to transfer the ratatouille to a serving platter.

GREEN BEAN SALAD WITH MAPLE-TAHINI DRESSING

serves 4	gluten-free, nut-free option, soy-free, refined sugar–free

There is nothing I like less than soggy vegetables, and green beans often turn out this way. Just a minute too long and they turn to mush.

I've tried cooking green beans in the Instant Pot at several different time and pressure combinations, ranging from 4 minutes at high pressure (complete mush) to zero minutes at low pressure (a bit undercooked). I settled on 1 minute at low pressure, as it yields a firm yet cooked bean that retains its bright green bean color and crunchy texture. If you like your beans a bit more well-done, you can cook them for 2 minutes at low pressure.

The crispness of the green beans, the creaminess of the maple-tahini dressing, the juicy acidity of the cherry tomatoes, and the slightly smoky crunch from the toasted almonds all work together to make this a refreshing and balanced salad.

GREEN BEANS

1 pound green beans, ends trimmed

¾ teaspoon kosher salt

Freshly cracked black pepper

1 tablespoon olive oil

2 garlic cloves, minced

2 shallots, diced

MAPLE-TAHINI DRESSING

2½ tablespoons tahini

2 tablespoons fresh lemon juice

1½ tablespoons extra-virgin olive oil

1 tablespoon pure maple syrup

1 garlic clove, finely minced

¼ teaspoon kosher salt, plus more to taste

¼ teaspoon freshly cracked black pepper

2 tablespoons warm water

SALAD ADD-ONS

½ cup cherry tomatoes or grape tomatoes, halved

⅓ cup toasted almonds, roughly chopped (omit for a nut-free option)

1 small bunch of fresh mint leaves torn into pieces

recipe continues

1. Cook the green beans: Place the green beans in the Instant Pot. Add ½ cup water, the salt, and pepper to taste.

2. Secure the lid and set the Pressure Release to Sealing. Select the Steam setting at *low pressure* and set the cook time to 1 minute.

3. Meanwhile, make the maple-tahini dressing: In a small bowl, combine the tahini, lemon juice, extra-virgin olive oil, maple syrup, garlic, salt, and pepper and whisk together until smooth and creamy. Then add the warm water and whisk until you have a pourable consistency. Taste for seasonings and adjust accordingly.

4. Once the 1-minute timer has completed and beeps, perform a quick pressure release by carefully switching the Pressure Release knob from Sealing to Venting.

5. Open the pot and, using oven mitts, carefully remove the inner pot and drain the green beans in a colander. If you prefer your beans on the crisp side of crisp-tender, transfer the cooked beans to a large bowl of cold water with ice to halt the cooking process.

6. Return the inner pot to the Instant Pot. Select the Sauté setting and, after a few minutes, add the olive oil, followed by the garlic and shallots. Cook until browned, about 3 minutes. Return the green beans to the pot, stir to combine, and cook for 1 minute.

7. Transfer the green bean mixture to a serving dish and drizzle with the dressing, tossing to coat. Sprinkle on the cherry tomatoes, almonds, and torn mint leaves and serve.

5

COMFORT FOOD FAVORITES

This is my favorite chapter in this book. It is loaded with comfort food classics and hearty dinner options that debunk all of the vegan myths floating out there—that vegans can't get enough protein, that vegan food isn't filling enough, that vegans are self-depriving weirdos who just eat salads (that last one is especially offensive!). Each meal is satisfying and decadent, and many are inspired by diverse global cuisines. This chapter has a mix of casual weeknight eats and more elaborate meals that are perfect for weekend entertaining, but every dish is big on both flavor and comfort.

MACARONI AND CHEESE

serves 6 to 8	no added sugar

It's no secret that macaroni and cheese is the ultimate American comfort food. For me, that first bite envelops me with a visceral nostalgia—I can see myself at the family kitchen table eating mac and cheese by the bowlful as a child.

I'm proud to report that you, too, can experience the childhood delight of biting into a forkful of ooey-gooey cheesiness without using (a) dairy (or neon-orange processed cheese) or (b) a stove or an oven. The end result is remarkably similar in taste and texture to the classic, thanks to an umami-rich vegan cheese sauce and a crunchy bread crumb topping that contrasts perfectly with the creamy cheese sauce. Even your omnivorous, cheese-loving friends and family will love this mac and cheese.

One caveat is that this recipe doesn't use the traditional elbow macaroni pasta. I prefer a larger macaroni-style pasta like cavatappi or medium-size shells, as the larger surface size tends to cook better in the Instant Pot.

Olive oil, for the pot and breadcrumbs

Vegan Cheese Sauce (page 49)

1 teaspoon garlic powder

1 teaspoon onion powder

1 teaspoon mustard powder (optional, but adds a nice tangy sharpness)

¼ teaspoon smoked paprika

¾ teaspoon kosher salt

½ teaspoon crushed red pepper flakes (optional)

16 ounces cavatappi pasta, medium-size shells, or other medium-size pasta with a cook time of 9 to 11 minutes (if your pasta has a different cook time, see Tip for how to calculate)

3 tablespoons vegan butter, cut into small pieces

1 cup panko or fresh bread crumbs

Freshly cracked black pepper

TIP *To calculate the precise cook time for your pasta, consult the instructions on the back of the box. Take the minimum cook time (if it's an odd number, round down to the nearest even number), divide that by 2, and then subtract 1. For example, for a range of 9 to 11 minutes, round 9 down to 8, divide it by 2 to get 4, then subtract 1, for a cook time of 3 minutes. A range of 11 to 13 minutes would be 4 minutes, etc.*

1. Generously grease the inner pot of the Instant Pot with the olive oil. Don't skip this step, as it prevents the pasta from sticking to the pot and burning.

2. Pour 3½ cups warm water into the Instant Pot (adding warm water helps the Instant Pot come to pressure more quickly and prevents the pasta from overcooking). Add the vegan cheese sauce, garlic powder, onion powder, mustard powder (if using), smoked paprika, salt, and pepper flakes (if using). Stir well to combine the ingredients. Add the pasta and stir to submerge it. Dot the mixture with the vegan butter.

3. Secure the lid and set the Pressure Release to Sealing. Select the Pressure Cook setting at high pressure and set the cook time to 3 minutes (or the cook time your calculations worked out to; see Tip).

4. Once the pasta has come to pressure and the timer begins, toast the bread crumbs. Heat a skillet over medium heat and add 1 teaspoon olive oil. Once the oil is hot, add the bread crumbs and toast, tossing occasionally, until golden brown, 2 to 3 minutes. Set aside.

5. Once the 3-minute timer has completed and beeps, perform a quick pressure release by carefully switching the Pressure Release knob from Sealing to Venting. I have experienced a little splattering at this stage, so you may want to cover the vent with a kitchen towel.

6. Open the pot and stir. If the cheese sauce appears thin, select the Sauté setting and heat the pasta, stirring to prevent sticking, for 1 to 3 minutes to thicken the sauce. The cheese sauce will also thicken considerably as it rests.

7. Transfer the macaroni and cheese to a serving bowl. Top with the toasted bread crumbs and black pepper to taste.

MISO MUSHROOM RISOTTO

serves 4 to 6	gluten-free, nut-free, no added sugar

I was a college student the first time I made mushroom risotto. I still remember the exquisite creaminess, the lingering richness, the earthy smell of mushrooms permeating my tiny 1960s-era kitchen in Berkeley. My friends and I hovered around the stove, taking turns tasting the risotto straight from the skillet, giddy with our culinary success.

When I became vegan, my love for risotto grew only stronger. I learned that the secret to creamy risotto is not butter or cheese but the starch in Arborio rice and that the savory quality I loved about risotto could be replicated with ingredients like miso paste.

While I think there is something special about the traditional process of making risotto, which involves standing over the stove for 30 minutes while gradually adding ladles of warm broth, I very much appreciate being able to make risotto in the Instant Pot with half the effort and time.

The miso butter and mushroom broth take this risotto over the top. But if you don't feel like making mushroom broth, this risotto is still heavenly with store-bought vegetable broth.

1½ cups Arborio rice

4 cups vegetable broth or Mushroom Broth (page 44)

¼ cup olive oil (or substitute vegan butter for up to 2 tablespoons of the oil), or more as needed

4 shallots, finely diced

4 garlic cloves, minced

20 ounces mixed mushrooms (see Tip), sliced

1½ teaspoons dried thyme

½ teaspoon freshly cracked black pepper

1 teaspoon kosher salt, plus more to taste

⅓ cup dry white wine (such as Pinot Grigio or Sauvignon Blanc)

¼ cup white or yellow miso paste

1 tablespoon reduced-sodium tamari or soy sauce

2 tablespoons vegan butter

¼ cup fresh Italian flat-leaf parsley, chopped

TIP *Feel free to use any combination of mushrooms you like. To keep the cost of ingredients low but still make this dish exciting, I use 75 percent brown button mushrooms or cremini mushrooms and 25 percent exotic mushrooms like shiitake, chanterelle, or oyster.*

recipe continues

1. Place the Arborio rice in a large bowl and pour the broth over it. Whisk the mixture for 15 seconds to release the starch from the rice, which helps the risotto become creamier. Pour the mixture through a fine-mesh sieve set over a bowl to catch the broth. The broth might appear cloudy, which is normal—that is the starch.

2. Select the Sauté setting on the Instant Pot and, after a few minutes, add the olive oil, followed by the shallots and garlic. Cook for 1 minute, tossing frequently. Add the sliced mushrooms, thyme, and pepper and cook until the mushrooms are browned and most of their liquid has evaporated, about 8 minutes. Add the salt during the last minute of cooking. If the mushrooms still have a lot of liquid after 8 minutes, remove the inner pot and tip it over the sink to drain off some of the excess liquid.

3. Add the drained Arborio rice to the Instant Pot and stir to coat, ensuring every grain of rice is coated in oil. If needed, add a bit more olive oil at this stage to prevent the rice from burning. Cook until the edges of the rice have turned translucent but the center is still opaque, 2 to 3 minutes.

4. Pour in the wine to deglaze the pan, using a wooden spoon to scrape up any browned bits on the bottom of the pot. Cook, stirring occasionally, until the liquid has mostly evaporated and the smell of alcohol has dissipated, about 2 minutes. Select the Cancel setting.

5. Add 2 tablespoons of the miso and the tamari and stir into all of the rice grains. Add the reserved broth and stir well to combine, scraping any final browned bits from the bottom of the pot.

6. Secure the lid and set the Pressure Release to Sealing. Select the Pressure Cook setting at high pressure and set the cook time to 5 minutes.

7. Once the 5-minute timer has completed and beeps, allow a natural pressure release for 10 minutes and then switch the Pressure Release knob from Sealing to Venting to release any remaining steam.

8. While the pot is depressurizing, in a small saucepan, add the vegan butter over medium heat. Once the butter begins to melt, add the remaining 2 tablespoons miso and heat until the ingredients have melted together into a loose paste, about 1 minute.

9. Open the pot and stir to combine the rice and cooking liquid. There may be some liquid sitting on top of the risotto. Stir thoroughly and the risotto will thicken and become creamy. Stir in the miso butter and taste for seasonings, adding additional salt or pepper as needed. Serve the risotto immediately and top each bowl with chopped parsley.

THREE-BEAN VEGETABLE CHILI

serves 6	gluten-free, nut-free, soy-free, refined sugar–free

This chili is hearty, chock-full of beans and vegetables, and the perfect balance of spicy, sweet, and bitter. You might be surprised to see chocolate in the ingredient list, but cocoa powder adds an underlying richness and depth of flavor without tasting like chocolate, and along with the blackstrap molasses, it intensifies the warmth of the spices and imbues the chili with subtly sweet and bitter undertones.

Feel free to substitute your favorite beans or vegetables or add more or less spices, but don't skip the masa harina, a traditional Mexican corn flour (you can find it in most grocery stores). It imparts a slight corn flavor and thickens the chili, giving it a smooth, velvety body. While I slightly prefer using dried beans (the beans get creamy but stay intact), canned beans work just fine. And like all chili recipes, this one tastes considerably better once it has rested for a few hours or overnight.

Since this recipe makes a huge quantity of chili, I like to freeze several servings in mason jars and reheat them whenever I arrive home, chilled to the bone from a cold winter's day and in need of a warm meal.

TIP *You can substitute 1 ounce of roughly chopped bittersweet chocolate for the cocoa powder and blackstrap molasses (or coconut sugar or brown sugar). Add it before you add the crushed tomatoes.*

4½ ounces (about ⅔ cup) dried black beans or 1 (15-ounce) can black beans

4½ ounces (about ⅔ cup) dried pinto beans or 1 (15-ounce) can pinto beans

4½ ounces (about ⅔ cup) dried kidney or cannellini beans or 1 (15-ounce) can kidney or cannellini beans

2 tablespoons olive oil

1 large onion, diced

4 garlic cloves, minced

2 jalapeño peppers, diced (seeded for a mild version)

2 small carrots, finely diced

1½ teaspoons kosher salt, plus more to taste

1 small red bell pepper, diced

8 ounces mushrooms, sliced and then chopped

2½ tablespoons chili powder

2 tablespoons unsweetened cocoa powder

1 tablespoon ground cumin

2 teaspoons dried oregano

2 teaspoons smoked paprika

¼ to ½ teaspoon cayenne pepper, to taste (omit for mild heat)

½ teaspoon freshly cracked black pepper

1½ to 2½ cups low-sodium vegetable broth (the smaller amount if using canned beans)

1 (15-ounce) can corn kernels, drained

1 tablespoon blackstrap molasses (or 2 teaspoons coconut sugar or brown sugar)

2 canned chipotle peppers in adobo sauce (optional for a smoky flavor and more heat)

1 (14.5-ounce) can crushed fire-roasted tomatoes

recipe and ingredients continue

2 tablespoons tomato paste

3 tablespoons masa harina (or cornmeal)

1 tablespoon fresh lime juice

OPTIONAL GARNISHES

Chopped scallions or fresh cilantro

Vegan sour cream

Vegan cheddar cheese, Vegan Cheese Sauce (page 49), or Vegan Queso (page 51)

1. If using dried beans, place them all in a large bowl and cover with 8 cups water. Soak the beans for 8 hours. Soaking the beans in the same bowl might change the color of the beans (but not the taste). Drain and rinse the soaked beans under cold water. If you are using canned beans, drain and rinse them.

2. Select the Sauté setting on the Instant Pot and let the pot heat up for a few minutes before adding the olive oil. Once the oil is hot, add the onion, garlic, jalapeños, and carrots. Add a pinch of salt and cook, stirring frequently, until the onion is translucent, about 5 minutes.

3. Add the bell pepper and mushrooms with another pinch of salt and cook until the mushrooms begin to release their liquid, 3 to 4 minutes.

4. Add the chili powder, cocoa powder, cumin, oregano, smoked paprika, cayenne (if using), black pepper, and the 1½ teaspoons salt. Stir vigorously to coat the vegetables in the spices and cook for 30 to 60 seconds to evaporate the liquid.

5. Add the beans, 2½ cups vegetable broth (1½ cups if using canned beans), corn, molasses, and chipotle peppers (if using). Stir well to combine. Select the Cancel setting.

6. Carefully pour the crushed tomatoes and tomato paste on top of the chili, but do not stir the mixture, allowing the tomatoes and paste to sit on top (this prevents the tomatoes from blocking the Instant Pot's heat sensor and burning).

7. Secure the lid and set the Pressure Release to Sealing. Select the Pressure Cook setting at high pressure and set the cook time to 12 minutes for dried beans or 6 minutes for canned beans.

8. Once the timer has completed and beeps, allow a natural pressure release for 10 minutes and then switch the Pressure Release knob from Sealing to Venting to release any remaining steam.

9. Open the pot and select the Sauté setting. In a slow, steady stream, add the masa harina and stir until the chili has thickened, 2 to 3 minutes. Add the lime juice and stir well to combine. Allow the chili to cool slightly before serving and garnish as desired.

JAMAICAN JERK JACKFRUIT TACOS

serves 4	gluten-free, nut-free, refined sugar–free

If you want to transport yourself to a Caribbean island without the expensive airfare, I highly recommend making these jackfruit tacos. Canned jackfruit is shredded until it has the consistency of pulled pork (gasp!) and is then quickly cooked in a blend of Jamaican jerk spices. Don't let the habanero pepper dissuade you from making this dish, as its citrusy, floral heat is well balanced by the juicy sweetness of mango and creaminess of avocado in the salsa. And a touch of liquid smoke adds a rich but subtle smokiness reminiscent of barbecue, making this the perfect dish to make for meat eaters, too.

TIP *You can find canned jackfruit at Asian markets, specialty or natural foods stores, Trader Joe's, or online. You want to buy the kind canned in water or brine, not syrup.*

MANGO-AVOCADO SALSA

2 cups peeled and diced mango (about 2 medium)

1 medium ripe avocado, diced

¾ cup diced red onion

½ cup diced cucumber

3 tablespoons fresh orange juice

3 tablespoons fresh lime juice (about 1½ limes)

½ cup loosely packed fresh cilantro, finely chopped

Kosher salt and freshly cracked black pepper

JACKFRUIT

2 (20-ounce) cans jackfruit in brine or water (see Tip)

2 tablespoons grapeseed oil or other neutral cooking oil

6 scallions (white and light-green parts only), sliced

4 garlic cloves, minced

1½-inch piece fresh ginger, grated or minced

1 habanero or Scotch bonnet pepper, seeded and minced (use only ½ pepper for less heat or substitute with a milder pepper such as serrano or jalapeño)

Jamaican Jerk Seasoning, store-bought or homemade (recipe follows)

2 tablespoons coconut sugar, coconut nectar, or agave nectar

2 tablespoons tomato paste

¼ cup reduced-sodium tamari or soy sauce

3 tablespoons fresh lime juice (about 1½ limes)

½ teaspoon liquid smoke (optional)

FOR SERVING

12 corn tortillas

Vegan sour cream (optional)

recipe continues

1. Make the mango-avocado salsa: In a medium bowl, combine the mango, avocado, onion, cucumber, orange juice, lime juice, and cilantro and mix gently. Season to taste with salt and pepper. (Preparing the salsa in advance gives it some time to marinate and will deepen the flavor.)

2. Prepare the jackfruit: Drain the canned jackfruit and lightly rinse under water, shaking off excess water. Use your fingers to remove any thick cores and pull the pieces apart so that it resembles shredded pork.

3. Select the Sauté setting on the Instant Pot and, after a few minutes, add the oil. Once the display reads "HOT," add the scallions and cook until browned, 1 to 2 minutes. Add the garlic, ginger, and chile pepper and cook for 1 minute, stirring frequently to prevent burning.

4. Add all of the Jamaican jerk seasoning, stir to coat, and cook for 30 seconds, stirring constantly, until very fragrant. Select the Cancel setting.

5. Add the shredded jackfruit, along with the coconut sugar, tomato paste, tamari, lime juice, and liquid smoke (if using). Stir well. Pour in ½ cup water and mix again.

6. Secure the lid and set the Pressure Release to Sealing. Select the Pressure Cook setting at high pressure and set the cook time to 4 minutes.

7. Once the 4-minute timer has completed and beeps, allow a natural pressure release.

8. Open the pot and stir well. Transfer the jackfruit to a serving bowl.

9. To serve: Heat the tortillas over an open flame (I place them directly on the burner of my gas stove) and use tongs to flip them after 30 to 45 seconds or when small brown spots appear, and cook for another 15 to 30 seconds. Stack them in a clean kitchen towel or in foil to keep them warm.

10. Serve the jackfruit with the warmed corn tortillas, mango avocado salsa, and vegan sour cream (if using).

Jamaican Jerk Seasoning
Makes about 2 tablespoons

1½ teaspoons onion powder
1 teaspoon sweet or hot paprika
1 teaspoon freshly cracked black pepper
1 teaspoon dried thyme
½ teaspoon ground allspice
½ teaspoon ground cumin
¼ to ½ teaspoon cayenne pepper, to taste
¼ teaspoon ground cinnamon
¼ teaspoon freshly grated or ground nutmeg

Combine all of the spices together in a small bowl.

LENTIL SHEPHERD'S PIE

serves 6	gluten-free, no added sugar

With a saucy red wine lentil and mushroom ragu, baked under a layer of creamy mashed potatoes, this vegan shepherd's pie is the ultimate comfort food: hearty, savory, and filling.

Typically, when you make a shepherd's pie, you need to boil the potatoes and cook the filling separately, but the Instant Pot makes it possible to cook them simultaneously. To ensure that the potatoes get fully cooked, you'll need to use small potatoes that are 4 to 5 ounces each. If you can't find small potatoes, be sure to use potatoes of roughly equal size and cut them in half.

This is an excellent dish to make around the holidays, when leftover mashed potatoes are abundant. Just prepare the lentil filling on its own and, since refrigerated mashed potatoes tend to dry out a bit, simply add a little nondairy milk to loosen them up and creamify them (creamify is a word, yes?).

TIP *This is one of those dishes where cooking with wine really enhances the flavors. Red wine brings out the uniquely earthy, rich flavors of mushrooms and lentils in a way that other liquids (such as broth or water) simply cannot.*

LENTIL FILLING

2 tablespoons olive oil

1 medium yellow onion, diced

2 large carrots, finely diced

1½ teaspoons kosher salt, plus more to taste

4 garlic cloves, minced

3 ounces cremini mushrooms, finely chopped (about 1 cup)

⅓ cup dry red wine (such as Pinot Noir)

1 cup dried green or brown lentils

1 cup low-sodium vegetable broth

2 tablespoons reduced-sodium tamari or soy sauce

2 bay leaves

8 sprigs fresh thyme

1 teaspoon sweet paprika

½ teaspoon freshly cracked black pepper

1 (14.5-ounce) can crushed fire-roasted tomatoes

MASHED POTATOES

6 small Yukon Gold potatoes (see headnote), peeled

¼ cup vegan butter or extra-virgin olive oil

¼ to ½ cup unsweetened plain almond milk or other nondairy milk

1 teaspoon kosher salt, plus more to taste

⅓ cup finely chopped chives (optional)

OPTIONAL GARNISHES

Chopped fresh herbs, such as thyme, Italian flat-leaf parsley, or chives

Extra-virgin olive oil, for drizzling

recipe continues

1. Make the lentil filling: Select the Sauté setting on the Instant Pot and let the pot heat up for a few minutes before adding the olive oil. Once the oil is hot, add the onion and carrots. Season with a pinch of salt and cook until the onion is beginning to brown, 5 to 6 minutes. Add the garlic and mushrooms and cook for another 2 minutes.

2. Pour in the red wine and cook, stirring occasionally, until the liquid has mostly evaporated and the smell of alcohol has dissipated, 3 to 4 minutes.

3. Add the lentils, vegetable broth, tamari, bay leaves, thyme, paprika, 1½ teaspoons of the salt, the pepper, and the crushed tomatoes. Stir to combine. Select the Cancel setting.

4. Cook the potatoes: Lower the Instant Pot steamer rack, with the handles facing up, into the lentil mixture. Carefully position the potatoes on top of the steamer rack.

5. Secure the lid and set the Pressure Release to Sealing. Select the Pressure Cook setting at high pressure and set the cook time to 12 minutes.

6. While the Instant Pot is coming to pressure, preheat the oven to 425°F.

7. Once the 12-minute timer on the Instant Pot has completed and beeps, perform a quick pressure release by carefully switching the Pressure Release knob from Sealing to Venting.

8. Open the pot and use a large spoon to carefully lift the potatoes out of the pot, leaving the steamer rack and lentil filling inside the pot. (The bottoms of the potatoes may be slightly red from the lentil mixture—this is OK!) Transfer the potatoes to a large bowl.

9. If you are using a ricer or a food mill, set it over the bowl and pass the potatoes through. Or, if you are using a potato masher, mash the potatoes. Then add the vegan butter, ¼ cup of the almond milk, and salt. Fold gently with a silicone spatula to combine until the potatoes are smooth and creamy. If the potatoes are too thick, add more of the almond milk. Stir in the chopped chives (if using) and taste for seasonings.

10. Carefully lift out the steamer rack (it will have some of the lentil mixture on the bottom of it). Spoon the lentil mixture into a 9-inch square baking dish, discarding the bay leaves and thyme sprigs. Top the lentils with the mashed potatoes and use a silicone spatula to smooth the surface. If desired, make small indents or waves in the mashed potatoes with a fork or spoon.

11. Transfer the baking dish to the oven and bake until the casserole is hot throughout and the potatoes are lightly browned, about 15 minutes. If desired, finish under the broiler for a few minutes to brown the top.

12. Serve warm and, if desired, top the shepherd's pie with fresh herbs and a drizzle of extra-virgin olive oil.

CHICKPEA VEGETABLE BIRYANI

serves 4 to 6	gluten-free, soy-free, no added sugar

I'm embarrassed to admit this, but as a child, I did not like Indian food except for a few select dishes. Happily, biryani was one of them.

As with many Indian dishes, there are countless regional variations of biryani, but there are a few universal principles. First, biryani is best when made with long-grain basmati rice, which you can find in nearly any grocery store. Second, the complexity of biryani is created through layers of spices, both ground and whole spices, as well as fresh herbs, nuts, and dried fruits. Don't let the long ingredient list scare you away—it's actually a simple dish to make, and a must-try if you enjoy Indian food. It's perfectly spiced, warm, and deeply saturated with fragrance and flavor.

Typically, vegetarian biryani is made with just vegetables, but I add chickpeas to turn it into a main course. My favorite part of this dish is how the creamy, cooling raita (a cucumber-yogurt sauce) mellows out the biryani slightly so that you can better taste each distinct flavor. For the raita, any nondairy yogurt will do, but a thicker yogurt works best if you can find one. I recommend my Homemade Coconut Yogurt (page 71), or for store-bought, Kite Hill Foods Greek-style yogurt or COYO's plain coconut yogurt.

1 cup white basmati rice

RAITA
¼ medium cucumber, unpeeled

1 cup unsweetened nondairy yogurt or Homemade Coconut Yogurt (page 71)

1 garlic clove, crushed through a press

1-inch piece fresh ginger, grated or finely minced

½ cup fresh cilantro, chopped

¼ cup fresh mint leaves, chopped

Juice of ½ lime

½ teaspoon ground cumin

½ teaspoon garam masala

¼ teaspoon kosher salt, plus more to taste

SPICES AND AROMATICS
3 tablespoons grapeseed oil or other neutral, high-heat cooking oil

6 whole green cardamom pods

1½ teaspoons cumin seeds or 1½ teaspoons ground cumin

3 whole cloves

3 bay leaves

8 whole black peppercorns or ⅛ teaspoon freshly cracked black pepper

1 large cinnamon stick or ½ teaspoon ground cinnamon

½ teaspoon fennel seeds

1 medium yellow onion, thinly sliced

5 garlic cloves, minced

1½-inch piece fresh ginger, grated or minced

recipe and ingredients continue

1 serrano pepper, diced (seeded and membranes removed for less heat)

1 teaspoon ground coriander

1 teaspoon ground turmeric

1 teaspoon garam masala

¼ to ½ teaspoon Indian red chile powder or cayenne pepper, to taste (optional, for a spicy version)

¼ teaspoon kosher salt

VEGETABLES AND CHICKPEAS

1 cup water

1¾ cups cooked chickpeas or 1 (15-ounce) can chickpeas, drained and rinsed

2 small Roma or plum tomatoes, chopped

3 cups mixed frozen vegetables (I like cauliflower and carrots)

2 teaspoons kosher salt

MIX-IN INGREDIENTS

1 tablespoon unrefined virgin coconut oil

¼ cup cashews, halved or roughly chopped

¼ cup golden raisins

1 tablespoon fresh lemon juice

¾ cup fresh cilantro, roughly chopped

¼ cup fresh mint leaves, roughly chopped

1. Prepare the rice: Place the rice in a large bowl and wash it under cold water until the water turns clear. This washes away the excess starch and prevents the biryani from becoming sticky. Drain the rice in a fine-mesh sieve and then soak the rice in a bowl with 2 cups cold water for 30 minutes. Thoroughly drain the soaked rice and allow it to dry out in the sieve for 15 minutes.

2. While the rice is soaking, make the raita: Use a box grater to finely grate the unpeeled cucumber. Place the grated cucumber in a fine-mesh sieve or wrap it in a clean, thin kitchen towel (or several paper towels) and squeeze out the excess water. Place the yogurt in a medium bowl and add the grated cucumber, garlic, ginger, cilantro, mint, lime juice, cumin, garam masala, and salt. Stir to combine. Taste for seasonings, adding more salt as needed or more lime juice for acidity. Refrigerate the raita until ready to use.

3. Prepare the spices: Select the Sauté setting on the Instant Pot and, after a few minutes, add 2 tablespoons of the grapeseed oil. Once the display reads "HOT," add the cumin, cloves, bay leaves, peppercorns, and cinnamon stick, and toss frequently until very aromatic, about 45 seconds. If using ground spices instead of whole spices, you may need to add a tablespoon of water to prevent the spices from drying out.

4. Add the onion and cook until just beginning to turn golden, 3 to 4 minutes. Add the garlic, ginger, serrano, coriander, turmeric, garam masala, red chile powder (if using), and ¼ teaspoon salt. Stir vigorously for 30 seconds to ensure the spices coat the mixture evenly. If the mixture is sticking to the bottom of the pot, add 2 tablespoons water and stir to scrape up any browned bits from the bottom of the pot.

5. Push the onion mixture to one side of the pot and add the remaining 1 tablespoon grapeseed oil. Pour in the soaked and drained rice and stir to coat the rice in the oil and onion mixture for 1 minute. Select the Cancel setting.

6. Prepare the vegetables and chickpeas: Add 1 cup water to the rice mixture in the pot along with the chickpeas, tomatoes, mixed frozen vegetables, and 2 teaspoons salt. Mix with a large spoon to incorporate all of the ingredients. The vegetables do not need to be completely submerged in the liquid, as they will get steamed.

7. Secure the lid and set the Pressure Release to Sealing. Select the Pressure Cook setting at high pressure and set the cook time to 4 minutes.

8. Meanwhile, prepare the mix-in ingredients: In a skillet, heat the coconut oil over medium-low heat. Once shimmering, add the cashews and golden raisins. Cook, stirring frequently to prevent burning, until they are both golden brown, 3 to 5 minutes. Set aside.

9. Once the 4-minute timer has completed and beeps, allow a natural pressure release for 5 minutes and then switch the Pressure Release knob from Sealing to Venting to release any remaining steam.

10. Open the pot and discard the bay leaves and cinnamon stick. Using a fork, fluff the rice and then add the lemon juice, cilantro, and mint, stirring to incorporate all of the ingredients. Taste for seasonings and add the fried cashews and golden raisins on top. Transfer the biryani to a serving dish and serve with the raita.

TEX-MEX BROWN RICE AND LENTILS

serves 6 to 8	gluten-free, nut-free option, soy-free option, no added sugar

This is one of my go-to meals when I want to make something healthy yet super easy. I keep coming back to it because the reward-to-work ratio is as high as it gets. The only work required is chopping a few vegetables and measuring out some spices. The reward? A hearty and nourishing bowl of comfort food that makes excellent leftovers throughout the week.

Typically, brown rice takes 45 to 55 minutes to cook on the stove. The Instant Pot speeds up the process considerably and delivers a complete, satisfying meal in less time. And the generous amount of Tex-Mex taco seasoning ensures that each bite is infused with layers of bold, smoky flavor.

This dish is superb on its own, but it might be even better when scooped into warm corn tortillas. And maybe even topped with a dollop of vegan sour cream.

TEX-MEX TACO SEASONING

1 tablespoon chili powder

1½ teaspoons ground cumin

½ teaspoon dried oregano

½ teaspoon sweet paprika

¼ teaspoon garlic powder

¼ teaspoon onion powder

⅛ teaspoon cayenne pepper

1 teaspoon kosher salt

1 teaspoon freshly cracked black pepper

RICE AND LENTILS

1 medium yellow onion, diced

1 small green bell pepper, diced

1 small red bell pepper, diced

6 garlic cloves, minced

1½ cups green or brown lentils

1½ cups long-grain brown rice

4 cups low-sodium vegetable broth

1½ teaspoons kosher salt

1 (4-ounce) can diced or chopped green chiles (mild or hot)

1 (14.5-ounce) can crushed fire-roasted tomatoes

2 medium tomatoes, diced

½ cup chopped fresh cilantro, plus more for serving

2 cups shredded vegan cheese (use a soy-free or nut-free variety as needed) or Vegan Queso (page 51; not soy-free or nut-free)

recipe continues

1. Make the Tex-Mex taco seasoning: In a small bowl, combine the chili powder, cumin, oregano, paprika, garlic powder, onion powder, cayenne, salt, and pepper until well combined.

2. Make the rice and lentils: Place the onion, bell peppers, garlic, lentils, rice, vegetable broth, salt, canned chiles, canned tomatoes, fresh tomatoes, and taco seasoning in the Instant Pot and stir well to combine.

3. Secure the lid and set the Pressure Release to Sealing. Select the Pressure Cook setting at high pressure and set the cook time to 12 minutes.

4. Once the 12-minute timer has completed and beeps, allow a natural pressure release for 15 minutes and then switch the Pressure Release knob from Sealing to Venting to release any remaining steam.

5. Open the pot and stir in the cilantro and vegan cheese or queso until well mixed. Put the lid back on and let rest for 5 to 10 minutes to allow the cheese to melt and the flavors to meld together. When ready to serve, serve with additional chopped cilantro, if desired.

HEARTY TEMPEH CHILI

serves 4 to 6	nut-free, refined sugar-free option

Occasionally, I meet someone who feels obligated to inform me that vegans simply can't get enough protein and/or that vegan food is not filling enough. Usually I ignore such babble, but if I really like the person, I make them this tempeh chili and debunk their misconceptions.

The combination of savory pinto beans, chewy tempeh, and hearty sweet potatoes makes this a triple-threat chili that is guaranteed to satisfy even the heartiest of appetites. The cocoa powder and chipotle chiles create layers of richness and warmth, while the masa harina (Mexican corn flour) gives it a thick, glossy texture.

If you're not familiar with tempeh, it's made from fermented whole soybeans that are formed into firm patties or blocks. Unlike tofu, it is naturally firm, with a nutty, earthy, almost mushroom-y taste. Plus, it's rich in protein, fiber, iron, and calcium; and thanks to the fermentation, it's also a good source of probiotics. To grate tempeh, use a box grater or crumble it finely with your hands.

This chili is fantastic on its own, but you can take it to the next level by spooning on some Vegan Cheese Sauce or Vegan Queso (page 49).

TIP *For an even richer flavor, replace up to half of the vegetable broth with a light-flavored beer like a pilsner when deglazing the pan. Cook for 3 to 4 minutes until the smell of alcohol is no longer as pungent before adding the rest of the ingredients.*

1 tablespoon olive oil

1 large yellow onion, chopped

2 medium carrots, diced

1 teaspoon kosher salt, plus more to taste

Freshly cracked black pepper

5 garlic cloves, minced

1 tablespoon chili powder

1 tablespoon ground cumin

1 teaspoon ground coriander

1 teaspoon sweet paprika

¼ to ½ teaspoon cayenne pepper, to taste

2 bay leaves

2 tablespoons unsweetened cocoa powder

2 cups low-sodium vegetable broth

1 (4-ounce) can diced or chopped green chiles (mild or hot)

1 tablespoon reduced-sodium tamari or soy sauce

1 tablespoon coconut sugar, maple syrup, or organic brown sugar

3 cups cooked pinto beans or 2 (15-ounce) cans, drained and rinsed

1 (8-ounce) block tempeh, grated or finely crumbled (see headnote)

2 medium sweet potatoes (6 ounces each), peeled and cut into a large dice (about 2 cups)

2 canned chipotle peppers in adobo sauce (optional, but adds a rich, smoky flavor)

1 (14.5-ounce) can crushed fired-roasted tomatoes

2 tablespoons tomato paste

3 tablespoons masa harina (or cornmeal)

recipe and ingredients continue

Vegan Cheese Sauce (page 49) or Vegan Queso (page 51)

Chopped scallions or fresh cilantro

1. Select the Sauté setting on the Instant Pot and let the pot heat up for a few minutes before adding the olive oil. Once the oil is hot, add the onion and carrots. Add a pinch each of salt and black pepper and cook until the onion is translucent and the carrots begin to soften, 4 to 5 minutes. Add the garlic and cook for 1 minute, tossing frequently to prevent burning.

2. Add the chili powder, cumin, coriander, paprika, cayenne, bay leaves, and cocoa powder and stir frequently until very fragrant and the vegetables are well coated with the spices, about 30 seconds.

3. Pour in the vegetable broth to deglaze the pan, using a wooden spoon to scrape up any browned bits on the bottom of the pot. Add the canned green chiles, tamari, coconut sugar, pinto beans, tempeh, sweet potatoes, chipotle peppers (if using), 1 teaspoon salt, and black pepper to taste. Stir well to combine and select the Cancel setting. Next, pour in the crushed tomatoes and tomato paste on top, but do not stir, allowing the tomatoes and paste to sit on top (this prevents the tomatoes from blocking the Instant Pot's heat sensor and burning).

4. Secure the lid and set the Pressure Release to Sealing. Select the Pressure Cook setting at high pressure and set the cook time to 8 minutes.

5. Once the 8-minute timer has completed and beeps, allow a natural pressure release for 10 minutes and then switch the Pressure Release knob from Sealing to Venting to release any remaining steam.

6. Open the pot, stir the chili, and discard the bay leaves. Select the Sauté setting and add the masa harina in a slow, steady stream and stir until the chili has thickened, 2 to 3 minutes.

7. Allow the chili to cool slightly before serving and garnish as desired.

VEGETABLE LASAGNA WITH BASIL RICOTTA

serves 4	nut-free, sugar-free

A lasagna in the Instant Pot sounds a bit kooky, and you might be wondering why you would want to do such a thing. For starters, the look of a round, layered lasagna is unique and eye-catching. Second, you can enjoy lasagna in the summer without turning on your oven (though there is the option to broil it for a few minutes if you wish). Finally, it's perfect if you don't have a lot of mouths to feed and don't want to make a huge casserole.

This recipe calls for no-boil lasagna noodles, which speeds things up. To ensure there is enough moisture to cook the noodles, remember to thin out the marinara sauce with some water.

The tofu "ricotta" works perfectly in this lasagna, lending a comforting, cheesy feel, along with a protein punch. I blend the ricotta in a food processor, which gives it a luxurious creamy texture, but you can also use a fork to mash everything up (and save yourself some dishes). Not a fan of tofu or want to keep this dish super quick and easy? Substitute your favorite store-bought vegan cheese—just be sure to use a variety that can melt nicely.

VEGETABLE FILLING

2 tablespoons olive oil

1 small yellow onion, diced

4 garlic cloves, minced

1 cup finely chopped zucchini

¾ cup finely chopped red bell pepper

1 cup chopped mushrooms

⅓ cup fresh basil leaves, chopped, plus more for garnish

1 teaspoon kosher salt

Freshly cracked black pepper

LASAGNA ASSEMBLY

1½ cups marinara sauce of choice or Fiery Arrabbiata Sauce (page 59)

6 to 8 individual no-boil or oven-ready lasagna sheets (see headnote)

Basil Ricotta (recipe follows) or 2 cups shredded vegan mozzarella or other cheese

1 cup chopped spinach or shredded Tuscan (lacinato) kale

½ cup shredded vegan mozzarella, for finishing (optional)

recipe continues

1. Make the vegetable filling: Select the Sauté setting on the Instant Pot and, after a few minutes, add the olive oil, followed by the onion. Cook the onion for 3 minutes, then add the garlic, zucchini, bell pepper, and mushrooms. Cook for an additional 3 minutes, tossing frequently to prevent the garlic from burning.

2. Add the basil, salt, and pepper to taste. Stir to combine and cook for 30 seconds. Select the Cancel setting and remove the inner pot.

3. To assemble the lasagna: Pour the marinara sauce into a large measuring cup and add ½ cup water to equal 2 cups, stirring to incorporate (thinning out the sauce with water ensures the noodles will cook evenly).

4. Pour ½ cup of the marinara sauce into the bottom of a 7-inch springform pan, spreading evenly with a silicone spatula. Top the sauce with half of the oven-ready lasagna noodles, breaking them into pieces and fitting them to cover the sauce in a mosaic-like pattern.

5. Add another ½ cup of the marinara sauce on top of the noodles. Using a silicone spatula, spread one-third of the basil ricotta (or shredded cheese) on top of the marinara sauce, followed by half of the vegetable filling and half of the spinach or kale.

6. Repeat the layers: Add ½ cup of the marinara sauce, followed by one-third of the basil ricotta (or shredded cheese), the remaining vegetable filling, and the remaining spinach or kale.

7. Finish with the remaining lasagna noodles (broken into pieces), the final ½ cup marinara sauce, and the final one-third of the basil ricotta (or shredded cheese). If you can't fit all of the lasagna noodles, just leave a few pieces out. You don't want to layer them on top of each other because that might cause them to cook unevenly.

8. Spray a piece of foil with nonstick cooking spray and tightly cover the pan.

9. Wipe out the inner pot of any remaining vegetables and give it a rinse. Add 1½ cups water to the inner pot.

10. For easy removal of the pan from the Instant Pot, create a foil sling following the instructions on page 21. (Alternatively, you can use oven mitts to carefully remove the pan.)

11. On the counter, place the pan on top of the steamer rack (with the handles facing up) and arrange the foil sling (if using) underneath the steamer rack. Carefully lower the steamer rack and pan into the inner pot using the foil sling or steamer rack handles.

12. Secure the lid and set the Pressure Release to Sealing. Select the Pressure Cook setting at high pressure and set the cook time to 20 minutes.

13. Once the 20-minute timer has completed and beeps, allow a natural pressure release. If you want to broil the lasagna in your oven, turn on your oven's broiler.

14. Open the pot and, wearing oven mitts, grasp the foil sling or steamer rack handles and carefully lift the pan out of the Instant Pot. Carefully remove the foil cover, taking care to not drip any condensation on the lasagna.

15. If desired, top the lasagna with the ½ cup shredded vegan mozzarella and place the lasagna under the broiler for 1 to 3 minutes (depending on the strength of your broiler and the distance between the heat and oven rack) to brown the top. You can also broil the lasagna without adding the vegan mozzarella. Garnish with fresh basil.

Basil Ricotta

Makes about 2 cups

- 1 (14-ounce) block extra-firm tofu
- ¼ cup nutritional yeast
- 2 garlic cloves, roughly chopped
- 2 tablespoons white or yellow miso paste
- ¾ teaspoon onion powder
- 1 teaspoon kosher salt, plus more to taste
- ½ teaspoon freshly cracked black pepper
- 1 tablespoon extra-virgin olive oil
- 15 fresh basil leaves
- 1½ teaspoons grated lemon zest
- 3 tablespoons fresh lemon juice

Drain the tofu and blot away the excess water with a few paper towels. For a smooth ricotta, crumble the tofu into a food processor. Add the nutritional yeast, garlic, miso, onion powder, salt, pepper, olive oil, basil, lemon zest, and lemon juice and blend until you have a creamy, smooth texture. Taste for salt, acidity, and cheesiness, adding more salt, lemon juice, or nutritional yeast, respectively, as needed. For a chunkier ricotta, place the tofu in a large bowl and break it into smaller chunks using a fork. Add the remaining ingredients and mix together until the consistency resembles ricotta cheese.

VEGETABLE PAELLA

serves 4 to 6	gluten-free option, soy-free, nut-free, no added sugar

This recipe has the bold flavors and intense aroma typical of paella, but the Instant Pot makes it less laborious to prepare. I add vegan sausage, both to mimic traditional paella and to make it hearty enough for a main dish. I love the gluten-free and soy-free sausages from Beyond Meat, as well as the grain-based, soy-free sausages from Field Roast, especially the Italian flavor. If you can't find a vegan sausage that crumbles, just dice it up.

Another star ingredient is saffron. If you soak the saffron threads in vegetable broth before cooking, it releases even more color and flavor, so you can use just a tiny bit of this expensive spice. Unfortunately, there is no proper substitute for the uniquely floral yet earthy flavor of saffron, but you can use turmeric to achieve the same golden color.

Traditional paella uses a short-grain rice called bomba rice, which is very absorbent and tends to not stick together. Since it can be hard to find, you can use another short-grain rice like Arborio or a medium-grain rice like Calrose.

2½ cups low-sodium vegetable broth

¼ teaspoon saffron threads (optional but highly recommended)

3 tablespoons olive oil

1 large yellow onion, chopped

4 garlic cloves, minced

9 ounces vegan sausage (see headnote) (about 3 sausage links), crumbled or diced

8 ounces cremini mushrooms, sliced

2 red, yellow, or orange bell peppers, chopped

1 teaspoon kosher salt

½ teaspoon freshly cracked black pepper

1½ cups bomba rice or another short-grain or medium-grain white rice (see headnote)

¾ cup dry white wine (such as Pinot Grigio or Sauvignon Blanc)

1 (14-ounce) jar or can artichoke hearts (packed in water), drained and quartered

2 bay leaves

1 tablespoon smoked paprika

½ teaspoon cayenne pepper

½ teaspoon crushed red pepper flakes (omit for a mild version)

½ teaspoon ground turmeric (for color only; omit if using saffron)

1 (14.5-ounce) can diced fire-roasted tomatoes

Grated zest of 1 small lemon

¼ cup chopped fresh Italian flat-leaf parsley, plus more for garnish

½ cup green or Kalamata olives, pitted and halved (optional)

recipe continues

1. Pour the vegetable broth into a measuring cup and stir in the saffron threads. Allow the saffron to soak while you prepare the other ingredients. If not using saffron, skip this step.

2. Select the Sauté setting on the Instant Pot and let the pot heat up for a few minutes before adding 1½ tablespoons olive oil. Once the oil is hot, add the chopped onion. Cook for 2 minutes to just slightly soften the onion. Add the garlic and cook for 1 minute, tossing frequently.

3. Mix in the sausage and cook for another 2 minutes, tossing frequently to prevent sticking. Add the mushrooms, bell peppers, ½ teaspoon of the salt, and the black pepper. Cook until the mushrooms begin to release their liquid, about 4 minutes. Select the Cancel setting and transfer the sausage-vegetable mixture to a bowl and set aside. There's no need to rinse the inner pot, but be sure to scrape up any browned bits stuck to the bottom so they won't burn during pressure cooking.

4. Return the inner pot to the Instant Pot and select the Sauté setting. Add the remaining 1½ tablespoons olive oil and, once the oil is shimmering, add the rice. Mix well to ensure all of the grains are coated in oil and toast the rice for 2 minutes, stirring frequently to prevent sticking.

5. Add the wine to deglaze the pan, using a wooden spoon to scrape up any browned bits on the bottom of the pot. Cook until the liquid has mostly evaporated and the smell of alcohol has dissipated, about 2 minutes. Select the Cancel setting.

6. Pour in the saffron-infused vegetable broth and stir to combine, scraping any remaining bits from the bottom of the pan. Return the sausage-vegetable mixture to the pot. Add the quartered artichokes, bay leaves, smoked paprika, cayenne, pepper flakes (if using), turmeric (if using), and remaining ½ teaspoon salt, stirring well to combine. Pour the diced tomatoes on top, but do not stir, allowing the tomatoes to sit on top (this prevents the tomatoes from blocking the Instant Pot's heat sensor and burning).

7. Secure the lid and set the Pressure Release to Sealing. Select the Pressure Cook setting at high pressure and set the cook time to 6 minutes.

8. Once the 6-minute timer has completed and beeps, allow a natural pressure release for 5 minutes and then switch the Pressure Release knob from Sealing to Venting to release any remaining steam.

9. Open the pot and discard the bay leaves. Stir in the lemon zest and parsley, and allow the paella to rest for 10 minutes before serving. Transfer the paella to a serving dish and top with extra chopped parsley and olives, if using.

PUMPKIN FARROTTO
(FARRO RISOTTO)

serves 4	nut-free option, soy-free option, no added sugar

Farro is one of those underappreciated ancient grains. It has a nutty earthiness and uniquely satisfying chew, lending itself beautifully to a diverse range of dishes including risotto. Or farrotto.

Farro's springy yet tender bite is the perfect contrast to the softer textures in this dish. With its bold wheat-y presence, farrotto boasts a heartier, more robust flavor than classic risotto, plus you get more fiber, protein, and nutrients.

The subtly sweet leeks, creamy pumpkin puree, and aromatic herb-infused oil will make you feel like you are eating a bowl of Thanksgiving flavors (without consuming 6,000 calories and having to put on your stretchy pants).

When buying farro, you want to look for pearled or semi-pearled farro, as the whole-grain variety requires overnight soaking and a much longer cooking time. You can find farro in the bulk foods section of well-stocked natural foods stores or in the whole grains section of most grocery stores.

TIP *While farro is wheat and therefore not gluten-free, it is relatively low in gluten and easier to digest than modern wheat varieties, so if you avoid gluten but don't have an allergy or serious sensitivity, you may be able to enjoy farro.*

2 tablespoons olive oil

2 large leeks, dark green tops discarded, thoroughly cleaned, trimmed, and diced

4 garlic cloves, minced

1½ cups pearled or semi-pearled farro

½ cup dry white wine (such as Pinot Grigio or Sauvignon Blanc)

1¾ cups low-sodium vegetable broth

1 (15-ounce) can unsweetened pumpkin puree

1 bay leaf

¼ teaspoon freshly grated or ground nutmeg

1 heaping teaspoon kosher salt, plus more to taste

Freshly cracked black pepper

HERB-INFUSED OIL

1½ tablespoons extra-virgin olive oil

1½ tablespoons vegan butter (use a soy-free variety to keep soy-free) or extra-virgin olive oil

12 fresh sage leaves

6 sprigs fresh thyme

2 sprigs fresh rosemary

FOR SERVING

¼ cup hazelnuts or walnuts, toasted (omit for a nut-free option)

¼ cup vegan parmesan cheese (optional)

recipe continues

1. Select the Sauté setting on the Instant Pot and let the pot heat up for a few minutes before adding the olive oil. Once the oil is hot, add the leeks. Cook, stirring occasionally, until the leeks are softened, about 3 minutes. Add the garlic and cook for 1 minute, stirring frequently to prevent burning.

2. Slowly add the farro, coating the grains in the leeks and olive oil, and cook for 1 minute.

3. Pour in the wine to deglaze the pan, using a wooden spoon to scrape up any browned bits on the bottom of the pot. Simmer until the liquid has mostly evaporated and the smell of alcohol has dissipated, about 3 minutes.

4. Pour in the vegetable broth, then add the pumpkin puree, bay leaf, nutmeg, salt, and pepper to taste. Select the Cancel setting.

5. Secure the lid and set the Pressure Release to Sealing. Select the Pressure Cook setting at high pressure and set the cook time to 10 minutes.

6. Once the 10-minute timer has completed and beeps, allow a natural pressure release for 10 minutes and then switch the Pressure Release knob from Sealing to Venting to release any remaining steam.

7. While the pot is depressurizing, make the herb-infused oil: Heat a skillet over medium heat and add the extra-virgin olive oil and vegan butter (or simply use a total of 3 tablespoons extra-virgin olive oil) over medium heat. Once melted and frothy (or shimmering if just using oil), add the sage, thyme, and rosemary. Allow the herbs to cook for a bit, tossing them around occasionally, until the oil is bubbling and smells very fragrant, 2 to 3 minutes. Discard the herbs using a slotted spoon.

8. Open the Instant Pot, discard the bay leaf, and stir the farrotto well. Select the Sauté setting and simmer for 3 minutes to thicken. Then pour the herb-infused oil over the farrotto and stir to incorporate.

9. To serve, scoop the farrotto into individual bowls and, if desired, garnish each with the hazelnuts and vegan parmesan. Serve immediately.

FOR SERVING

4 or 6 gyro-style wraps, pocketless pitas, or flatbread

Shredded red cabbage

Diced tomatoes and cucumbers

1. Make the lentil-walnut ragu: Select the Sauté setting on the Instant Pot and let the pot heat up for a few minutes before adding the oil. Once the oil is hot, add the onion. Cook until the onion is beginning to brown, 4 to 5 minutes. Add the garlic and cook for 1 minute, tossing frequently to prevent burning.

2. Add the za'atar, cumin, oregano, paprika, and cayenne and stir frequently for 30 seconds until the onion is well coated in the spices. Select the Cancel setting.

3. Pour in the vegetable broth to deglaze the pan, using a wooden spoon to scrape up any browned bits on the bottom of the pot. Add the lentils, walnuts, salt, and black pepper to taste. Pour the diced tomatoes on top, but do not stir, allowing the tomatoes to sit on top (this prevents the tomatoes from blocking the Instant Pot's heat sensor and burning).

4. Secure the lid and set the Pressure Release to Sealing. Select the Pressure Cook setting at high pressure and set the cook time to 16 minutes.

5. Meanwhile, make the tzatziki: Use a box grater to finely grate the unpeeled cucumber. Place the grated cucumber in a fine-mesh sieve or wrap it in a clean, thin kitchen towel (or several paper towels) and squeeze out the excess water. Place the nondairy yogurt in a medium bowl and add the grated cucumber, garlic, dill, salt, lemon juice, olive oil, and black pepper to taste. Stir to combine. Taste for seasonings, adding more salt as needed, more lemon for acidity, or more dill for fresh herb flavor.

6. Once the 16-minute timer has completed and beeps, allow a natural pressure release for 10 minutes and then switch the Pressure Release knob from Sealing to Venting to release any remaining steam.

7. Open the pot and stir well. To serve, spoon the ragu onto the wraps or pita and top with shredded cabbage, diced tomatoes and cucumber, and the tzatziki.

Za'atar Seasoning
Makes about 2 tablespoons

1 tablespoon white sesame seeds

1 tablespoon minced fresh thyme leaves

1 teaspoon ground sumac (available at gourmet grocery stores, spice shops, or online)

¼ teaspoon coarse or flaked sea salt

In a small dry skillet, toast the sesame seeds, tossing occasionally, until golden, 3 to 5 minutes. Pour into a small bowl and add the thyme, sumac, and salt and stir to combine. Store in an airtight container in a cool, dry place.

KHICHDI
(INDIAN LENTIL AND RICE PORRIDGE)

serves 6	gluten-free, nut-free option, soy-free, sugar-free

As a child, whenever I had a tummy ache, my mother would serve me *khichdi*, an Indian rice and lentil porridge. I would hover my face over a hot bowl of *khichdi*, inhaling its aroma and feeling the steam warm my cheeks, and after eating, I would feel better instantly. *Khichdi* feels like a hug in a bowl, which explains why many Indians treat it as a panacea.

Khichdi involves cooking white rice and yellow lentils (split yellow mung beans) until they get creamy and thick, almost like risotto. If you open your Instant Pot to find a big bowl of mush, don't be alarmed—*khichdi* should look mushy!

There are many regional variations throughout India. My version combines a bit of what I love from the various *khichdi* recipes I've tried over the years, and like all *khichdis*, it's the ultimate comfort food.

1 cup white basmati rice

1 cup yellow lentils (split yellow mung beans) or red lentils

2 tablespoons refined coconut oil

2½ teaspoons cumin seeds

2 bay leaves

1-inch piece fresh ginger, grated or minced

4 garlic cloves, minced

1 serrano pepper, diced (optional)

6½ cups water

½ teaspoon ground turmeric

2½ teaspoons kosher salt, plus more to taste

½ teaspoon freshly cracked black pepper or whole black peppercorns

2 tablespoons unrefined coconut oil or vegan butter

½ cup cashews, roughly chopped (omit for a nut-free option)

¼ to ½ teaspoon Indian red chile powder or cayenne pepper, to taste (omit for a mild version)

6 tablespoons unsweetened shredded coconut

recipe continues

1. Place the rice and lentils in a large bowl and cover with a generous amount of cold water. Soak, covered, for 30 minutes. Drain the rice and lentils in a fine-mesh sieve.

2. Select the Sauté setting on the Instant Pot and, after a few minutes, add the refined coconut oil. Once the display reads "HOT," add 2 teaspoons of the cumin seeds and the bay leaves. Fry until the cumin seeds turn brown, 60 to 90 seconds.

3. Add the ginger, garlic, and serrano and cook until very fragrant and the garlic is lightly golden, about 1 minute, then select the Cancel setting.

4. Add the soaked rice and lentils to the Instant Pot, along with 6½ cups water, the turmeric, salt, and black pepper. Stir to combine all of the ingredients.

5. Secure the lid and set the Pressure Release to Sealing. Select the Pressure Cook setting at high pressure and set the cook time to 12 minutes.

6. Once the 12-minute timer has completed and beeps, allow a natural pressure release for 20 minutes and then switch the Pressure Release knob from Sealing to Venting to release any remaining steam.

7. Open the pot and discard the bay leaves. Taste the *khichdi* for salt and adjust accordingly. Don't be alarmed if the *khichdi* is mushy—it should be mushy, similar to an oatmeal texture. The *khichdi* will absorb the remaining liquid as it rests.

8. In a skillet, heat the unrefined virgin coconut oil or vegan butter over medium-low heat. Once shimmering (or melted, if using butter), add the cashews and cook, stirring frequently to prevent burning, until golden brown, 3 to 4 minutes. Add the remaining ½ teaspoon cumin seeds and the red chile powder (if using) and cook until very fragrant, 20 to 30 seconds. Remove the pan from the heat.

9. Transfer the *khichdi* to a serving bowl and stir in the shredded coconut. Pour the spiced cashews over the *khichdi*.

ONE-POT BOLOGNESE PASTA

serves 6	no added sugar

While your Italian *nonna* might not approve of the changes I've made to his classic Italian dish, this Bolognese pasta is perfect for those nights when you want to throw everything in one pot but still enjoy a satisfying, gourmet meal.

To replicate the rich flavor and heartiness of traditional Bolognese, this recipe uses a traditional Italian *soffritto* of onion, carrots, and celery, along with meaty shiitake mushrooms and walnuts, protein-rich lentils, and plump sun-dried tomatoes.

To make this meal as simple as possible, do the prep work before bed or in the morning before you leave for work: Slice the veggies, crush the walnuts, and measure out the spices. Then, when you wake up or get home, the dish comes together in no time!

TIP *To crush walnuts, pulse them in a food processor until they are the texture of bread crumbs. Or, place them in a resealable plastic bag and use a rolling pin or a meat (gasp!) mallet to crush them.*

¾ cup red lentils

2½ tablespoons olive oil

1 medium yellow onion, diced

1 large carrot, diced

2 celery stalks, diced

2 teaspoons kosher salt, plus more to taste

4 garlic cloves, minced

8 ounces shiitake mushrooms caps, finely chopped

2 teaspoons dried oregano

2 teaspoons dried thyme

¾ teaspoon freshly grated or ground nutmeg

½ teaspoon crushed red pepper flakes (omit for a mild version)

¼ teaspoon cayenne pepper

Freshly cracked black pepper

½ cup dry red wine (such as Pinot Noir)

3½ cups low-sodium vegetable broth or water

½ cup walnuts, finely crushed (see Tip)

1 tablespoon reduced-sodium tamari or soy sauce

1 tablespoon white or yellow miso paste

1½ tablespoons high-quality balsamic vinegar

10 oil-packed sun-dried tomato halves, excess oil blotted away, chopped

8 ounces penne pasta, or other medium-size pasta with a cook time of 9 to 11 minutes (if your pasta has a different cook time, see Tip on page 180 for how to calculate)

1 (14.5-ounce) can diced fire-roasted tomatoes

2 tablespoons tomato paste

recipe and ingredients continue

2 cups marinara sauce of choice, or Fiery Arrabbiata Sauce (page 59)

1 cup fresh basil, finely slivered

½ cup fresh Italian flat-leaf parsley, chopped

½ cup vegan parmesan cheese (optional)

---

1. Place the lentils in a bowl and cover with water. Soak while you prep the other ingredients, or for 30 minutes, and then drain.

2. Select the Sauté setting an the Instant Pot and let the pot heat up for a few minutes before adding the oil. Once the oil is hot, add the onion, carrot, and celery. Add a pinch of salt and cook until the vegetables have softened, about 4 minutes. Add the garlic and shiitake mushrooms and cook for 3 minutes until the mushrooms begin to release their liquid, tossing frequently to prevent the garlic from burning.

3. Add the oregano, thyme, nutmeg, pepper flakes (if using), cayenne, 2 teaspoons salt, and black pepper to taste and stir for 1 minute to coat the vegetables with the spices.

4. Pour in the wine to deglaze the pan, using a wooden spoon to scrape up any browned bits on the bottom of the pot. Simmer until the liquid has mostly evaporated and the smell of alcohol has dissipated, 4 to 5 minutes. Select the Cancel setting.

5. Add the broth, the soaked and drained lentils, walnuts, tamari, miso, 1 tablespoon of the vinegar, the sun-dried tomatoes, and pasta. Stir to combine, submerging the pasta underneath the liquid as much as possible. Pour the canned diced tomatoes and tomato paste on top, but do not stir, allowing the tomatoes and paste to sit on top (this prevents the tomatoes from blocking the Instant Pot's heat sensor and burning).

6. Secure the lid and set the Pressure Release to Sealing. Select the Pressure Cook setting at high pressure and set the cook time to 3 minutes.

7. While the pasta is pressure cooking, gently warm the marinara sauce in a saucepan or in a microwave-safe bowl.

8. Once the 3-minute timer has completed and beeps, perform a quick pressure release by carefully switching the Pressure Release knob from Sealing to Venting.

9. Open the pot and pour in the warm marinara sauce and the remaining ½ tablespoon vinegar, gently stirring to combine, until the sauce is warmed throughout. Add the basil and parsley and gently toss. Sprinkle on the vegan parmesan (if using) and serve immediately.

PASTA PRIMAVERA ALFREDO

serves 4 to 6	nut-free option, no added sugar

Growing up in a small town, sit-down restaurant meals were reserved for the rare family weekend outing, when we'd drive to the next town thirty minutes away. We usually ended up at the Olive Garden, the one place where my vegetarian parents could eat something besides a baked potato. My favorite dish there was the pasta primavera, which was drowning in butter and cream but ostensibly balanced by a sprinkling of vegetables.

This pasta primavera Alfredo is a tribute to my family's memories at Olive Garden—a dairy-free, more grown-up version of the pasta primavera of my teen years. Nostalgia aside, it's one of my favorite dishes because it's indulgent and rich but also light, thanks to the generous amount of vegetables and bright lemon zest. While edamame aren't typical in pasta primavera, I use them in place of peas since they add a generous amount of protein. And if you'd like to add more protein, stir in some cooked white beans at the end as well.

1 medium head broccoli, cut into very small florets

2 tablespoons olive oil

2 tablespoons vegan butter or olive oil

1 large yellow onion, finely diced

2 medium carrots, finely diced

1½ teaspoons kosher salt, plus more to taste

6 garlic cloves, minced

¼ cup dry white wine (such as Pinot Grigio or Sauvignon Blanc)

3 tablespoons nutritional yeast

1 tablespoon fresh lemon juice

Freshly cracked black pepper

1 (13.5-ounce) can "lite" or reduced-fat coconut milk

2½ cups unsweetened plain nondairy milk (I suggest something a little creamier than your standard almond milk, such as coconut milk ["drinking milk" from a carton, not a can], oat milk, or cashew milk)

8 ounces farfalle or other medium-size pasta with a cook time of 11 to 13 minutes or less (if your pasta has a different cook time, see Tip on page 180 for how to calculate)

16 ounces frozen shelled edamame, thawed, or 1 cup unthawed frozen peas

15 cherry tomatoes or grape tomatoes, halved

3 cups baby spinach or baby kale, roughly chopped

Grated zest of 1 medium lemon

⅓ cup fresh Italian flat-leaf parsley, finely chopped

⅓ cup fresh basil, finely slivered

½ cup vegan parmesan cheese (optional)

recipe continues

1. Set up a large bowl of ice and water to make an ice bath. Steam the broccoli on the stove while the pasta is cooking in the Instant Pot (this method saves time but requires extra dish washing), or steam it in the Instant Pot. If using the Instant Pot, select the Sauté setting and add ½ cup water to the inner pot. Once the water is gently simmering, add the broccoli florets with a pinch of salt. Place the Instant Pot lid on top (set the Pressure Release to Venting; the lid won't lock into place), or use a glass lid that fits your Instant Pot, and let the broccoli steam. After 5 minutes, check to see if the broccoli is done, and if it's still too crisp, let it steam for 1 more minute. Select the Cancel setting. Remove the inner pot, drain, and transfer the broccoli to the ice bath to stop cooking (this helps the broccoli retain its bright green color). Wipe away any remaining water from the inner pot.

2. Select the Sauté setting on the Instant Pot and, after a few minutes, add the olive oil and vegan butter. Once the mixture is melted and frothy, add the onion and carrots with a pinch of salt and cook until the onion is completely soft, 6 to 7 minutes.

3. Add the garlic and cook for 1 minute, then pour in the wine. Cook, stirring occasionally, until the liquid has mostly evaporated and the smell of alcohol has dissipated, 2 to 3 minutes. Select the Cancel setting.

4. Add the nutritional yeast, lemon juice, 1½ teaspoons salt, and pepper to taste and stir to combine with the vegetables. Pour in the canned coconut milk and the nondairy milk. Add the pasta, submerging it to ensure even cooking.

5. Secure the lid and set the Pressure Release to Sealing. Select the Pressure Cook setting at high pressure and set the cook time to 4 minutes (or the cook time your calculations worked out to; see Tip, page 180).

6. Once the 4-minute timer has completed and beeps, allow a natural pressure release for 5 minutes and then switch the Pressure Release knob from Sealing to Venting to release any remaining steam.

7. Open the pot and stir the pasta. The pasta should be al dente or almost al dente, and will become more tender during this next sauté step. Select the Sauté setting and press the Sauté button again until you reach Less heat. Cook, gently stirring occasionally to prevent sticking, for 3 to 4 minutes to slightly thicken the sauce (the sauce will also thicken considerably while resting).

8. Stir in the steamed broccoli, edamame, tomatoes, spinach, lemon zest, parsley, and basil. Stir the mixture for 1 minute, then select the Cancel setting. Let the pasta sit for a few minutes for all the flavors to meld together and for the sauce to thicken. Season to taste with salt and pepper and serve with vegan parmesan, if desired.

6

SOUPS, STEWS, AND CURRIES

The first meals I made in my Instant Pot were soups and stews, and I've never looked back. The Instant Pot is able to achieve the depth of flavor and richness associated with hours of slow simmering, but in considerably less time and with zero babysitting. Whether you're looking for a traditional lentil soup or a complex, aromatic curry, there is something cozy for you in this chapter. After trying a few of these dishes, you'll get into a comfortable rhythm and be able to craft your own soup recipes on the fly.

CREAMY DREAMY CAULIFLOWER SOUP

serves 6	gluten-free option, nut-free option, soy-free, sugar-free

One of the easiest dishes to make in the Instant Pot is soup. Just lightly sauté aromatics, toss in some vegetables and broth, perhaps some legumes, close the lid, and voilà. For most pureed soups, like this one, you can even puree the soup directly in the Instant Pot using an immersion blender. Or, if you're fond of washing extra dishes (some people find washing dishes to be meditative; I am not one of those people), you can always transfer your soup in batches to a blender.

In the fall and winter, I make soup nearly every week, and cauliflower often makes it into the rotation. Once cooked and pureed, cauliflower transforms from crunchy to creamy, and, in this soup, it gets an even creamier upgrade from potatoes and a little splash of full-fat coconut milk.

1½ tablespoons olive oil

1 medium yellow onion, diced

1¾ teaspoons kosher salt, plus more to taste

4 garlic cloves, minced

1 large head cauliflower (2½ to 3 pounds), cut into large florets

1 pound Yukon Gold potatoes, peeled and cut into cubes

4 cups low-sodium vegetable broth

8 sprigs fresh thyme

½ teaspoon freshly cracked black pepper, plus more to taste

¼ teaspoon freshly grated or ground nutmeg

¼ cup canned full-fat or "lite" coconut milk

GARNISHES

1 cup panko or fresh bread crumbs (omit if gluten-free) + 1 teaspoon olive oil

¼ cup roasted or toasted almonds, chopped (omit for a nut-free option)

Grated zest of 1 small lemon

2 tablespoons capers, drained

2 tablespoons finely chopped fresh Italian flat-leaf parsley

recipe continues

1. Select the Sauté setting on the Instant Pot and let the pot heat up for a few minutes before adding the olive oil. Once the oil is hot, add the onion and a pinch of salt. Cook until the onion has started to brown, about 5 minutes. Add the garlic and cook for 1 minute, stirring frequently to prevent burning.

2. Add the cauliflower, potatoes, vegetable broth, thyme sprigs, 1¾ teaspoons salt, the pepper, and nutmeg. Stir to combine. Select the Cancel setting.

3. Secure the lid and set the Pressure Release to Sealing. Select the Soup setting at high pressure and set the cook time to 5 minutes.

4. Once the 5-minute timer has completed and beeps, allow a natural pressure release for 10 minutes and then switch the Pressure Release knob from Sealing to Venting to release any remaining steam.

5. While the pot is depressurizing, prepare the garnishes: Heat a skillet over medium-high heat and add the 1 teaspoon olive oil. Once the oil is hot, add the panko and toast, tossing occasionally, until golden brown, 3 to 4 minutes.

6. Open the pot and, using an immersion blender, puree for a few minutes until you have a thick and creamy soup. (Alternatively, blend the soup in batches in a high-powered blender. Be sure to remove the center cap from the blender lid to vent steam, but cover the hole with a kitchen towel.) Taste for seasonings and add salt and pepper to taste.

7. Serve in bowls and top with the toasted bread crumbs, almonds, lemon zest, capers, and parsley.

RED LENTIL ALMOND CURRY

serves 4 to 6	gluten-free, soy-free, no added sugar

My recipe for red lentil almond curry is one of my most popular, and each time someone makes the recipe, she usually adds "I can't believe this is vegan!" I can't blame them, as I had the same thoughts the first time I made this dish. It's one of the few recipes I make on a regular basis but still dream about. It's aromatic, perfectly spiced, and coconut-y. And despite its decadent taste, it packs in a lot of nutrition from the lentils and anti-inflammatory trio of ginger, turmeric, and garlic.

This curry is particularly amazing when eaten Indian-style—ditch the utensils and use your hand to fold a piece of naan or roti over the curry and eat the whole morsel in one scoop. It tastes better this way, trust me, and is a full sensory experience.

2 tablespoons unrefined virgin coconut oil

1 large yellow onion, diced

2 medium carrots, diced

4 garlic cloves, minced

2-inch piece fresh ginger, grated or minced

1 to 2 serrano peppers, to taste, diced (seeded and membranes removed for less heat)

1 tablespoon grated or minced fresh turmeric or 1 teaspoon ground turmeric

1 tablespoon curry powder

1 teaspoon ground cumin

1 teaspoon garam masala

½ teaspoon ground coriander

½ teaspoon Indian red chile powder or ¼ teaspoon cayenne pepper

1½ teaspoons kosher salt

½ teaspoon freshly cracked black pepper

1½ cups water

1 cup red lentils, rinsed

1 (13.5-ounce) can full-fat coconut milk

3 tablespoons no-added-sugar almond butter

2 medium tomatoes, finely chopped

Juice of ½ lemon

½ cup fresh cilantro, roughly chopped

FOR SERVING (OPTIONAL)

Cooked white basmati rice

Naan or roti

Homemade Coconut Yogurt (page 71) or store-bought coconut yogurt

recipe continues

1. Select the Sauté setting on the Instant Pot and let the pot heat up for a few minutes before adding the coconut oil. Once the oil is hot, add the onion and carrots. Cook, stirring occasionally, until the onions have softened, about 5 minutes.

2. Add the garlic, ginger, serranos, and the fresh turmeric (if using) and cook for 90 seconds, stirring frequently to prevent sticking.

3. Stir in the ground turmeric (if using), curry powder, cumin, garam masala, coriander, red chile powder, salt, and black pepper. Add 2 tablespoons water to prevent burning. Stir the spices into the vegetables to coat evenly, stirring constantly for 30 seconds. Select the Cancel setting.

4. Pour in the water to deglaze the pan, using a wooden spoon to scrape up any browned bits on the bottom of the pot. Add the red lentils, coconut milk, almond butter, and chopped tomatoes, stirring to combine.

5. Secure the lid and set the Pressure Release to Sealing. Select the Pressure Cook setting at high pressure and set the cook time to 10 minutes.

6. Once the 10-minute timer has completed and beeps, allow a natural pressure release for 10 minutes and then switch the Pressure Release knob from Sealing to Venting to release any remaining steam.

7. Open the pot and stir in the lemon juice and cilantro. Serve the curry over white basmati rice or with naan bread (or roti) and add a dollop of coconut yogurt on top, if desired.

FRENCH LENTIL SOUP

serves 6	gluten-free, nut-free, soy-free, no added sugar

This is one of the simpler recipes in the book, but you'll come back to it time and time again. It's made with inexpensive ingredients, many of which you almost certainly keep in your pantry, and it's easy enough to make for a weeknight dinner. But don't confuse simple with boring.

There are many reasons why this humble lentil soup is extra special. The onions cook down until they are sticky-sweet and browned, adding a rich umami flavor, while the bouquet garni (or bundle of fresh herbs) saturates the entire soup with a fragrance that I can only describe as "rustic French home cooking." A splash of balsamic vinegar at the end really dials up the flavors. And the best part? The soup gets better the next day, becoming heartier and more harmonious in flavor.

I use French green lentils because they hold their texture nicely and don't completely break down in the soup. Plus, they have a distinct light, peppery flavor that I adore. If you can't find them, you can substitute standard green or brown lentils, though the soup will be a bit mushier.

3 tablespoons olive oil

1 medium yellow onion, finely diced

3 medium carrots, diced

3 celery stalks with leaves, diced

4 garlic cloves, minced

1 medium Yukon Gold potato, peeled and diced

1 teaspoon kosher salt, plus more to taste

½ teaspoon freshly cracked black pepper

1 teaspoon sweet or hot paprika

1½ cups French green (Puy) lentils

Bouquet garni: 2 bay leaves + a few sprigs *each* of Italian flat-leaf parsley, rosemary, oregano, and thyme, tied tightly together with kitchen twine

4 cups low-sodium vegetable broth

1 (28-ounce) can fire-roasted crushed tomatoes

2 to 3 teaspoons high-quality balsamic vinegar or lemon juice, to taste

FOR SERVING

Baguette or rustic bread, sliced

recipe continues

1. Select the Sauté setting on the Instant Pot and let the pot heat up for a few minutes before adding the olive oil. Once the oil is hot, add the onion and a pinch of salt. Cook until the onion is browned and completely soft, 6 to 8 minutes.

2. Add the carrots, celery, garlic, potato, salt, and the pepper and cook until the carrots are just starting to soften, 2 to 3 minutes.

3. Add the paprika and lentils and cook for 30 seconds, stirring to coat the lentils with the spices and seasonings. Select the Cancel setting.

4. Add the bouquet garni and vegetable broth, then pour the crushed tomatoes on top. Stir gently.

5. Secure the lid and set the Pressure Release to Sealing. Select the Pressure Cook setting at high pressure and set the cook time to 12 minutes.

6. Once the 12-minute timer has completed and beeps, allow a natural pressure release.

7. Open the pot and remove the bouquet garni. The soup will be quite thick at this point. If you like the soup to have a stew-like consistency, leave as is, or pour in 1 cup water to thin it out a bit. Add more water until you achieve your desired consistency.

8. Stir in the vinegar and taste for seasonings. I usually add a large pinch of salt at this point. Transfer the soup to bowls and serve with bread.

THAI VEGETABLE GREEN CURRY

serves 4	gluten-free, nut-free, refined sugar–free

The smell of this fragrant curry transports me to Thailand, to the busy city streets lined with food vendors churning out warm bowls of soup and curry day after day. This curry is rich but not oily and the perfect balance between spicy, sweet, and sour. For a unique spin, I add lemongrass, a tropical grass with a distinct mint, lemon, and ginger taste.

The Thai basil brings a wonderful scent of lemon and licorice, but you can substitute Italian basil if needed. Also, there is some variability in curry paste brands, so you may need less or more curry paste depending on your taste and spice preference. I like the brand Thai Kitchen for its strong flavor and minimal ingredient list.

TIPS *Make this curry easier by replacing the fresh vegetables with frozen mixed vegetables.*
To cut lemongrass, remove the knobby ends and the tough upper stem, bisect the remaining stalk, and remove the tough outer layers (but reserve them). Once you reach the fleshy interior, finely dice it up. And for even more lemongrass flavor, add the tough outer layers of the lemongrass stalks to the curry, but discard after cooking.

1 (14-ounce) block extra-firm tofu or firm tofu

2 tablespoons unrefined virgin coconut oil

4 scallions (white and light-green parts only), sliced

4 garlic cloves, minced

1½-inch piece fresh ginger, grated or finely minced

1 to 3 Thai green chiles, to taste, thinly sliced (seeded for a milder heat or omit entirely)

5 tablespoons green curry paste (I recommend Thai Kitchen brand)

1 (13.5-ounce) can full-fat coconut milk, well stirred

3 tablespoons reduced-sodium tamari or soy sauce

1 tablespoon coconut sugar

4 to 5 cups mixed vegetables, such as: 1 cup halved green beans or 1 cup asparagus pieces (1½-inch); 2 medium carrots, sliced ¼ inch thick; ½ cup diced red bell pepper; ¾ cup diced zucchini; 1 cup diced Japanese eggplant

1 (8-ounce) can water chestnuts or sliced bamboo shoots (optional but adds a nice crunchy texture)

3 lemongrass stalks (optional but highly recommended), trimmed and finely diced (see Tips)

1 tablespoon fresh lime juice

10 to 20 Thai basil leaves (or Italian basil leaves), finely slivered, plus more for garnish

¼ cup chopped fresh cilantro, plus more for garnish

FOR SERVING

White jasmine rice

recipe continues

1. Drain the tofu and blot away the excess water with a few paper towels. Cut the tofu into cubes.

2. Select the Sauté setting on the Instant Pot and, after a few minutes, add the coconut oil, followed by the scallions, garlic, ginger, and Thai chiles (if using). Cook for 2 minutes, tossing frequently to prevent sticking. Carefully add the green curry paste and stand back, as the paste might sputter up. Cook until the mixture is very fragrant, about 30 seconds. Select the Cancel setting.

3. Pour in the coconut milk to deglaze the pan, using a wooden spoon to scrape up any browned bits on the bottom of the pot. Stir in the tamari and coconut sugar.

4. Add the mixed vegetables, water chestnuts (if using), tofu, and lemongrass and gently stir to incorporate all of the ingredients. If you saved the lemongrass outer layers (see Tip), add them to the curry as well. It might not appear that there is enough liquid to bring the Instant Pot to pressure, but the vegetables will also release water.

5. Secure the lid and set the Pressure Release to Sealing. Select the Pressure Cook setting at high pressure and set the cook time to 2 minutes.

6. Once the 2-minute timer has completed and beeps, perform a quick pressure release by carefully switching the Pressure Release knob from Sealing to Venting.

7. Open the pot, and if you'd like the curry to be a little thicker, select the Sauté setting and press the Sauté button again until you reach Less heat. Bring the curry to a boil and cook for 2 to 3 minutes to thicken slightly.

8. Stir in the lime juice, basil, and cilantro. Serve the curry over white jasmine rice and garnish with additional Thai basil or cilantro if desired.

THE BEST CORN CHOWDER

serves 4 to 6	gluten-free, soy-free, no added sugar

I settled on the name "the best corn chowder" for this recipe because it really is the best. It's so creamy that you'll have to double-check you didn't add a carton of heavy cream.

This recipe is entirely dairy-free (obviously) and gluten-free, but still incredibly lush thanks to cashews, coconut milk, and potatoes.

The secret flavoring agent in this soup is celery salt. It's one of those quintessential ingredients in American cuisine, more specifically New England cuisine, that is used quite frequently but rarely talked about. Celery salt adds a grassy and salty, almost tangy flavor that enhances this soup and gives it a distinctively delicious taste. If you don't have celery salt, you can substitute ¼ teaspoon celery seeds and ½ teaspoon salt.

I love making this chowder in late summer, when fresh corn is incredibly sweet. But if you prefer your soup on a cold winter night while cuddled in a blanket by the fireplace, you can use canned corn or thawed frozen corn.

TIP *To enhance the flavor of the soup, before cutting the kernels off the ears of fresh corn, place the husked ears over an open flame and turn occasionally until the kernels are lightly charred, then shave off the kernels.*

1 cup raw cashews

4 large ears sweet corn, husked, or 3 cups canned or frozen corn kernels

2 tablespoons olive oil

1 medium yellow onion, chopped

4 garlic cloves, minced

2 jalapeño peppers, diced (seeded and membranes removed for less heat)

1 medium carrot, diced

1 cup diced celery (2 to 3 medium stalks)

1 teaspoon kosher salt, plus more to taste

Freshly cracked black pepper

1 pound Yukon Gold potatoes, peeled and diced

2 bay leaves

1 teaspoon smoked paprika

½ teaspoon ground cumin

½ teaspoon celery salt

2 to 4 cups low-sodium vegetable broth

1 (13.5-ounce) can full-fat coconut milk

3 tablespoons nutritional yeast

1 lime, halved

GARNISHES

Reserved corn kernels

¼ cup chopped chives

Diced tomatoes or red bell pepper (optional)

Chopped cilantro or finely slivered basil leaves (optional)

recipe continues

1. Place the cashews in a bowl and cover with boiling water while you prepare the other ingredients. Drain after 20 to 30 minutes.

2. Hold an ear of corn upright in a large bowl and shave off the kernels with a sharp knife. (If you charred the ears of corn, wait until the corn is cool enough to handle.) Repeat with the remaining ears. Place the kernels in a bowl and reserve a tablespoon or two for garnish.

3. Select the Sauté setting on the Instant Pot and let the pot heat up for a few minutes before adding the olive oil. Once the oil is hot, add the onion. Cook until the onion is translucent, 4 to 5 minutes.

4. Add the garlic and jalapeños and cook for 1 minute, stirring frequently. Add the carrot and celery with a pinch each of salt and black pepper and cook for 2 minutes. Add the potatoes and cook for 2 more minutes, tossing frequently to prevent the potatoes from sticking. Select the Cancel setting.

5. Add the corn kernels, drained cashews, 1 teaspoon salt, black pepper to taste, bay leaves, smoked paprika, cumin, celery salt, 2 cups of the vegetable broth, the coconut milk, and nutritional yeast. Stir well to combine.

6. Secure the lid and set the Pressure Release to Sealing. Select the Pressure Cook setting at high pressure and set the cook time to 6 minutes.

7. Once the 6-minute timer has completed and beeps, allow a natural pressure release for 5 minutes and then carefully switch the Pressure Release knob from Sealing to Venting to release any remaining steam.

8. Open the pot and discard the bay leaves. Squeeze the juice of ½ lime into the soup, stir, and taste for seasonings. Add more lime juice or salt and black pepper as needed. The soup will be very thick at this point, so I like to thin it out a bit with additional vegetable broth during the blending stage (see next step).

9. Transfer the soup in two or three batches to a high-powered blender (don't fill the blender to capacity). Be sure to remove the center cap from the blender lid to vent steam, but cover the hole with a kitchen towel. Start at low speed and gradually work your way up and blend until the soup is thick and creamy. I typically add a total of 1 additional cup of broth to the batches to thin the soup during blending, but if you prefer a slightly thinner soup, add more broth. Alternatively, use an immersion blender directly in the Instant Pot to blend the soup for a few minutes until the soup is pureed and thick, thinning with the additional broth as you blend.

10. Transfer the pureed soup to bowls and top each bowl with the reserved corn kernels, chives, and other garnishes as desired.

WEST AFRICAN PEANUT STEW

serves 6	gluten-free, soy-free, no added sugar

Peanut stews are common across West Africa, with many regional variations. Some are thin and soup-like, others are thick stews served over grains; some contain okra, others collard greens. But the star ingredient is always peanut butter. Whether creamy or crunchy, it blends harmoniously with the spices and aromatics and adds a rich creaminess that will warm your soul. Just be sure to use a natural peanut butter with minimal ingredients (e.g., nothing but peanuts and salt).

The peanut butter flavor can be quite intense when you first taste the stew, but the flavors will mellow out the next day. And if the addition of peanut butter wasn't peanutty enough for you, the stew gets finished with roasted peanuts, which bring a crunchy contrast to the creamy stew.

1½ tablespoons refined coconut oil or a neutral cooking oil such as grapeseed oil

1 large yellow onion, diced

6 garlic cloves, minced

2-inch piece fresh ginger, grated or minced

1 habanero or Scotch bonnet pepper, seeded and minced (use ½ pepper for less heat or a less spicy pepper, such as a jalapeño or serrano)

1½ teaspoons ground cumin

1 teaspoon ground coriander

1 teaspoon ground turmeric

½ teaspoon dried thyme

½ teaspoon freshly cracked black pepper

¼ teaspoon cayenne pepper (optional)

¼ teaspoon ground cinnamon

¼ teaspoon ground cloves

2 cups low-sodium vegetable broth

1 pound sweet potatoes, peeled and cut into ¾-inch cubes

1½ teaspoons kosher salt

½ cup no-added-sugar peanut butter

1¾ cups cooked chickpeas or 1 (15-ounce) can chickpeas, drained and rinsed

1 (28-ounce) can crushed tomatoes

3 tablespoons tomato paste

4 cups kale or collard greens, stems and midribs removed and sliced into strips (very finely sliced if using collard greens)

½ cup fresh cilantro, roughly chopped, plus more (optional) for garnish

recipe and ingredients continue

1 tablespoon fresh lime juice

⅓ cup roasted peanuts, roughly chopped

FOR SERVING

Couscous, white or brown rice, or fonio
(a West African ancient grain)

1. Select the Sauté setting on the Instant Pot and let the pot heat up for a few minutes before adding the oil. Once the oil is hot, add the onion. Cook until the onion is softened, 3 to 4 minutes. Add the garlic, ginger, and chile pepper and cook for 1 minute, tossing frequently.

2. Add the cumin, coriander, turmeric, thyme, black pepper, cayenne (if using), cinnamon, and cloves. Stir the spices into the vegetables and cook until the mixture is fragrant, about 30 seconds.

3. Pour in the vegetable broth to deglaze the pan, using a wooden spoon to scrape up any browned bits on the bottom of the pot. Add the sweet potatoes, salt, peanut butter, and chickpeas. Stir to combine and select the Cancel setting. Pour the crushed tomatoes and tomato paste on top, but do not stir, allowing the tomatoes and paste to sit on top (this prevents the tomatoes from blocking the Instant Pot's heat sensor and burning).

4. Secure the lid and set the Pressure Release to Sealing. Select the Pressure Cook setting at high pressure and set the cook time to 5 minutes.

5. Once the 5-minute timer has completed and beeps, allow a natural pressure release.

6. Open the pot and stir in the greens. Select the Sauté setting and cook until the greens are wilted and cooked through, 2 to 4 minutes (collards will take slightly longer than kale). Select the Cancel setting. Stir in the cilantro and lime juice and taste for seasonings.

7. Transfer the stew to individual bowls and garnish with the roasted peanuts and more cilantro if desired. Serve over couscous, white or brown rice, or fonio.

TOFU CAULIFLOWER TIKKA MASALA

serves 4 to 6	gluten-free, refined sugar–free

I have met more than one stranger who has asked me: "You're Indian? Do you like chicken tikka masala? I LOVE chicken tikka masala." As absurd as this line of questioning is, I do not blame them because the creamy, gravy-like masala sauce is nothing short of amazing.

Typically, the spiced tomato cream sauce gets its richness from some combination of heavy cream, ghee, and whole milk yogurt. To mimic this luscious consistency without the dairy, this recipe relies on two substitutes: full-fat coconut milk and cashew cream. Unlike most cashew cream recipes, which require you to soak raw cashews overnight, this one can come together while you prep the rest of the ingredients. It adds a rich mouthfeel and creamy texture that will have your guests convinced they're eating the traditional dairy-heavy version.

A few notes: Refrigerating the coconut cream for 24 hours (or more) allows the thick cream to separate from the liquid so it's easy to scoop out. The rest of the coconut milk is saved for the tikka masala. Be sure to cut the cauliflower into large florets; otherwise, the high pressure of the Instant Pot will overcook them. Finally, you can make the Cashew Cream (recipe follows) while the tikka masala is being pressure-cooked, or make ahead and store in the fridge.

MARINATED TOFU

1 (14-ounce) block extra-firm tofu

1 (13.5-ounce) can full-fat coconut milk, refrigerated for at least 24 hours (see headnote)

1 teaspoon ground cumin

1 teaspoon garam masala

1 teaspoon ground turmeric

½ teaspoon Indian red chile powder or ¼ teaspoon cayenne pepper

¾ teaspoon kosher salt

TIKKA MASALA

2½ tablespoons grapeseed oil or refined coconut oil

1½ teaspoons cumin seeds

1 medium yellow onion, diced

6 garlic cloves, minced

1½-inch piece fresh ginger, grated or minced

1 or 2 serrano peppers, to taste, finely diced (seeded and membranes removed for less heat)

2 teaspoons garam masala

1½ teaspoons sweet paprika

1 teaspoon ground coriander

½ teaspoon ground turmeric

¼ teaspoon Indian red chile powder or cayenne pepper (optional)

1¼ teaspoons kosher salt

½ teaspoon freshly cracked black pepper, or to taste

1 cup water

2 Roma or plum tomatoes, diced

recipe and ingredients continue

1 tablespoon coconut sugar

1 medium head cauliflower, cut into large florets (about 5 cups)

1 (15-ounce) can tomato sauce

Cashew Cream (recipe follows)

1 tablespoon fresh lemon juice or lime juice

½ cup fresh cilantro, roughly chopped

FOR SERVING

Cooked white basmati rice and/or naan

1. Marinate the tofu: Drain the tofu and cut into 4 slabs. Place the tofu on a cutting board lined with paper towels. Place more paper towels on top of the tofu and weight them down with a few heavy cookbooks or a heavy skillet filled with a few cans of beans. Let sit for at least 30 minutes, changing the paper towels in between to drain all of the moisture. (This is a good time to start soaking the cashews for the Cashew Cream; recipe follows.)

2. Cut the pressed tofu into cubes. Remove the coconut milk from the refrigerator, scoop out ⅓ cup coconut cream from the top, and reserve the remaining coconut milk for the tikka masala. Place the coconut cream in a wide shallow bowl or pie plate and whisk in the cumin, garam masala, turmeric, chile powder, and salt until smooth. Stir in the pressed tofu cubes and gently mix with a silicone spatula until all of the tofu is coated with the marinade. Refrigerate while you make the tikka masala.

3. Make the tikka masala: Select the Sauté setting on the Instant Pot and let the pot heat up for a few minutes before adding the oil. Once the oil is hot, add the cumin seeds. Fry the seeds, stirring occasionally, until lightly toasted and aromatic, about 1 minute. Add the onion, garlic, ginger, and serrano and cook, stirring frequently to avoid burning, until the onion has softened, about 3 minutes.

4. Add the garam masala, paprika, coriander, turmeric, chile powder (if using), ¼ teaspoons kosher salt, and black pepper and cook for 30 seconds, stirring frequently to avoid burning. Select the Cancel setting.

5. Pour in the water to deglaze the pan, using a wooden spatula or spoon to scrape up any browned bits on the bottom of the pot. Add the reserved canned coconut milk, tomatoes, and coconut sugar. Stir to combine. Top with the cauliflower florets and spread the marinated tofu on top of the cauliflower, but do not stir (you want the tofu to sit on top of everything).

6. Secure the lid and set the Pressure Release to Sealing. Select the Pressure Cook setting at high pressure and set the cook time to 3 minutes. (This is a good time to finish preparing the Cashew Cream.)

7. Once the 3-minute timer has completed and beeps, perform a quick pressure release by carefully switching the Pressure Release knob from Sealing to Venting.

8. Open the pot, add the tomato sauce and cashew cream, and stir to incorporate. Select the Sauté setting, bring to a boil, and cook until the sauce has thickened and evenly warmed throughout, 2 to 3 minutes.

9. Taste for seasonings, stir in the lemon juice and cilantro, and serve with white basmati rice.

Cashew Cream
Makes about 1 cup

¾ cup raw cashews

¾ cup unsweetened plain almond milk or other nondairy milk

1 tablespoon fresh lemon juice

Heaping ¼ teaspoon kosher salt

1. Place the cashews in a heatproof bowl and cover with boiling water. Soak for at least 30 minutes, then drain.

2. Transfer the soaked cashews to a high-powered blender or food processor, along with the almond milk, lemon juice, and salt. Process until smooth and thick, and all bits of cashews have been pulverized, 2 to 3 minutes.

CREAMY CARROT-GINGER SOUP

serves 4	gluten-free, soy-free, no added sugar

This is a great recipe for novice cooks to try. While the ingredients and cooking steps are basic, the flavor of the soup is complex. It's velvety smooth, naturally sweet, and has lots of zing from fresh ginger and citrus.

It's also one of those plant-based dishes that is deceptively decadent. Carrots are inherently creamy, and when paired with coconut milk and nut butter, the result is a rich, luxurious soup that is equal parts indulgent and nourishing. The addition of orange juice and zest intensifies the flavor of carrots while simultaneously adding a kiss of freshness to this soup.

Since this is a very creamy soup, it will thicken in the fridge. To serve leftovers, heat the soup on the stovetop, adding vegetable broth or water as needed until it reaches your desired consistency.

1 tablespoon olive oil

1 large yellow onion, diced

2 pounds carrots, peeled and roughly chopped

1½ teaspoons kosher salt

Freshly cracked black pepper

4 garlic cloves, roughly chopped

2-inch piece fresh ginger, grated or minced

1 teaspoon ground cumin

¼ to ½ teaspoon cayenne pepper, to taste (optional)

2½ cups low-sodium vegetable broth

1 bay leaf

¼ cup no-added-sugar cashew butter or almond butter

1 (13.5-ounce) can full-fat coconut milk

1 teaspoon grated orange zest, plus more to taste

2 tablespoons fresh orange juice, plus more to taste

OPTIONAL GARNISHES

Chopped chives and/or cilantro

recipe continues

1. Select the Sauté setting on the Instant Pot and let the pot heat up for a few minutes before adding the olive oil. Once the oil is hot, add the onion, carrots, ½ teaspoon of the salt, and a few grinds of black pepper. Cook until the vegetables are beginning to soften, about 5 minutes.

2. Add the garlic, ginger, cumin, cayenne (if using), the remaining 1 teaspoon salt, and black pepper to taste. Cook for 1 to 2 minutes, coating the vegetables in the spices.

3. Select the Cancel setting and pour in the vegetable broth to deglaze the pan, using a wooden spoon to scrape up any browned bits on the bottom of the pot. Add the bay leaf, nut butter, and coconut milk (reserve a few spoons of coconut milk for the garnish, if desired). Stir to combine.

4. Secure the lid and set the Pressure Release to Sealing. Select the Soup setting at high pressure and set the cook time to 10 minutes.

5. Once the 10-minute timer has completed and beeps, allow a natural pressure release for 5 minutes and then carefully switch the Pressure Release knob from Sealing to Venting to release any remaining steam.

6. Open the pot and discard the bay leaf. Taste the soup for seasonings and adjust accordingly. Using an immersion blender, puree for a few minutes until you have a thick and creamy soup. (Alternatively, blend the soup in batches in a high-powered blender. Be sure to remove the center cap from the blender lid to vent steam, but cover the hole with a kitchen towel.)

7. Stir the orange zest and orange juice into the soup. Taste and add more orange juice and/or orange zest if desired.

8. Transfer the soup to bowls and, if desired, garnish with chopped chives and cilantro.

SPICED LENTIL, KALE, AND SAUSAGE SOUP

serves 6 to 8	gluten-free option, nut-free, soy-free option, no added sugar

This soup is hearty and robust, and a great remedy for those wintry days that leave you craving something warm and comforting. Both lentils and plant-based sausage make this a protein-rich dish that will keep you full for hours. And there's a generous amount of kale thrown in at the end because, well, greens are good for you. This soup is designed to be chunky and thick, but if you prefer it soupier, add an extra cup of water before pressure cooking, or afterward, when you add the kale.

If you've never tried vegan "sausages," you have quite a bit to explore! There are new plant-based meat alternatives hitting grocery stores each month, with different textures, tastes, and flavors. My favorites are the Beyond Meat sausages (gluten- and soy-free) or the grain-based, soy-free sausages from Field Roast, both of which can be crumbled like traditional sausage, but a firmer sausage (such as those from Tofurky) also works great.

4 links (12 to 14 ounces) vegan sausage (see headnote)

3 tablespoons olive oil

1 medium yellow onion, diced

2 celery stalks, diced

3 medium carrots, diced

6 garlic cloves, chopped

1 tablespoon ground cumin

2 teaspoons chili powder

1 teaspoon ground turmeric

½ teaspoon ground coriander

¼ teaspoon cayenne pepper (optional)

½ to 1 teaspoon crushed red pepper flakes, to taste (omit for a mild version)

1 teaspoon kosher salt, plus more to taste

4 cups low-sodium vegetable broth

2 cups water or low-sodium vegetable broth

2 bay leaves

1½ cups brown or green lentils

1 (14.5-ounce) can crushed fire-roasted tomatoes

1 tablespoon apple cider vinegar or red wine vinegar

5 ounces baby kale or baby spinach

Freshly cracked black pepper

¼ cup chopped fresh Italian flat-leaf parsley, for garnish

recipe continues

1. Depending on the texture of your vegan sausage, crumble it in a bowl or slice each link into rounds.

2. Select the Sauté setting on the Instant Pot and press the Sauté button again until you reach More heat. After a few minutes, add 1½ tablespoons of the olive oil. Once the display reads "HOT," add the vegan sausage and toss occasionally until it begins to brown, 3 to 5 minutes. The exact time will depend on your brand of sausage. Select the Cancel setting. Using a slotted spoon, transfer the sausage to a plate and wipe out the inner pot of the Instant Pot.

3. Return the inner pot and select the Sauté setting. Add the remaining 1½ tablespoons olive oil, followed by the onion, celery, carrots, and garlic. Cook until the vegetables are softened, 4 to 5 minutes.

4. Add the cumin, chili powder, turmeric, coriander, cayenne, if using, pepper flakes (if using), and salt. Cook, stirring frequently to prevent burning, until fragrant, 30 to 60 seconds. Select the Cancel setting.

5. Pour in the vegetable broth to deglaze the pan, using a wooden spoon to scrape up any browned bits on the bottom of the pot. Return the sausage to the pot, along with the 2 cups water, bay leaves, and lentils. Stir to combine all of the ingredients. Pour the crushed tomatoes on top, but do not stir, allowing the tomatoes to sit on top (this prevents the tomatoes from blocking the Instant Pot's heat sensor and burning).

6. Secure the lid and set the Pressure Release to Sealing. Select the Pressure Cook setting at high pressure and set the cook time to 15 minutes.

7. Once the 15-minute timer has completed and beeps, allow a natural pressure release for 5 minutes and then carefully switch the Pressure Release knob from Sealing to Venting to release any remaining steam.

8. Open the pot, discard the bay leaves, and stir in the vinegar and kale (or spinach). Select the Sauté setting and cook for 2 to 3 minutes to wilt the greens. Season to taste with salt and black pepper and garnish with the parsley.

PHO (VIETNAMESE NOODLE SOUP)

serves 4	gluten-free, nut-free, refined sugar–free

My first date with my partner was at a Vietnamese restaurant. I had never tasted pho, and he insisted that I try it. I became hooked immediately. Nearly five years later, we found ourselves crouched on tiny plastic stools in the alleyways of Hanoi's Old Quarter, devouring bowls of steaming broth and noodles that were remarkably light yet complex in flavor. The richness of the broth was perfectly balanced by the endless array of toppings—fresh herbs, spicy chile peppers, tangy lime wedges, and crunchy bean sprouts.

To achieve this depth of flavor, pho broth is traditionally simmered for hours. However, with pressure cooking, you can achieve a richly flavored broth in a fraction of the time. Begin by charring onions and ginger for smokiness and sweetness. And some tips about this step: Don't skimp on the oil, or you'll have a mess to scrape up; and you may want to wear long sleeves or gloves, as the hot oil can splatter.

When topping the pho, tear up the fresh herbs, as it releases their essential oils and perfumes the soup with an intoxicating aroma.

TIPS *You can find pho noodles in well-stocked grocery stores or any Asian market, and they come in various thickness, ranging from 1/16 inch (narrow) to 1/4 inch (wide).*

For the baked tofu, I recommend a five-spice flavor.

12 ounces dried rice noodles, dried rice sticks, or banh pho (see Tip)

BROTH

2 tablespoons grapeseed oil or other neutral, high-heat cooking oil

2 medium yellow onions, peeled and halved

4-inch piece fresh ginger, thinly sliced

3 cardamom pods, lightly smashed with the back of a knife

3 whole star anise pods

4 whole cloves

1 cinnamon stick

1 tablespoon coriander seeds

1 teaspoon fennel seeds

½ teaspoon whole black peppercorns

1 Fuji apple, peeled and cut into large chunks

½ cup fresh cilantro, roughly chopped

2 tablespoons reduced-sodium tamari or soy sauce

1 tablespoon coconut sugar

2 cups sliced shiitake mushroom caps (5 to 6 ounces)

8 cups low-sodium vegetable broth (you can substitute water for up to 4 cups)

1 teaspoon kosher salt, plus more to taste

TOPPINGS

1 (6- or 8-ounce) block baked tofu (see Tips), cut into cubes

3 scallions, sliced on the diagonal

recipe and ingredients continue

1 cup Thai basil leaves, torn up

1 cup cilantro leaves, torn up

2 limes, cut into wedges

2 cups bean sprouts

Thinly sliced hot chile peppers or Sriracha

1. Place the dried rice noodles in a large bowl, cover with warm water, and soak until the noodles are pliable and opaque, 30 to 45 minutes. Drain the noodles and rinse them to remove excess starch. (Alternatively, cook the noodles according to the instructions on the package.)

2. Meanwhile, prepare the broth: Select the Sauté setting on the Instant Pot and, after a few minutes, add the oil. Once the display reads "HOT," add the onions and ginger slices, cut side down. Do not toss and allow to cook until charred and deeply browned, about 4 minutes.

3. Add the whole spices (cardamom pods through black peppercorns) and cook for 1 minute, stirring the mixture frequently. Add the apple, cilantro, tamari, coconut sugar, and shiitakes. Pour the vegetable broth and/or water on top and stir to combine. Select the Cancel setting.

4. Secure the lid and set the Pressure Release to Sealing. Select the Pressure Cook setting at high pressure and set the cook time to 15 minutes.

5. Once the 15-minute timer has completed and beeps, allow a natural pressure release for 10 minutes and then switch the Pressure Release knob from Sealing to Venting to release any remaining steam.

6. Open the pot and, using oven mitts, remove the inner pot. Carefully strain the broth into a fine-mesh sieve set over a large bowl (discard the solids). Season the broth with 1 teaspoon salt, stir, and taste. Add more salt as needed. Select the Cancel setting.

7. Place the cooked rice noodles in individual bowls. Pour over the strained broth and add the baked tofu cubes. Top the pho with the scallions, basil, cilantro, lime wedges, bean sprouts, and chiles or Sriracha.

BUTTERNUT SQUASH CHICKPEA TAGINE

serves 4	gluten-free, nut-free, soy-free

This is one of those dishes that's impossible not to love. A lightened-up spin on a classic North African stew, it's comforting yet healthy, feels hearty but has a fresh flair, and boasts flavors that are sublimely balanced.

Saffron lends a very subtle floral aroma that contrasts nicely with the earthiness of chickpeas and butternut squash, while the lemon zest and juice bring a welcome freshness. And like a good tagine, there is a pleasant sweetness from dried fruit. The spicy pickled golden raisins are my favorite component of this dish. When you bite into one, you get the perfect hit of sweetness, spiciness, and acidity.

If you can't find saffron, there is no real substitute. Fortunately, I've tried this dish without saffron, and I can vouch that it's still very delicious. This tagine is satisfying enough to serve on its own, but it's also wonderful served over a bed of couscous. Finally, be sure to soak the chickpeas in advance to cut the cook time and to prevent the butternut squash from overcooking.

TIP *While I prefer using dried chickpeas for the best texture, you can make this dish with 2½ cups cooked chickpeas (equivalent to one 15-ounce can plus two-thirds of another 15-ounce can). Simply reduce the pressure-cook time to 7 minutes.*

1 cup dried chickpeas (see Tip)
2 teaspoons kosher salt

SPICY PICKLED RAISINS
⅓ cup golden raisins
2½ tablespoons organic cane sugar
⅓ cup apple cider vinegar or white wine vinegar
¼ to ½ teaspoon crushed red pepper flakes, to taste

TAGINE
2 tablespoons olive oil
1 large yellow onion, diced
2 medium carrots, diced
5 garlic cloves, minced
2 teaspoons ground cinnamon
2 teaspoons ground coriander
1 teaspoon cumin seeds or ground cumin
1 teaspoon sweet paprika
¼ to ½ teaspoon cayenne pepper, to taste (optional)
2 bay leaves
1½ teaspoons kosher salt, plus more to taste
1¼ cups low-sodium vegetable broth or water
3 cups peeled and finely diced peeled butternut squash (from one 1½-pound butternut squash)
¼ cup finely diced dried apricots (about 8 apricots)
1 (14.5-ounce) can crushed tomatoes
3 to 4 ounces Tuscan (lacinato) kale, stems and midribs removed, roughly chopped
¼ cup roughly chopped fresh cilantro, plus more (optional) for garnish
Grated zest and juice of 1 small lemon

recipe continues

1. Cover the chickpeas with 6 cups water and stir in the 2 teaspoons salt. Soak for 8 hours or overnight, then drain and rinse them under cold water.

2. Make the spicy pickled raisins: Place the raisins in a glass jar. In a small saucepan, combine the sugar, vinegar, and pepper flakes and bring to a boil over medium-high heat, whisking until the sugar is dissolved. Remove from the heat and carefully pour the hot vinegar mixture over the raisins. Leave the jar uncovered and allow the mixture to come to room temperature.

3. Cook the tagine: Select the Sauté setting on the Instant Pot and let the pot heat up for a few minutes before adding the olive oil. Once the oil is hot, add the onion and carrots. Cook until the vegetables have softened, 4 to 5 minutes. Add the garlic and cook for 1 minute, stirring frequently.

4. Add the cinnamon, coriander, cumin seeds, paprika, cayenne (if using), bay leaves, and salt. Stir the spices into the vegetables for 30 seconds until the mixture is fragrant. Select the Cancel setting.

5. Pour in the broth, followed by the drained chickpeas, butternut squash, and dried apricots. Stir to combine all of the ingredients. Pour the crushed tomatoes on top, but do not stir, allowing the tomatoes to sit on top (this prevents the tomatoes from blocking the Instant Pot's heat sensor and burning).

6. Secure the lid and set the Pressure Release to Sealing. Select the Pressure Cook setting at high pressure and set the cook time to 12 minutes.

7. Once the 12-minute timer has completed and beeps, allow a natural pressure release.

8. Open the pot, discard the bay leaves, and stir in the kale. Select the Sauté setting and cook for 2 to 3 minutes to wilt the kale. Select the Cancel setting.

9. Add the cilantro and a bit of the lemon zest and half of the lemon juice. Stir and give it a taste. Add more lemon juice and/or lemon zest as desired. Taste for seasonings and add more salt as needed.

10. Transfer the tagine to bowls and add a few spoons of the spicy pickled raisins to each bowl. Garnish with fresh cilantro if desired.

TUSCAN RIBOLLITA

serves 4 to 6

nut-free, soy-free, no added sugar

As a teenager, I watched Giada De Laurentiis's show *Everyday Italian*, well, every day, and it taught me everything I needed to know about Italian cooking—the importance of fresh herbs, the perfect pasta and sauce pairings, and how to pronounce *ciabatta* and *spaghetti* like a real Italian. Thanks, Giada.

Originating in Tuscany, possibly as early as the Middle Ages, ribollita is a soup that was originally made by reboiling the previous day's leftover minestrone or vegetable soup (made with inexpensive ingredients like onions, carrots, and beans) and thickening it up with bread. Fast-forward many centuries, and the Instant Pot enables you to achieve those deep flavors in a fraction of the time. The bouquet garni also helps. A bundle of fresh herbs tied together with string, a bouquet garni infuses the entire soup with a rich aroma and depth of flavor. This is hearty, warming Italian comfort food that would make any Italian chef proud. I hope you're reading this, Giada!

Ribollita should be a very thick, almost stew-like soup. But if you prefer a slightly more liquidy soup, feel free to add more broth or water after cooking. I usually add 1 cup during the final simmering step, but you can add up to 2 cups.

2 tablespoons olive oil

1 large yellow onion, finely diced

2 large carrots, finely diced

3 celery stalks, finely diced

1 teaspoon kosher salt, plus more to taste

Freshly cracked black pepper

8 garlic cloves, thinly sliced

¼ to 1 teaspoon crushed red pepper flakes, to taste

3 to 4 cups low-sodium vegetable broth

Bouquet garni: 2 bay leaves + a few sprigs *each* of Italian flat-leaf parsley, sage, rosemary, and thyme, tied tightly together with kitchen twine

1 (14.5-ounce) can crushed tomatoes, preferably San Marzano

1 tablespoon tomato paste

2 cups cooked cannellini beans or 1 (15-ounce) can cannellini beans, drained and rinsed

1 large bunch of Tuscan (lacinato) kale (10 to 14 ounces), thick stems removed and sliced into thick ribbons

6 large slices ciabatta bread or other hearty, rustic bread, cut or torn into 1-inch pieces (about 4 cups)

½ cup vegan parmesan cheese (optional)

1. Select the Sauté setting on the Instant Pot and let the pot heat up for a few minutes before adding the olive oil. Once the oil is hot, add the onion, carrots, and celery. Season lightly with salt and black pepper and cook until the vegetables are beginning to soften, 3 to 4 minutes. Add the garlic and pepper flakes and cook for 1 minute, tossing frequently.

2. Add 2 cups of the vegetable broth, the bouquet garni, 1 teaspoon salt, black pepper to taste, crushed tomatoes, and tomato paste and stir to combine. Top the mixture with the cannellini beans and sliced kale, but do not stir. Select the Cancel setting.

3. Secure the lid and set the Pressure Release to Sealing. Select the Pressure Cook setting at high pressure and set the cook time to 5 minutes.

4. Once the 5-minute timer has completed and beeps, allow a natural pressure release for 10 minutes and then switch the Pressure Release knob from Sealing to Venting to release any remaining steam.

5. Open the pot and discard the bouquet garni. Select the Sauté setting and add the pieces of bread and stir to combine. Simmer for 10 minutes, stirring frequently, until the soup has thickened. Add the remaining 1 to 2 cups vegetable broth while it's simmering to thin out the soup slightly.

6. Transfer the soup to bowls and garnish each bowl with a few sprinkles of vegan parmesan if desired.

LEMONGRASS-GINGER KABOCHA SQUASH SOUP

serves 4	gluten-free, nut-free, no added sugar

September 1 marks an important day in food culture: It's the day it becomes socially acceptable to put pumpkin in everything. But, the real star of fall should be kabocha squash. Its light, velvety texture and sweet, nutty notes make it the perfect mash-up between a sweet potato and a pumpkin.

You can find this underrated winter squash (also known as a Japanese pumpkin) at farmers' markets, Asian grocers, and stores like Trader Joe's and Whole Foods. Its peak season is late summer and fall, though you may find it year-round.

The sweetness of the kabocha squash shines in this soup and is underscored by a sweetness from juicy Fuji apples. There's a little heat from Thai chile peppers and a pungency from fresh ginger and lemongrass. The result is a harmoniously flavored soup that is light yet creamy, making it the ideal starter at your Thanksgiving table.

TIP *As much as I love kabocha squash in this soup, if you can't find it, you can replace it with butternut squash or sweet potatoes. Butternut squash is earthier and less sweet than kabocha, so I recommend adding either a tablespoon of maple syrup or 2 more Fuji apples. Sweet potatoes are sweeter, so you can omit the apples.*

1 kabocha squash (2 to 2¼ pounds) (see Tip)

1½ tablespoons grapeseed oil or other neutral, high-heat cooking oil

1 large yellow onion, diced

2 medium carrots, diced

4 garlic cloves, minced

2-inch piece fresh ginger, grated or minced

3 Thai green chile peppers, thinly sliced (seeded for a milder heat or omit entirely)

4 cups low-sodium vegetable broth

2 large Fuji apples, unpeeled and roughly chopped

1½ teaspoons kosher salt

1 (13.5-ounce) can full-fat coconut milk

1 tablespoon reduced-sodium tamari or soy sauce

2 lemongrass stalks (optional but highly recommended), tough outer layers removed and stalks cut into 6-inch pieces (see Tip, p. 237)

1 to 2 teaspoons fresh lime juice, to taste

OPTIONAL GARNISHES

Roasted peanuts

Sautéed shiitake mushrooms

Fresh cilantro, chopped

recipe continues

1. Using a large, sharp knife, halve the squash through the stem and cut off the stem. You may need to microwave the whole squash for 2 to 3 minutes to soften it and make it easier to slice. Once halved, use a large spoon to scoop out the seeds and gunk. Cut each half into 3 or 4 wedges, lay each wedge flat on its side, and use a knife to cut the peel off. Then, cut the squash into 1½-inch chunks. You should end up with about 5 cups of squash.

2. Select the Sauté setting on the Instant Pot and, after a few minutes, add the oil. Once the display reads "HOT," add the onion and carrots and cook for 5 minutes, stirring occasionally, until the onion begins to brown.

3. Add the garlic, ginger, and chiles (if using) and cook for 1 minute, stirring frequently.

4. Pour in the vegetable broth to deglaze the pan and use a wooden spoon to scrape up any browned bits on the bottom of the pot. Add the kabocha squash, apples, salt, coconut milk, tamari, and lemongrass. Stir to combine well. Select the Cancel setting.

5. Secure the lid and set the Pressure Release to Sealing. Select the Soup setting at high pressure and set the cook time to 12 minutes.

6. Once the 12-minute timer has completed and beeps, allow a natural pressure release for 5 minutes and then switch the Pressure Release knob from Sealing to Venting to release any remaining steam.

7. Open the pot and discard the lemongrass stalks. Using an immersion blender, puree the soup for a few minutes until you have a thick and creamy soup. (Alternatively, blend the soup in batches in a high-powered blender. Be sure to remove the center cap from the blender lid to vent steam, but cover the hole with a kitchen towel.)

8. Stir in 1 teaspoon lime juice and taste. Add another teaspoon of lime juice, if desired, and adjust the seasonings accordingly. Transfer the soup to bowls and garnish as desired.

WHITE BEAN AND BROCCOLI SOUP

serves 4	gluten-free, nut-free option, no added sugar

While a dairy-free, cheese-free broccoli soup might not sound very exciting, this soup will pleasantly surprise you. Cannellini beans, with their lush and creamy texture, lend a richness while packing a protein punch; crushed red pepper flakes add an unexpected bite and sharpness; and basil imparts a flair of freshness. While the soup is plenty creamy on its own, you can make it even more luxurious by adding some coconut milk at the end. The almond crumble is a delightful savory topping, bringing a nutty flavor and a textural contrast to the creaminess of the soup, though you can easily omit it to make this recipe nut-free.

With a rather minimal ingredient list and quick cook time, this is a great soup to make for an easy weeknight dinner, served alongside a crunchy vegetable salad. Pack the leftovers for lunch and bring along a crusty whole-grain bread for dunking.

1½ tablespoons olive oil

1 small yellow onion, diced

3 garlic cloves, minced

¼ to ½ teaspoon crushed red pepper flakes, to taste

¼ cup dry white wine (such as Pinot Grigio or Sauvignon Blanc)

1 pound broccoli, cut into florets and stems thinly sliced

1¾ cups cooked cannellini beans or 1 (15-ounce) can cannellini beans, drained and rinsed

6 sprigs fresh thyme

½ cup loosely packed fresh basil leaves, roughly chopped

2½ cups low-sodium vegetable broth

1½ teaspoons kosher salt, plus more to taste

Freshly cracked black pepper

ALMOND CRUMBLE (OMIT FOR A NUT-FREE OPTION)

¼ cup raw almonds

1½ tablespoons nutritional yeast

¼ teaspoon kosher salt

¼ teaspoon extra-virgin olive oil

FOR FINISHING

1 teaspoon reduced-sodium tamari or soy sauce

1 teaspoon Dijon or whole-grain mustard

¼ cup nutritional yeast

1 cup canned "lite" or reduced-fat coconut milk (optional)

Kosher salt and freshly cracked black pepper

2 tablespoons finely slivered fresh basil, for garnish

recipe continues

1. Select the Sauté setting on the Instant Pot and let the pot heat up for a few minutes before adding the olive oil. Once the oil is hot, add the onion and cook until the onion has softened, about 4 minutes. Add the garlic and pepper flakes and cook for 1 minute, tossing frequently to prevent sticking.

2. Pour in the wine to deglaze the pan, using a wooden spoon to scrape up any browned bits on the bottom of the pot. Simmer until the liquid has mostly evaporated and the smell of alcohol has dissipated, about 3 minutes.

3. Add the broccoli florets and stems and cook for 1 to 2 minutes. Select the Cancel setting.

4. Add the cannellini beans, thyme sprigs, the chopped basil, vegetable broth, salt, and black pepper to taste. Stir to combine all of the ingredients.

5. Secure the lid and set the Pressure Release to Sealing. Select the Pressure Cook setting at high pressure and set the cook time to 5 minutes.

6. Meanwhile, make the almond crumble: In a food processor, combine the almonds, nutritional yeast, salt, and extra-virgin olive oil and pulse repeatedly for about 30 seconds, or until the mixture has a fine, crumbly texture. Don't overpulse or you'll end up with almond butter.

7. Once the 5-minute timer has completed and beeps, allow a natural pressure release for 5 minutes and then carefully switch the Pressure Release knob from Sealing to Venting to release any remaining steam.

8. Open the pot and discard the thyme sprigs. To finish the soup, stir in the tamari, mustard, nutritional yeast, and coconut milk (if using). Using an immersion blender, puree for a few minutes until you have a thick and creamy soup. (Alternatively, blend the soup in batches in a high-powered blender. Be sure to remove the center cap from the blender lid to vent steam, but cover the hole with a kitchen towel.) Taste the soup for seasonings and add salt and black pepper as needed.

9. Garnish each bowl with a few spoons of almond crumble and the slivered basil.

CHANA MASALA

| serves 4 to 6 | gluten-free, nut-free, soy-free, no added sugar |

As an embarrasingly picky child, *chana masala* was one of the few dishes my mother could coax me into eating, and to this day, it is still my favorite Indian dish. While I am proud of this recipe and have served it to countless happy friends, it somehow never tastes as good as when my mother makes it. When you've been making something for 30 years, you just have a leg up. However, I am proud to report that my mother referred to this dish as "first class," which is an Indian mother's ultimate seal of approval.

Chana masala, or *chole masala*, as it's sometimes called (depending on the type of chickpea used), is an Indian chickpea curry. There are very few ingredients in this dish aside from spices and aromatics so it's important to not skimp on these. If you can't find black mustard seeds, you can use the more commonly available brown mustard seeds instead (they are a tad less spicy). Many traditional *chana masala* recipes call for amchur powder, which is dried mango powder made from unripe mangos, but it's difficult to find outside of Indian grocery stores, and lemon juice makes a good substitute (just stir it in at the end).

12 ounces (1½ cups) dried chickpeas (see Tip)

3 tablespoons neutral cooking oil (such as grapeseed oil) or coconut oil

2 teaspoons black mustard seeds

1½ teaspoons cumin seeds

2 medium yellow onions, finely diced

6 garlic cloves, minced

1½-inch piece fresh ginger, grated or minced

1 serrano pepper, minced (seeded and membranes removed for less heat)

3 bay leaves

1 tablespoon garam masala

2 teaspoons ground coriander

1½ teaspoons amchur powder or 1½ tablespoons fresh lemon juice

1 teaspoon ground turmeric

½ teaspoon Indian red chile powder or ¼ teaspoon cayenne pepper (omit for a mild version)

½ teaspoon freshly cracked black pepper

1¼ cups low-sodium vegetable broth or water

1 (14.5-ounce) can diced tomatoes

1½ teaspoons kosher salt

1 cup fresh cilantro, roughly chopped

FOR SERVING
White basmati rice, roti, or naan

1. Cover the chickpeas with plenty of water and soak for 8 hours or overnight, then drain and rinse them under cold water.

2. Select the Sauté setting on the Instant Pot and after a few minutes, add the oil. Once the display reads "HOT," add the mustard seeds and cumin seeds and fry for 45 seconds, tossing frequently, until very aromatic. Add the onions and cook, stirring frequently, until the onions are softened and start to turn golden, 5 to 6 minutes.

3. Add the garlic, ginger, serrano, and bay leaves and cook until the garlic is golden brown, 1 to 2 minutes.

4. Add the garam masala, coriander, amchur powder (if using lemon juice instead, do not add yet), turmeric, chile powder (if using), and black pepper and stir until very fragrant, about 30 seconds. You may need to add a tablespoon of water to prevent the mixture from drying out and/or burning.

5. Select the Cancel setting and pour in the vegetable broth to deglaze the pan, using a wooden spoon to scrape up any browned bits on the bottom of the pot. Then add the soaked and drained chickpeas, tomatoes, and salt. Stir well to combine.

6. Secure the lid and set the Pressure Release to Sealing. Select the Pressure Cook setting at high pressure and set the cook time to 35 minutes.

7. Once the 35-minute timer beeps, allow a natural pressure release.

8. Open the pot and discard the bay leaves. Stir in the fresh lemon juice (if not using amchur powder) and cilantro. Taste for seasonings, and adjust accordingly. Serve over white basmati rice.

TIPS *I've made this recipe using dried chickpeas and canned chickpeas, and while they both taste delicious, I prefer the texture of dried chickpeas. But if you're looking to save time, use 3 (15-ounce) cans of chickpeas, drained and rinsed. Reduce the pressure-cook time to 8 minutes.*

Curious why a dish that uses soaked chickpeas has a cook time of 35 minutes? A long cook time is necessary to fully soften the chickpeas so they almost melt into the curry. If you skimp on the cook time, the chickpeas will be cooked through, but the sauce won't thicken up to its characteristic gravylike texture.

RED CURRY RICE NOODLE SOUP

serves 6 to 8	gluten-free, nut-free, refined sugar–free

Perhaps it is fitting that I first made this soup on a hot and humid day, as I first fell in love with noodle soups during a hot and humid month I spent in Thailand a few years ago. Inspired by those nights spent slurping soups at little plastic tables on the streets of Chiang Mai, I developed this recipe with a key principle of traditional Thai cooking in mind—carefully balancing spiciness, saltiness, sourness, and sweetness in each bite.

Traditional Thai cooking is an instinctive way of cooking. It relies less on measuring cups and teaspoons and more on your taste buds and experience. If you taste the soup and find it to be too sour, add a bit more sugar, or if it's too spicy for you, add more soy sauce, miso paste, and lime juice. Because this is a lentil soup, it gets very thick and creamy, so you may want to thin it out slightly with water or vegetable broth at the end or if you're heating up leftovers.

- 2½ tablespoons grapeseed oil or other neutral, high-heat cooking oil
- 1 large sweet onion, diced
- 3 carrots, diced
- 1 large red bell pepper, diced
- 6 garlic cloves, minced
- 2-inch piece fresh ginger, grated or minced
- 2 to 3 Thai bird's eye chiles or 2 serrano peppers (seeded for less heat or omit peppers entirely)
- ¼ cup red curry paste (I recommend Thai Kitchen brand)
- 4 cups low-sodium vegetable broth
- 2 cups water
- 3 tablespoons Sriracha or similar chili-garlic sauce (use less for mild heat)
- 2 bay leaves
- ½ teaspoon kosher salt
- 1 tablespoon reduced-sodium tamari or soy sauce
- 1 tablespoon white or yellow miso paste
- 1½ cups red lentils, rinsed
- 2½ tablespoons fresh lime juice
- ¾ cup fresh cilantro, roughly chopped, plus more for garnish
- ½ cup fresh basil, finely slivered, plus more for garnish
- 2 tablespoons coconut sugar
- 1 (13.5-ounce) can full-fat coconut milk
- 6 ounces thin rice noodles (vermicelli)
- White or black sesame seeds, for garnish

recipe continues

1. Select the Sauté setting on the Instant Pot and, after a few minutes, add the oil. Once the display reads "HOT," add the onion, carrots, and bell pepper and cook until the onion is softened and begins to become translucent, 4 to 5 minutes.

2. Add the garlic, ginger, chiles (if using), and red curry paste and cook for 1 minute until the mixture is very fragrant, stirring constantly.

3. Add the vegetable broth, water, Sriracha, bay leaves, salt, tamari, miso, and red lentils. Stir to combine. Select the Cancel setting.

4. Secure the lid and set the Pressure Release to Sealing. Select the Pressure Cook setting at high pressure and set the cook time to 10 minutes.

5. Once the 10-minute timer has completed and beeps, allow a natural pressure release for 10 minutes and then switch the Pressure Release knob from Sealing to Venting to release any remaining steam.

6. Open the pot and discard the bay leaves. Add the lime juice, cilantro, basil, coconut sugar, and coconut milk. Stir to combine all of the ingredients and select the Sauté setting.

7. Add the thin rice noodles, submerge them in the liquid, and allow the soup to come to a simmer. If you have a glass lid that fits your Instant Pot, cover the Instant Pot with the glass lid. (Alternatively, you can place the Instant Pot lid on top and set the Pressure Release to Venting; the lid won't lock into place.) Cook the noodles in the soup, covered, until they have softened, 3 to 5 minutes.

8. If you find the soup to be a bit thick, pour in ½ cup water and stir, adding more as needed.

9. Taste the soup for salt, acidity, and sweetness, adding more salt, lime juice, or coconut sugar as needed. Transfer the soup to bowls and garnish with additional basil, cilantro, and sesame seeds.

EASY SWEET POTATO DAL

serves 4	gluten-free, nut-free, soy-free, no added sugar

Sweet potatoes give this dal a modern twist. With the earthiness of a traditional Indian dal and the creaminess and sweetness of a coconut milk curry, this is one of my favorite comfort foods. Pressure cooking the lentils, along with sweet potatoes and coconut milk, yields a rich, thick dal that will coat your belly with happiness.

Many traditional recipes for dal call for finishing the dal with spiced oil, sometimes referred to as *tadka*. However, I think this version is insanely good as is and doesn't need the *tadka*. But, if you want to take this dish over the top, you can finish it with the *tadka* recipe found in my Basic (But Oh-So-Delicious) Indian Dal (page 109).

When you first open the pot after the pressure has been released, the dal might look watery. Not to worry, it will thicken up while you bring it to a boil on the Sauté setting, and will continue to thicken while it rests.

1½ tablespoons unrefined virgin coconut oil

1 large yellow onion, chopped

1 teaspoon kosher salt, plus more to taste

5 garlic cloves, minced

2-inch piece fresh ginger, grated or finely minced

1 to 2 serrano peppers, to taste (seeded and membranes removed for less heat), diced

1 teaspoon ground coriander

1 teaspoon ground cumin

1 teaspoon ground turmeric

½ teaspoon Indian red chile powder or ¼ teaspoon cayenne pepper (omit for a mild version)

2 bay leaves

1 cup red lentils, rinsed

1½ pounds sweet potatoes, peeled and cut into ¾-inch cubes

2 large or 3 small tomatoes, chopped, or 1 (15-ounce) can diced tomatoes

1 (13.5-ounce) can "lite" or reduced-fat coconut milk

2 cups water

½ cup fresh cilantro, roughly chopped

1 to 2 tablespoons fresh lemon juice, to taste

recipe continues

1. Select the Sauté setting on the Instant Pot and, after a few minutes, add the coconut oil, followed by the onion. Add a tiny pinch of salt and cook until the onion is slightly softened, 3 to 4 minutes.

2. Add the garlic, ginger, serranos, coriander, cumin, turmeric, chile powder (if using), and bay leaves. Stir and cook until the mixture is very aromatic, 30 to 60 seconds.

3. Add the lentils, sweet potatoes, tomatoes, coconut milk, water, and 1 teaspoon salt and stir to combine all of the ingredients. Select the Cancel Setting.

4. Secure the lid and set the Pressure Release to Sealing. Select the Pressure Cook setting at high pressure and set the cook time to 12 minutes.

5. Once the 12-minute timer has completed and beeps, allow a natural pressure release.

6. Open the pot and stir the dal well. Select the Sauté setting, bring the dal to a boil, and cook for 3 to 4 minutes to slightly thicken. The dal will continue to thicken as it rests. Discard the bay leaves.

7. Add the cilantro and 1 tablespoon lemon juice. Taste for seasonings and, if needed, add more lemon juice for acidity or more salt.

7

DESSERTS

I first fell in love with food when I began
baking for others as a teenager. There's
nothing like seeing someone you love bite
into a warm brownie you've just baked and
then tell you how much they love it (hello,
self-confidence!). My love for sweets, both
making and eating, has not subsided over time,
and my desserts are usually my most popular
recipes, so I particularly love this chapter.

Whether you're a chocolate lover (you must
try the Double-Fudge Chocolate Cake on
page 281) or more into fruity desserts, you will
find decadent and divine treats to please every
palate. While there are a few lighter options,
most of these desserts aren't pretending to be
healthy, so just go find your second stomach
and indulge in these mouthwatering desserts.

DOUBLE-FUDGE CHOCOLATE CAKE

serves 10 to 12	nut-free option, soy-free

There are some people who like their brownies cakey as opposed to fudgy. I am not one of those people. In fact, I prefer the opposite: I like my cake to be fudgy, almost like a brownie. And this double-fudge chocolate cake is one step removed from eating pure fudge. As one of my coworkers put it when she tried it, "This is insane."

There are a few secrets to the fudgy texture and taste. The pressure cooker pot-in-pot method essentially steams the chocolate cake, helping it retain a rich, pudding-like interior while still cooking it through, so there's no risk of overbaking or ending up with a dry texture. Also, there's a generous amount of high-quality cocoa powder and dark chocolate chunks in this cake. The chocolate chunks slowly melt into the cake so that every time you get a bite with one, it's like you're eating a molten lava cake. Finally, I find that using cake flour instead of all-purpose makes for cakes that are much lighter and less dense when baking in the Instant Pot.

To balance this chocolate decadence, I suggest pairing it with something tart and acidic, like the raspberry coulis or simply fresh raspberries.

Cooking spray, for the pan

1¼ cups + 2 tablespoons unbleached cake flour

¾ teaspoon baking soda

½ teaspoon fine sea salt

½ teaspoon ground cinnamon

½ cup unsweetened cocoa powder

½ cup organic cane sugar

⅓ cup packed organic brown sugar

¼ cup sunflower oil or melted coconut oil

¾ cup unsweetened plain almond milk or other nondairy milk (at room temperature if using coconut oil)

1 teaspoon apple cider vinegar

1 teaspoon pure vanilla extract

1 teaspoon espresso powder or other dark-roast instant coffee powder

2 tablespoons boiling water

4 ounces 65% to 80% dark chocolate chunks or chips

RASPBERRY COULIS (OPTIONAL, BUT RECOMMENDED)

1 cup fresh or thawed frozen raspberries

2 tablespoons organic cane sugar

1½ teaspoons fresh lemon juice

TIP *Make this a triple chocolate cake by drizzling melted dark chocolate on top of the cake before adding the raspberry coulis.*

recipe continues

1. Use the bottom of a 7-inch springform pan to trace a circle on a piece of parchment paper and cut out the round of paper. Line the bottom of the pan with the parchment paper (or generously grease with cooking spray or oil) and lightly grease the sides to prevent sticking.

2. For easy removal of the pan from the Instant Pot, create a foil sling following the instructions on page 21. (Alternatively, you can use oven mitts to carefully remove the pan.)

3. In a medium bowl, sift together the cake flour, baking soda, salt, cinnamon, and cocoa powder. Sifting ensures that there are no dry clumps in the batter.

4. In a large bowl, whisk together the cane sugar, brown sugar, and oil until well combined. Then whisk in the almond milk, vinegar, vanilla, and espresso powder until the mixture is smooth and no clumps remain.

5. Gradually add half of the flour mixture to the wet mixture and whisk together until almost smooth. Add the remaining flour mixture and the boiling water. Switch to a silicone spatula and mix until just smooth.

6. Fold in the dark chocolate chunks or chips with a silicone spatula. Pour the batter into the prepared springform pan. Spray a piece of foil with cooking spray and loosely cover the pan.

7. Pour 1 cup of water in the inner pot of the Instant Pot. On the counter, place the pan on top of the steamer rack with the handles facing up and arrange the foil sling (if using) underneath the steamer rack. Carefully lower the steamer rack and pan into the inner pot using the foil sling or steamer rack handles.

8. Secure the lid and set the Pressure Release to Sealing. Select the Pressure Cook setting at high pressure and set the cook time to 45 minutes.

9. Once the 45-minute timer has completed and beeps, allow a natural pressure release for 10 minutes and then switch the Pressure Release knob from Sealing to Venting to release any remaining steam.

10. Open the pot and, using oven mitts, grasp the foil sling or steamer rack handles and carefully lift the pan out of the Instant Pot. Let the cake cool to room temperature on a wire rack. If making this into a triple chocolate cake (see Tip), drizzle the melted dark chocolate on the cake while it's cooling on the wire rack (put a sheet pan or plate underneath the wire rack for easy cleanup).

11. While the cake is cooling, make the raspberry coulis, if using: In a saucepan combine the raspberries, sugar, and lemon juice and cook over low heat, gently smashing down the raspberries as the mixture cooks, until the raspberries have broken down, about 10 minutes. Allow the mixture to simmer until thickened and reduced, an additional 10 minutes, then remove from the heat.

APPLE CRISP–STUFFED APPLES

makes 5 stuffed apples	gluten-free, soy-free option, refined sugar–free

As soon as the air starts to get crisp and the morning sunrise a little later, I develop a very primal craving for apples.

And when I want an easy yet satisfying fall dessert for guests, I make baked apples in my Instant Pot. This dish has the sweet, tart goodness of a traditional apple crisp (without the oven time!), stuffed and "baked" inside of juicy apples.

Use an apple variety that can withstand the heat of baking (Honeycrisp, Braeburn, Jonagold, and Pink Lady are good options) and choose the freshest apples you can find (look for apples with stems that are flexible and green). A 6-quart Instant Pot can fit 5 large apples.

After the apples are cooked, you may notice that some of the peels are starting to break away. Don't throw those peels out, as they are extra flavorful (and especially delicious when served with a scoop of vegan vanilla ice cream)!

APPLE CRISP FILLING

¾ cup golden raisins

¾ cup walnuts or pecans, finely chopped

½ cup almond flour (or all-purpose flour if not gluten-free)

1½ teaspoons ground cinnamon

¾ teaspoon ground ginger

¼ teaspoon freshly grated or ground nutmeg

2½ tablespoons pure maple syrup

½ teaspoon pure vanilla extract

Generous pinch of fine sea salt or kosher salt

APPLES

5 large apples (about 7 ounces each)

½ cup apple juice or water

2 tablespoons vegan butter or solid coconut oil, sliced into about 8 pieces (use a soy-free variety of vegan butter to keep soy-free)

½ teaspoon ground cinnamon

FOR SERVING (OPTIONAL)

Vegan vanilla ice cream, nondairy whipped topping, or coconut whipped cream

recipe continues

1. Make the apple crisp filling: In a medium bowl, combine the raisins, walnuts, almond flour, cinnamon, ginger, nutmeg, maple syrup, vanilla, and salt and mix with a spoon or fork until all of the ingredients are well coated.

2. Prepare the apples: Slice off the very top and stem of each apple. Then, using a melon baller or spoon, scoop out the inner core and some of the apple flesh to make a cavity for the streusel filling. Don't scoop too deeply into the apple because you don't want to cut a hole through the bottom.

3. Spoon the apple crisp filling into each apple and fill to the top, but do not overstuff. If you have extra filling, reserve it for the end and use it as a topping for the cooked apples.

4. Pour the apple juice into the inner pot of the Instant Pot. Add the sliced vegan butter or coconut oil and ½ teaspoon cinnamon to the apple juice.

5. Gently lower the stuffed apples into the inner pot of the Instant Pot, arranging them as needed to ensure they all fit.

6. Secure the lid and set the Pressure Release to Sealing. Select the Pressure Cook setting at *low pressure* and set the cook time to 3 minutes.

7. Once the 3-minute timer has completed and beeps, perform a quick pressure release by carefully switching the Pressure Release knob from Sealing to Venting.

8. Open the pot and, using a large spoon or slotted spoon, carefully remove the apples and transfer to a serving plate or to individual serving dishes. Pour a few spoons of the sauce at the bottom of the inner pot over each apple.

9. Serve the apples warm with ice cream, whipped topping, or coconut whipped cream, if desired. Top with any reserved apple crisp filling.

TIP *Freeze leftover compote in an ice cube tray. Pop out as many cubes as needed (each cube will hold about 2 tablespoons) and quickly thaw.*

MIXED BERRY COMPOTE

makes about 3 cups	gluten-free, nut-free, soy-free

Warm and fruity, perfectly sweet yet subtly tart, this compote is irresistible. And versatile. You can serve it over a bowl of ice cream for dessert or my Blackberry and Meyer Lemon Bread Pudding (page 309). Scoop it over the Overnight Sweet Potato French Toast (page 91) for a decadent weekend brunch, or spoon a little over a bowl of coconut yogurt and muesli for a healthy yet indulgent breakfast.

While compote is not difficult to make in a saucepan, it is certainly more convenient to throw everything in the Instant Pot instead of standing over the stove and periodically checking the fruit to make sure it comes out just right.

I like to use equal portions of raspberries, blackberries and blueberries, but feel free to use your favorite berries. If you use strawberries, chop them into roughly the same size as the other berries. You can use fresh or frozen berries, though frozen berries produce more liquid, so I usually add more of the cornstarch or arrowroot slurry to sufficiently thicken up the compote. And if you're lucky enough to have very sweet berries during the summer, you can reduce the amount of sugar by a few tablespoons.

1 medium lemon

4 cups mixed fresh or frozen (unthawed) berries

¾ cup organic cane sugar (reduce by a few tablespoons if your berries are very sweet)

2 tablespoons cornstarch or arrowroot powder

1. Grate the lemon to get 1 teaspoon zest and set aside. Squeeze the lemon to get 2½ tablespoons juice.

2. Add 3½ cups of the berries to the Instant Pot, reserving the remaining ½ cup. Add the sugar and lemon juice and stir to combine the ingredients. There's no need to add water, as the berries will exude enough liquid for the Instant Pot to come to pressure.

3. Secure the lid and set the Pressure Release to Sealing. Select the Pressure Cook setting at high pressure and set the cook time to 3 minutes.

4. Once the 3-minute timer has completed and beeps, allow a natural pressure release for 10 minutes and then switch the Pressure Release knob from Sealing to Venting to release any remaining steam.

5. In a small bowl, stir together the cornstarch or arrowroot and 2 tablespoons water until dissolved into a slurry. Open the pot and add half of the slurry to the compote. Select the Sauté setting and bring the compote to a boil, stirring constantly. Once the compote has come to a boil, check to see if it is sufficiently thick enough. If not, add the remaining slurry and stir until thickened. The compote will thicken considerably as it cools to room temperature.

6. Select the Cancel setting and add the reserved ½ cup berries and the lemon zest and stir to combine.

7. Once cool, transfer the compote to a glass jar or airtight container and store in the fridge for 1 to 2 weeks, or freeze for longer.

THAI MANGO STICKY RICE

serves 4	gluten-free, nut-free, soy-free

The best dessert I've eaten while traveling abroad is Thai mango sticky rice. It might be one of the best desserts I've eaten, period. Sweet, sticky rice and juicy mangos are smothered in a rich coconut sauce, creating an irresistible blend of sweet and salty, chewy and creamy.

Cooking this dessert usually requires the rice to be soaked for several hours or overnight, and then steamed in a tall aluminum pot and bamboo basket. The Instant Pot makes this process quicker, more easily accessible, and eliminates the soaking step.

Traditionally, mango sticky rice is topped with toasted or fried yellow mung beans (dry-toast them in a skillet for a few minutes until golden brown and crispy), but you can substitute toasted sesame seeds for an equally delicious crunch.

1 cup Thai sticky rice, sweet rice, or glutinous rice

1⅓ cups canned full-fat coconut milk, well stirred

7 tablespoons organic cane sugar

½ teaspoon fine sea salt or kosher salt, plus more to taste

1 tablespoon cornstarch

2 ripe Ataúlfo (honey) mangoes (about 6 ounces each), peeled, pitted, and thinly sliced or diced (see Tip)

2 tablespoons yellow mung beans, toasted, or 2 teaspoons toasted white sesame seeds or black sesame seeds

TIP *Ataúlfo (honey) mangos are the best variety of mango available in the West for this Thai dessert. Compared to the more common Tommy Atkins mangos (usually available year-round), they are smaller, sweeter, more flavorful, and less fibrous. They're available from late February to early August.*

You can find Thai sticky rice, sweet rice, or glutinous rice at well-stocked grocery stores, Asian markets, or online.

recipe continues

1. For easy removal of the pan from the Instant Pot, create a foil sling following the instructions on page 21. (Alternatively, you can use oven mitts to carefully remove the pan.)

2. Place the sticky rice in a large bowl and add water to cover. Gently stir the rice with your hands, then drain the water, and repeat 4 or 5 times until the water runs almost clear. This removes the excess starch and prevents the rice from becoming gummy. Place the rinsed rice in a heatproof glass or stainless steel bowl that fits inside the inner pot of your Instant Pot. Add ⅔ cup cold water to the bowl to cover the rice.

3. On the counter, place the bowl on top of the steamer rack with the handles facing up and arrange the foil sling (if using) underneath the steamer rack. Pour 1½ cups water into the inner pot of the Instant Pot. Carefully lower the steamer rack and bowl into the inner pot using the foil sling or steamer rack handles.

4. Secure the lid and set the Pressure Release to Sealing. Select the Pressure Cook setting at high pressure and set the cook time to 13 minutes.

5. Once the 13-minute timer has completed and beeps, allow a natural pressure release for 10 minutes and then switch the Pressure Release knob from Sealing to Venting to release any remaining steam.

6. While the pot is depressurizing, in a small saucepan, bring ⅔ cup of the coconut milk to a simmer over medium heat. Add 5 tablespoons of the cane sugar and ¼ teaspoon of the salt and whisk until the sugar is dissolved and the milk tastes salty-sweet. Keep the sauce warm.

7. Open the Instant Pot and, with oven mitts, transfer the cooked sticky rice to a large bowl and pour the warm coconut milk mixture on top. Stir well to combine and gently fluff with a fork. Cover and let it sit until the liquid is absorbed, about 20 minutes. You can let the rice rest at room temperature for up to 2 hours.

8. Meanwhile, set aside 2 tablespoons of the remaining coconut milk in a small bowl. Wipe out the saucepan and add the remaining coconut milk. Add the cornstarch to the small bowl and whisk until smooth, forming a slurry. Bring the coconut milk in the saucepan to a simmer over medium heat, whisking frequently. Whisk the slurry into the coconut milk on the stove and simmer until the mixture has thickened, about 2 minutes. Whisk in the remaining 2 tablespoons cane sugar and the remaining ¼ teaspoon salt until the sugar is dissolved. The coconut cream should be slightly saltier and less sweet than the coconut milk mixture used to cover the rice.

9. When ready to serve, use a 1-cup measuring cup to scoop the coconut rice into mounds on individual plates and arrange the sliced or diced mango alongside. Drizzle the warm coconut cream over the rice and garnish with the toasted yellow mung beans or sesame seeds. Serve immediately. Do not warm up or refrigerate, as the rice will turn rock hard.

PECAN PUMPKIN MOUSSE TART

makes one 7-inch tart	soy-free

My first cookbook would not be complete without a recipe for a pumpkin tart, a dessert I've been making since Thanksgiving 2002.

I've never enjoyed the traditional pumpkin pie because it's hard to do well. The crust can be soggy and the filling is often too grainy, usually because it's overbaked. In contrast, tarts—with their shallow sides and relatively thin bottom crust—lend themselves to more even baking and enable the pumpkin pie filling (when done right) to shine.

This pumpkin mousse filling is, without a doubt, the lightest and airiest yet creamiest pumpkin pie filling I've made in all these years. Using the Instant Pot instead of an oven essentially steams the tart, resulting in a soft, luscious mousse that literally melts in your mouth, just the way a custard pie should.

My secret pumpkin tart weapons are orange zest and fresh nutmeg. The orange zest adds a pop of freshness and enhances the natural pumpkin spice flavors, while the nutmeg brings a warm and spicy aroma. The sticky, sweet glaze and pecan topping is like eating pumpkin pie and pecan pie (another Thanksgiving favorite) at the same time (sort of).

PECAN-GINGER CRUST

Cooking spray or melted coconut oil, for the pan

½ cup pecans

15 gingersnap cookies (3½ to 4 ounces)

Pinch of fine sea salt

2 tablespoons coconut oil, melted

PUMPKIN PIE FILLING

1 cup canned unsweetened pumpkin puree

6 ounces silken tofu

¼ cup + 3 tablespoons pure maple syrup

2 tablespoons no-sugar-added almond butter

2 tablespoons arrowroot powder or cornstarch

1 teaspoon ground cinnamon

½ teaspoon nutmeg, preferably freshly grated

¼ teaspoon ground ginger

⅛ teaspoon ground cloves

⅛ teaspoon fine sea salt

1 teaspoon pure vanilla extract

1 teaspoon grated orange zest

TOPPING

¼ cup coconut nectar or brown sugar (or pure maple syrup, but the glaze will be a bit thin)

2 tablespoons coconut cream (from a can of full-fat coconut milk or a can of coconut cream)

1 tablespoon coconut oil

Pinch of fine sea salt

½ teaspoon pure vanilla extract

⅓ cup pecans, finely chopped

recipe continues

1. Make the pecan-ginger crust: Generously grease the bottom of a 7-inch springform pan with cooking spray or brush it with melted coconut oil.

2. In a food processor, combine the pecans, gingersnaps, and salt and blend until the nuts and cookies are mostly pulverized. With the machine running, pour in the melted coconut oil, scraping down the sides with a silicone spatula as needed. Once you have a slightly sticky texture that you can press together, press it into the bottom and 1 inch up the sides of the prepared springform pan, flattening it out with your fingers or a flat-bottomed glass as you go. Transfer the pan to the freezer to set (for at least 15 minutes) while you prepare the rest of the tart. Wipe out the processor bowl to make the filling.

3. For easy removal of the pan from the Instant Pot, create a foil sling following the instructions on page 21. (Alternatively, you can use oven mitts to carefully remove the pan.)

4. Make the pumpkin pie filling: Place the pumpkin puree, tofu, maple syrup, almond butter, arrowroot powder, cinnamon, nutmeg, ginger, cloves, salt, vanilla, and orange zest in the food processor (or a high-powered blender) and blend well until the mixture is completely smooth and creamy. Pour the filling on top of the frozen crust in the springform pan. Use a silicone spatula to smooth out the top and cover the pan with a piece of foil.

5. On the counter, place the pan on top of the steamer rack (with the handles facing up) and arrange the foil sling (if using) underneath the steamer rack. Pour 1 cup water into the inner pot of the Instant Pot. Carefully lower the steamer rack and pan into the inner pot using the foil sling or steamer rack handles.

6. Secure the lid and set the Pressure Release to Sealing. Select the Pressure Cook setting at high pressure and set the cook time to 35 minutes.

7. Once the 35-minute timer has completed and beeps, allow a natural pressure release for 15 minutes and then switch the Pressure Release knob from Sealing to Venting to release any remaining steam.

8. Open the pot and, using oven mitts, grasp the foil sling or steamer rack handles and lift the pan out of the Instant Pot. Carefully remove the foil, taking care to not drip any condensation on the cake. The surface should be smooth and mostly set to the touch. Allow the tart to cool to room temperature on a wire rack before unclasping the springform pan. Then refrigerate the tart for at least 3 hours before serving.

9. When ready to serve, prepare the topping: In a small saucepan, combine the coconut nectar, coconut cream, coconut oil, and salt and bring to a boil, whisking until smooth. Remove from the heat and whisk in the vanilla. Allow to slightly cool for 10 minutes before drizzling over the pumpkin tart. Then sprinkle the pie evenly with the chopped pecans.

TIP *To keep this tart gluten-free, omit the gingersnap cookies from the crust. Instead, increase the amount of pecans to 1¼ cups, add 1 tablespoon pure maple syrup, and a pinch of sea salt. Drizzle in 1 to 2 tablespoons melted coconut oil while the machine is running. And if you prefer a firmer, crispier crust, blind bake the crust in the oven for 15 minutes at 325°F before pressure cooking the filled tart.*

COOKIES 'N' CREAM CHEESECAKE

serves 8

If you think it's impossible to bake a cheesecake in the Instant Pot, let alone a vegan cheesecake, let me share some secrets. Since cheesecake is essentially a custard, it should be baked evenly and ideally in a water bath. This can be annoying to deal with in an oven. Luckily, the Instant Pot already acts as a huge water bath. The water at the bottom of the pot steams the cheesecake inside the cake pan and cooks it perfectly every time.

Now, for the vegan part. Soaked raw cashews and coconut cream bring the ultra-rich, creamy, and smooth texture characteristic of cheesecake. You can either soak the cashews in room-temperature water for 8 hours or overnight, or if you forget to soak them, you can do a quick soak in boiling water for 1 hour. Lemon juice adds the tangy bite typical of cheesecake without the cream cheese, but if you prefer a bit more of that tangy flavor, you can add ⅔ cup vegan cream cheese (I recommend the Tofutti brand) and reduce the amount of both the cashews and coconut cream to ⅔ cup each.

And if a vegan cheesecake in the Instant Pot wasn't enough to wow you, this cheesecake has cookies in the filling and the crust. You're welcome.

TIP *You'll need to refrigerate your can of coconut milk for 24 hours (or more) to solidify the cream. Depending on the brand, there is between ⅔ and ¾ cup of cream in a 13.5-ounce can of full-fat coconut milk. You can also buy canned coconut cream.*

CRUST

Cooking spray, for the pan

16 crème-filled chocolate sandwich cookies

2 tablespoons coconut oil, melted, or a neutral-flavored oil

CHEESECAKE FILLING

1¼ cups raw cashews, soaked for 8 hours and drained well

¾ cup coconut cream, refrigerated for at least 24 hours to solidify (see Tip)

2 tablespoons coconut oil, melted

2 tablespoons fresh lemon juice

¼ cup organic cane sugar or sweetener of choice

1 tablespoon arrowroot powder or cornstarch

1 teaspoon pure vanilla extract

⅛ teaspoon fine sea salt

8 crème-filled chocolate cookies, coarsely chopped

OPTIONAL GARNISHES

Nondairy whipped topping or coconut whipped cream

Crème-filled chocolate sandwich cookies, crushed

Melted dark chocolate

recipe continues

1. Use the bottom of a 7-inch springform pan to trace a circle on a piece of parchment paper and cut the paper into a round. Line the bottom of the pan with the parchment round for easy removal (or generously grease with cooking spray). Lightly grease the sides of the cake pan.

2. For easy removal of the pan from the Instant Pot, create a foil sling following the instructions on page 21. (Alternatively, you can use oven mitts to carefully remove the pan.)

3. Make the crust: Place the cookies in a food processor and blitz until pulverized. With the machine running, drizzle in the oil, scraping down the sides of the bowl with a silicone spatula as needed. Wipe out the processor bowl to prepare the filling. (Alternatively, you can crush the cookies by placing them in a zip-top plastic bag and crushing them with a rolling pin; transfer cookie crumbs to a medium bowl and pour in the oil, stirring to combine with a fork.) Press the cookie crust firmly onto the bottom of the prepared springform pan. Refrigerate the crust while you prepare the filling.

4. Make the cheesecake filling: Add the soaked and drained cashews and solid coconut cream to the food processor and blend until the mixture resembles ricotta cheese. Add the melted coconut oil, lemon juice, sugar, arrowroot, vanilla, and salt and blend until smooth and creamy, scraping down the sides as needed. Using a silicone spatula, fold the chopped cookies into the cheesecake batter.

5. Pour the cheesecake batter on top of the refrigerated crust, smooth out the top with a silicone spatula, and cover the pan tightly with foil.

6. On the counter, place the pan on top of the steamer rack (with the handles facing up) and arrange the foil sling (if using) underneath the steamer rack. Pour 1½ cups water into the inner pot of the Instant Pot. Carefully lower the steamer rack and pan into the inner pot using the foil sling or steamer rack handles.

7. Secure the lid and set the Pressure Release to Sealing. Select the Pressure Cook setting and set to high pressure for 35 minutes.

8. Once the 35-minute timer has completed and beeps, allow a natural pressure release.

9. Open the pot and, using oven mitts, grasp the foil sling or steamer rack handles and lift the pan out of the Instant Pot. Carefully remove the foil cover, taking care to not drip any condensation on the cake. Use the corner of a paper towel to soak up any water on the cake's surface.

10. Allow the cake to cool to room temperature on a wire rack, and then cover with plastic wrap and refrigerate for at least 4 hours. When ready to serve, garnish as desired.

LEMON POPPY SEED BUNDT CAKE

serves 8	nut-free option, soy-free

I am an admitted chocophile. However, this lemon poppy seed cake is one of those rare desserts that makes me forget about chocolate. It's tender, fluffy, and moist (everyone's favorite word!). Fresh lemon zest and lemon juice arouse your taste buds with a fragrant tanginess and the poppy seeds offer a deep, nutty flavor with a pleasant crunch. And the sweet lemony icing on top adds that sweet-tart combo that is so seductively delicious. Most of the sweetness in this cake comes from the icing, so if you omit it (but I highly recommend making it), you may want to increase the amount of sugar in the cake to ½ cup.

I use cake flour for an ultra-light texture and smooth mouthfeel. The tender texture, contrasted with the chewy bite from the poppy seeds, is irresistible. To top things off, this cake is so simple to make and stays perfectly moist (there it is again) when cooked in the Instant Pot.

TIP *If your yogurt is very thick, you'll want to reduce the amount from ⅔ cup to ½ cup and add 2½ tablespoons of plain almond milk or other nondairy milk.*

BUNDT CAKE

Cooking spray or neutral-flavored oil, for the pan

1 ½ cups unbleached cake flour

2 teaspoons aluminum-free baking powder

¼ teaspoon baking soda

Scant ½ teaspoon fine sea salt

⅔ cup coconut yogurt or other nondairy yogurt

⅓ cup organic cane sugar

½ cup unsweetened applesauce

¼ cup unsweetened plain almond milk or other nondairy milk

¼ cup sunflower oil or other neutral-flavored oil

½ teaspoon pure vanilla extract

1 tablespoon grated lemon zest (about 1 medium lemon)

¼ cup fresh lemon juice (about 1½ medium lemons)

1 tablespoon poppy seeds

LEMON ICING

1 cup organic powdered sugar

1½ teaspoons grated lemon zest

2 tablespoons fresh lemon juice

1 to 2 tablespoons unsweetened plain almond milk or other nondairy milk

recipe continues

1. Make the Bundt cake: Coat a 6-cup Bundt pan generously with cooking spray or grease lightly with the oil.

2. For easy removal of the pan from the Instant Pot, create a foil sling following the instructions on page 21. (Alternatively, you can use oven mitts to carefully remove the pan.)

3. In a medium bowl, sift together the cake flour, baking powder, baking soda, and salt. Sifting ensures that there are no dry clumps in the batter.

4. In a large bowl, whisk together the yogurt, sugar, applesauce, almond milk, sunflower oil, vanilla, lemon zest, and lemon juice. Gradually add the dry ingredients to the wet ingredients, whisking until smooth. Fold in the poppy seeds using a silicone spatula.

5. Pour the cake batter into the prepared Bundt pan and cover with a piece of foil.

6. On the counter, place the pan on top of the steamer rack (with the handles facing up) and arrange the foil sling (if using) underneath the steamer rack. Pour 1½ cups water into the inner pot of the Instant Pot. Carefully lower the steamer rack and pan into the inner pot using the foil sling or steamer rack handles.

7. Secure the lid and set the Pressure Release to Sealing. Select the Pressure Cook setting at high pressure and set the cook time to 30 minutes.

8. Once the 30-minute timer has completed and beeps, allow a natural pressure release.

9. Carefully remove the foil cover, taking care to not drip any condensation on the cake. Check the cake for doneness by inserting a toothpick in the center. If it comes out clean with just a few crumbs, the cake is done. If the cake is still very moist, re-cover the pan with foil, place it back on top of the steamer rack, and select the Pressure Cook setting at high pressure and cook for another 5 minutes; allow a natural pressure release for 5 minutes before performing a quick pressure release.

10. Wearing oven mitts, grasp the foil sling or steamer rack handles and carefully lift the pan out of the Instant Pot. Allow the cake to cool on a wire rack for 30 minutes. Run a paring knife around the edges to loosen the cake and carefully invert the cake pan onto the wire rack.

11. Make the lemon icing: In a small bowl, whisk together the powdered sugar, lemon zest, and lemon juice until smooth. Add the almond milk 1 tablespoon at a time, whisking until you have a pourable glaze. Once the cake has cooled, drizzle with the icing and cut into slices.

SWEET CORN ROSEMARY CAKE
WITH BALSAMIC SYRUP

serves 6 to 8	nut-free, soy-free

I would describe this cake as corn bread in cake form. It is sweet and savory, tender and light, and bursting with exciting flavors. It is rustic and casual, making it a perfect afternoon snack cake. In fact, every time I have baked this cake, I have found myself making frequent trips to the kitchen and lobbing off small bits of cake directly from the pan, snacking on it while I work away at my desk.

However, it is quite easy to dress up this cake. You can serve it with the rich, sticky balsamic syrup as I did here, or with a fruit compote such as my Mixed Berry Compote (page 287) or a citrus-based one. And of course, a dollop of non-dairy whipped cream would be fabulous. If you make the balsamic syrup, I insist that you avoid using a cheap balsamic vinegar. I've tried making it with $2 balsamic vinegar and it tastes like sour watered-down alcohol.

When you remove the cake from the Instant Pot, the surface might be a bit cracked, but remember, it's a rustic cake! And you can cover up the cracks with the aforementioned toppings. I recommend serving this cake warm, as it high-lights the cake's warm, corn bread–like flavors.

¾ cup canned full-fat coconut milk

½ tablespoon fresh lemon juice

¾ cup fine cornmeal

1 cup all-purpose flour

1 tablespoon aluminum-free baking powder

¼ teaspoon baking soda

1 teaspoon kosher salt

⅔ cup agave nectar (see Tip)

⅓ cup extra-virgin olive oil

1½ teaspoons grated lemon zest (about ½ medium lemon)

1 teaspoon pure vanilla extract

2 tablespoons fresh rosemary, finely chopped

BALSAMIC SYRUP

½ cup high-quality balsamic vinegar

¼ cup organic brown sugar or coconut nectar

1 small sprig fresh rosemary

FOR SERVING

Coconut whipped cream, nondairy whipped topping, or vegan vanilla ice cream

---

TIP *If you are avoiding agave nectar, you can substitute maple syrup but the cake will have a more robust, less neutral flavor.*

recipe continues

1. Use the bottom of a 7-inch springform pan to trace a circle on a piece of parchment paper and cut the paper into a round. Line the bottom of the pan with the parchment paper for easy removal (or grease generously with oil or cooking spray).

2. For easy removal of the pan from the Instant Pot, create a foil sling following the instructions on page 21. (Alternatively, you can use oven mitts to carefully remove the pan.)

3. Place the coconut milk in a measuring cup and stir well to remove any clumps. Stir in the lemon juice and set aside.

4. In a large bowl, whisk together the cornmeal, flour, baking powder, baking soda, and salt.

5. Make a well in the center of the dry ingredients. Pour in the agave nectar, olive oil, lemon zest, vanilla, and the coconut milk/lemon juice mixture. Gently mix the dry and wet ingredients together with a wooden spoon until the batter is just smooth, taking care to not overmix. Gently fold in the chopped rosemary using a silicone spatula. Pour the batter into the prepared springform pan.

6. On the counter, place the pan on top of the steamer rack (with the handles facing up) and arrange the foil sling (if using) underneath the steamer rack. Pour 1 cup water into the inner pot of the Instant Pot. Carefully lower the cake pan into the inner pot using the foil sling or steamer rack handles.

7. Secure the lid and set the Pressure Release to Sealing. Select the Pressure Cook setting at high pressure and set the cook time to 35 minutes.

8. Once the 35-minute timer has completed and beeps, allow a natural pressure release.

9. Open the pot and check the cake for doneness by inserting a toothpick in the center. If it comes out clean with just a few crumbs, the cake is done. If the cake is still very moist, select the Pressure Cook setting at high pressure and cook for another 5 minutes; allow a natural pressure release for 5 minutes before performing a quick pressure release.

10. Wearing oven mitts, grasp the foil sling or steamer rack handles and carefully lift the pan out of the Instant Pot. Allow the cake to cool in the pan for 10 minutes on a wire rack before loosening the clasp, then cool the cake for another 10 minutes before serving.

11. While the cake is cooling, make the balsamic syrup: In a small saucepan, combine the vinegar, brown sugar, and rosemary sprig. Bring to a simmer and cook until the sugar has melted and the syrup has thickened, 4 to 6 minutes. Discard the rosemary sprig.

12. Cut the cake into slices and serve warm with the balsamic syrup. If desired, also serve with coconut whipped cream, nondairy whipped topping, or vegan vanilla ice cream.

RED WINE–POACHED PEARS

serves 4	gluten-free, nut-free option, soy-free

This is one of the most elegant yet easiest desserts you can make. White-fleshed pears are bathed in a warming aroma of spices and red wine until perfectly tender and emerge in a gorgeous crimson coat. It's the kind of recipe that'll impress your dinner party guests but that requires very little effort on your part. Win-win.

When selecting pears, look for pears that are somewhat firm and not quite ripe; fruit that is ready to eat will disintegrate into mush under the heat of the Instant Pot. Regarding pear variety, I prefer Bosc pears, as they keep their shape while cooking and have a slender, elegant neck that makes for a lovely presentation, but Anjou pears also work very nicely. (Bartlett pears tend to get mushy.)

For a light and healthy dessert, serve these poached pears with coconut yogurt, or for something a bit more decadent, pair with vegan vanilla ice cream.

4 firm-ripe pears (see headnote)

Juice of ½ lemon

2 cups dry red wine (such as Pinot Noir, Malbec, or Cabernet Sauvignon)

1 (4-inch-long) strip of orange zest

Juice of 1 large orange (⅓ to ½ cup)

1 cup organic cane sugar

4 cinnamon sticks

4 whole cloves

¼ cup chopped pistachios (omit for a nut-free option)

1 teaspoon toasted white sesame seeds

FOR SERVING (OPTIONAL)

Vegan vanilla ice cream, coconut yogurt, or coconut whipped cream

recipe continues

1. Peel the pears, keeping them whole and leave the stems intact. Slice a small amount off the bottom of the pears to create a flat bottom so the pears can stand upright. Rub the pears with the lemon juice to prevent them from browning.

2. Add 1½ cups water, the wine, orange zest, orange juice, sugar, cinnamon sticks, and cloves to the Instant Pot. Select the Sauté setting and press the Sauté button again until you reach More heat. Bring the mixture to a low boil (it should take 5 to 7 minutes), stirring until the sugar is dissolved.

3. Select the Cancel setting and then select the Sauté setting again, and press the button until you reach Less heat. Gently lower the peeled pears into the poaching liquid and allow the pears to simmer for 5 minutes. Select the Cancel setting.

4. Secure the lid and set the Pressure Release to Sealing. Select the Pressure Cook setting at high pressure and set the cook time to 4 minutes.

5. Once the 4-minute timer has completed and beeps, perform a quick pressure release by carefully switching the Pressure Release knob from Sealing to Venting.

6. Open the pot and, using a slotted spoon, carefully remove the pears to a serving platter or to individual plates and allow to cool slightly, leaving the poaching liquid behind in the Instant Pot. Once the pears have slightly cooled, pour a few spoons of the poaching liquid on top of each pear and garnish each with a tablespoon of pistachios and a sprinkling of sesame seeds. If desired, dollop each pear with a scoop of vegan vanilla ice cream, coconut yogurt, or coconut whipped cream.

PEACH-RASPBERRY CRISP

serves 8 to 10	gluten-free, soy-free

Every summer, I carefully load up several pounds of peaches in my tote bags at the farmers' market, vowing to return home and bake peach cobbler, peach crisp, and peach pie. Living in New York City, however, has consistently thwarted these plans. I have to walk agonizingly long blocks of hot concrete to get home to my kitchen and by the time I arrive, I remember that it is a very bad idea to turn on the oven. The next day, I have eaten half of the juicy peaches, and I still do not want to turn on my oven.

Luckily, I can now make a peach crisp in my Instant Pot, no oven required! This recipe is a somewhat deconstructed peach crisp. The fruit cooks separately and then is topped with the crisp topping—but it is no less delicious than a traditional crisp.

To prevent the peaches from getting soggy, use peaches that are slightly firmer than you would use for snacking and use a serrated knife to slice them. If your peaches aren't overly sweet, you can use a tablespoon more of brown sugar in the peach filling. This crisp is easily customizable, so feel free to swap blueberries for raspberries, pecans for walnuts, or all-purpose flour for the almond flour. As long as your peaches are sweet, the end result will be exquisite.

PEACH-RASPBERRY FILLING

8 firm-ripe medium peaches (see headnote)

Cooking spray or neutral-flavored oil, for the pot

1 pint raspberries (about 2 cups)

2 tablespoons organic cane sugar

1 tablespoon organic brown sugar or organic cane sugar

½ teaspoon ground cinnamon

¼ teaspoon ground ginger

2 whole cloves or ⅛ teaspoon ground cloves (optional)

Pinch of kosher salt or fine sea salt

½ teaspoon pure almond extract (or pure vanilla extract)

1 teaspoon fresh lemon juice

1 tablespoon cornstarch or arrowroot powder

CRISP TOPPING

⅓ cup refined oconut oil

1 cup rolled oats (gluten-free if needed)

½ cup almond flour

½ cup walnuts, chopped

½ cup packed organic brown sugar

½ teaspoon ground cinnamon

½ teaspoon kosher salt

FOR SERVING (OPTIONAL)

Vegan vanilla ice cream

recipe continues

1. Leave the peaches unpeeled and use a serrated knife to slice them into ¾-inch-thick wedges. You will end up with about 6 cups of sliced peaches.

2. Coat the inner pot of the Instant Pot with cooking spray or lightly grease with oil.

3. Add the sliced peaches and raspberries to the inner pot. Top with the cane sugar, brown sugar, cinnamon, ginger, cloves (if using), salt, almond extract, and lemon juice. Stir gently to coat the fruit.

4. Secure the lid and set the Pressure Release to Sealing. Select the Pressure Cook setting at high pressure and set the cook time to 1 minute.

5. Meanwhile, prepare the crisp topping: In a large skillet, heat the coconut oil over medium heat. Once the oil is melted and hot, add the oats, almond flour, walnuts, brown sugar, cinnamon, and salt. Cook, tossing frequently to prevent burning, until toasted and lightly browned, 5 to 7 minutes. Carefully transfer the crisp topping to a large piece of parchment paper and spread out to cool slightly.

6. Once the 1-minute timer has completed and beeps, perform a quick pressure release by carefully switching the Pressure Release knob from Sealing to Venting.

7. In a small bowl, whisk together the cornstarch and 1 tablespoon water until dissolved into a slurry. Open the pot and pour the slurry into the peach-raspberry filling. Select the Sauté setting and bring to a boil, stirring gently until the filling has thickened, 1 to 2 minutes.

8. Transfer the peach-raspberry filling to a large serving bowl or individual dessert bowls and sprinkle generously with the crisp topping. Serve warm with vegan vanilla ice cream if desired.

BLACKBERRY AND MEYER LEMON
BREAD PUDDING

serves 6 to 8	nut-free option, soy-free, refined sugar–free option

The first time I tried this recipe, I ended up eating half of the pan in 15 minutes because it was just that good. It's pure comfort food with an elegant touch, making it the perfect dish to serve for a Mother's Day or holiday brunch. Plus, it's so easy to make that you really can't mess it up. Simply toss together bread, berries, and a blender-made batter, spread in a pan, and let the Instant Pot do the rest.

Meyer lemons, a cross between lemons and mandarin oranges, have an indescribably alluring aroma—sweet, sour, and floral, akin to bergamot. They are sweeter and less tangy than lemons, but you can use regular lemons with equally delectable results.

Because blackberries can be quite tart, I macerate half of them in a bit of sugar and serve them over the warm bread pudding. If fresh blackberries are hard to come by, you can substitute the frozen variety. Finally, be sure to use a crusty loaf of bread that isn't soft, or you'll end up with a sad, soggy mess.

MACERATED BLACKBERRIES

6 ounces fresh blackberries (1 small container)

2 tablespoons organic cane sugar, organic brown sugar, or coconut sugar

1 tablespoon fresh Meyer lemon juice (or regular lemon juice)

BREAD PUDDING

1 loaf crusty Italian bread or French bread (12 to 14 ounces)

6 ounces fresh blackberries (1 small container)

½ cup slivered almonds or chopped raw almonds (omit for a nut-free option)

1 cup canned full-fat coconut milk, well stirred

2 very ripe medium bananas

½ cup organic cane sugar, organic brown sugar, or coconut sugar

1½ teaspoons cornstarch or arrowroot powder

2 teaspoons pure vanilla extract

½ teaspoon aluminum-free baking powder

Grated zest of 1 Meyer lemon or regular lemon (about 1 tablespoon)

Cooking spray or neutral-flavored oil, for the pan

OPTIONAL GARNISHES

Coconut whipped cream or nondairy whipped topping

Meyer lemon zest (or regular lemon zest)

recipe continues

1. Macerate the blackberries: In a medium bowl, combine the blackberries, sugar, and lemon juice. Stir to combine, cover, and refrigerate until the bread pudding is ready to serve, stirring occasionally.

2. Make the bread pudding: Slice or tear the bread into bite-size pieces. Place the bread pieces in a large bowl along with the blackberries and almonds.

3. In a blender, combine the coconut milk, bananas, sugar, cornstarch, vanilla, baking powder, and lemon zest. Blend until the mixture is completely smooth.

4. Pour the coconut milk batter over the bread mixture and gently mix to coat all of the bread cubes. Set aside to soak for a few minutes.

5. While the bread is soaking, lightly grease a 7-cup round glass dish or 1½-quart soufflé dish with cooking spray or a bit of neutral oil. For easy removal of the dish from the Instant Pot, create a foil sling following the instructions on page 21. (Alternatively, you can use oven mitts to carefully remove the dish.)

6. Transfer the soaked bread to the greased dish. Gently press down on the bread to help it absorb the coconut milk batter. Spray a piece of foil with cooking spray and tightly cover the dish.

7. On the counter, place the dish on top of the steamer rack (with the handles facing up) and arrange the foil sling (if using) underneath the steamer rack. Pour 1½ cups water in the inner pot of the Instant Pot. Carefully lower the dish into the inner pot using the foil sling or steamer rack handles.

8. Secure the lid and set the Pressure Release to Sealing. Select the Pressure Cook setting at high pressure and select the cook time to 30 minutes.

9. Once the 30-minute timer has completed and beeps, allow a natural pressure release.

10. Open the pot and, wearing oven mitts, grasp the foil sling or steamer rack handles and carefully lift the dish out of the Instant Pot. Carefully remove the foil cover without dropping condensation on the bread pudding.

11. Serve the bread pudding warm and top each serving with a few spoons of the macerated blackberries and, if desired, a spoon of coconut whipped cream or nondairy whipped topping and lemon zest.

BANANA BREAD WITH WALNUT STREUSEL

serves 8	nut-free option, soy-free option

Every time I make this banana bread, no one can believe I did it in the Instant Pot. While the Instant Pot method won't save you time, it does offer many benefits over the traditional method. Most important, it's foolproof. When I bake banana bread in the oven, five out of ten times I end up with a middle that is undercooked and edges that have browned. The even and contained heat of the pressure cooker, in contrast, ensures that the banana bread bakes perfectly each time. Second, pressure cooking is akin to baking a cake in a water bath, so the loaf ends up moist and light, fluffy and tender. The surface might appear cracked, but I promise it doesn't interfere with the taste. And finally, you don't have to turn on your oven, which means you can enjoy banana bread in the summer without turning your house into a sweaty fire pit.

The recipe is designed for a 7¾ × 3¾-inch loaf pan, which fits inside a 6-quart Instant Pot. If you don't have such a loaf pan, a 7-inch springform pan also gets the job done (you just won't have the traditional loaf shape).

TIP *Want to keep this bread nut-free? Omit the walnut streusel (the bread is delicious on its own) and use a nut-free milk such as oat milk or soy milk instead of the almond milk.*

Cooking spray or neutral-flavored oil, for the pan

1¼ cups all-purpose flour, plus more for flouring the pan

1 teaspoon aluminum-free baking powder

¼ teaspoon baking soda

½ teaspoon fine sea salt or kosher salt

⅓ cup coconut oil, melted, or a neutral-flavored oil such as sunflower oil

½ cup organic cane sugar

⅓ cup unsweetened plain almond milk or other nondairy milk, at room temperature

2 tablespoons flaxseed meal

1 teaspoon pure vanilla extract

3 very ripe medium bananas, mashed with a fork

WALNUT STREUSEL

¼ cup rolled oats

⅓ cup chopped walnuts

2 tablespoons all-purpose flour or almond flour

½ teaspoon ground cinnamon

Scant ¼ teaspoon kosher salt

1½ tablespoons coconut oil, melted

1 tablespoon pure maple syrup

recipe continues

1. Grease a 7¾ × 3¾-inch loaf pan or a 7-inch springform pan with cooking spray or oil and sprinkle with a spoon of flour. Shake to evenly distribute the flour and set the pan aside.

2. For easy removal of the pan from the Instant Pot, create a foil sling following the instructions on page 21. (Alternatively, you can use oven mitts to carefully remove the pan.)

3. In a medium bowl, whisk together the 1¼ cups flour, baking powder, baking soda, and salt.

4. In a large bowl, whisk the melted coconut oil and sugar until incorporated. Stir in the room-temperature almond milk, flaxseed meal, and vanilla until well combined.

5. Gently stir the dry ingredients into the wet ingredients with a wooden spoon or silicone spatula until just combined, taking care to not overmix. Fold in the mashed bananas with a silicone spatula.

6. Pour the banana bread batter into the prepared pan and cover the pan tightly with foil. On the counter, place the pan on top of the steamer rack (with the handles facing up) and arrange the foil sling (if using) underneath the steamer rack. Pour 1 cup of water in the inner pot of the Instant Pot. Carefully lower the pan into the inner pot using the foil sling or steamer rack handles. A loaf pan will fit very snugly.

7. Secure the lid and set the Pressure Release to Sealing. Select the Pressure Cook setting at high pressure and increase the cook time to 50 minutes.

8. Meanwhile, prepare the walnut streusel: In a small bowl, mix together the oats, walnuts, flour, cinnamon, and salt. Pour in the melted coconut oil and maple syrup and fold in with a silicone spatula to evenly combine.

9. Once the 50-minute timer on the Instant Pot has completed and beeps, allow a natural pressure release.

10. Wearing oven mitts, grasp the foil sling or steamer rack handles and carefully lift the pan out of the Instant Pot. Carefully remove the foil cover without dropping condensation on the bread. Insert a toothpick to ensure the bread is done—it should come out with a few moist crumbs. If the bread needs more time, re-cover the pan with foil, place it back on top of the steamer rack, select the Pressure Cook setting at high pressure, and cook for another 5 minutes; allow a natural pressure release for 5 minutes before performing a quick pressure release.

11. Once the bread is cooked through, sprinkle the top evenly with the streusel and allow it to cool in the pan for 10 minutes on a wire rack. Then remove the bread from the pan and cool for another 10 minutes on the wire rack before cutting into slices.

ACKNOWLEDGMENTS

This book is my baby. Not just because I poured my heart and soul into it and not just because I don't have an actual human baby. But because it is the consummation of my decision to pursue my dreams (however unrealistic), to prioritize happiness, and live a life of purpose and fulfillment.

Of course, this book is also the result of the eternal love and support from my family. Mom, you may never fully understand what my job is, but your unwavering love and selflessness more than make up for it. Even if I thanked you for being the world's best mom every day for the next one hundred years, I would still never be able to repay you. Dad, thank you so much giving me the best life I could ask for and for sticking with me. I know you were nervous (terrified) when I first decided to quit lawyering, but it means so much to me that you are now my biggest fan, showing off my work to every unsuspecting stranger who will listen to you. Puja, your (mostly) unintentional humor and daily text messages kept me smiling during my longest days, and your generous gift cards to Whole Foods left my wallet smiling and less empty.

To my partner in life, Max, thank you. For your willingness to visit multiple farmers' markets and grocery stores to find me the perfect ingredient, for not complaining when I occupied the TV-watching area of the apartment with my photography gear, and for becoming my professional dishwasher and taste-tester. And of course, for always pushing me to keep following my dreams and to never give up.

To my editor, Lucia Watson, and the team at Penguin/Avery, thank you for believing in me, guiding me through the entire process, and honing my vision. I am so incredibly grateful for the opportunity you've given me to publish my first cookbook.

To my literary agent, Sharon Bowers, thank you for your welcome sense of humor and advice throughout this new and exciting process.

And finally, to the *Rainbow Plant Life* community. I cannot thank you enough for supporting me and for giving me a platform to share my passion for veganism and food photography. This book simply would not exist without you, so thank you from the bottom of my vegan heart.

INDEX

Page numbers in *italics* refer to photos.